To Orlene &
July '91
from the Joy-Full
Group -
Joanne & Ross
Karen & Jim
Ray & Wendy.

10/03
4

Lansdowne's Birds of the Forest

Lansdowne's
BIRDS
of the
FOREST

Paintings by J.F. LANSDOWNE
Text by JOHN A. LIVINGSTON

M&S

Published in 1989 by
Arrowood Press
A division of LDAP, Inc.
166 Fifth Avenue
New York, NY 10010

Published by arrangement with
McClelland & Stewart Inc.
The Canadian Publishers
481 University Avenue
Toronto, Ontario
M5G 2E9

Canadian Cataloguing in Publication Data
Lansdowne, J. F. (James Fenwick), 1937-
    Birds of the forest

Includes index.
ISBN 0-7710-4589-1

1. Birds — North America — Pictorial works.
I. Livingston, John A., 1923-   . II. Title.

QL681.L36   1989   598.297   C89-094539-X

Printed in Hong Kong.

Note From The Publisher

BROUGHT TOGETHER in one volume are two classic works: *Birds of the Northern Forest* and *Birds of the Eastern Forest* (originally published in two volumes). It has been our desire to reproduce these works intact; consequently, we have retained the original indexes and bibliographies for each of these titles. We hope that this new edition will bring the distinctive illustrations of J.F. Lansdowne to the attention of an even wider audience.

Contents

Birds of the Eastern Forest: 1

Contents

Introduction

WHEN we think of the forest, some of us immediately hark back to our childhood to conjure up a picture of a dense, gloomy, silent place fit only for solitary sorcerers and anti-social dragons. Our pioneer ancestors thought of the forest as an implacable enemy to be conquered at all costs, as a matter of survival. A naturalist may think of the forest in terms of the organ-like phrases of a wood thrush, or the distant muffled-drum of a ruffed grouse. Another may recall the springy squelch of sphagnum, or the pungency of skunk cabbage. All these concepts are equally fanciful, of course, because *the* forest as such simply does not exist. There are a number of forest *regions*; each has its own distinctive plant and animal life, and is thus a clearly discernible *biotic* region as well. Some, such as the area under discussion here, have experienced physical change since the time of settlement, and this has greatly influenced their natural history.

Thus, with the exception of mountains, sea-coasts, grasslands, and arctic barrens, which are still clearly identifiable as such and are exactly what their names imply, the regions of Canada are most conveniently catalogued by their forest cover, or by the forest cover they would have if they were in a natural state. Even in an unspoiled, primeval condition, of course, no area is entirely covered by forest. Woodlands are broken and interrupted by meadows and bogs; natural fires caused by lightning open great patches. Ponds, lakes, marshes, and other watercourses are abundant. But in general, and having these qualifications in mind, the landscape is dominated by trees, and the kinds of trees in an area allow us to describe it meaningfully from the naturalist's point of view.

This book's predecessor, *Birds of the Northern Forest* (McClelland and Stewart, Toronto; Houghton Mifflin, Boston; 1966)*, presented a selection of characteristic birds of the evergreen or boreal region – the great mantle of spruce, fir and larch that covers such a vast portion of Canada. To its north is the treeless tundra. To its south, in the eastern part of the country, is a transition zone of mixed evergreens and deciduous trees. This is the Great Lakes-St. Lawrence Valley region, where the most obvious trees are pine, spruce, yellow birch and maples. Farther east, the Maritime forest region consists mostly of spruces, balsam, yellow birch, maples and pine. The most restricted biotic area in Canada, in a geographic sense, is the Carolinian zone of southern Ontario, which extends along the north shore of Lake Erie and deep into the eastern U.S. This true hardwood forest features several kinds of oaks, with sycamore, tulip-tree, sassafras, hackberry, papaw, hickories and black walnut, none of which occurs elsewhere in Canada. Like the other regions, it has its own special complement of birds, as do the different sorts of habitat within it.

*Birds of the Northern Forest comprises Part III of the present volume.

In two volumes*, we now look at some of the birds of southeastern Canada and the eastern United States, where broad-leaved trees and mixed deciduous-evergreen woodlands form the characteristic forest landscape. (This includes the area I grew up in, and live in now, so personal reference will appear in much of what follows.) At one time, great stretches of the east were in pine, much of which has been cut off long since. Under normal conditions, pine is usually succeeded by maple, beech, hemlock, and yellow birch, and in many parts of our area those trees now make up the forest cover. In other places the forest is entirely gone, and fields and urban development have taken its place.

Changes in the face of the land are reflected in changes in animal populations and distributions, including those of birds. From the naturalist's point of view, the Great Lakes-St. Lawrence region is one of the most disturbed areas in North America; alterations in their environment have greatly affected the numbers and ranges of our native birds. During the same period when commercial hunting was draining off such huge numbers of passenger pigeons, the cutting and burning of oak and beech forests removed the habitat of the birds, and they quickly disappeared. The turkey, dependent on the same type of environment, was pushed out of Canada as a wild bird. But as the original forests gradually dwindled and agriculture took their place, new kinds of birds moved in to replace those that had been dispossessed – birds of orchards and "edges," such as eastern bluebirds, robins, and red-headed woodpeckers. Vast areas of cornfields encouraged the spread of the bobwhite and mourning dove.

Then came "clean farming," the general tidying-up of dead trees, old fence-posts and the like, which, together with the introduced European starling, sent several native birds into a precipitous decline. The removal of brushy hedgerows drove out others. Water pollution – by industrial and municipal wastes, and by oil – has reduced feeding, resting and breeding areas for many aquatic birds; marsh drainage and filling have eliminated others. Tourist trespass has crowded out still more.

But, on the credit side, the widespread appearance of mixed second-growth forest has encouraged certain species such as the redstart and the chestnut-sided warbler, which (with white-tailed deer) must be much more numerous today than they were in pioneer times. Human buildings and structures have helped birds such as the eastern phoebe, cliff swallow, chimney swift, and common nighthawk. Even our "scorched-earth" manner of dealing with so much of the landscape has proved of benefit to species such as the killdeer, the horned lark, and the mourning dove. Change is not necessarily good or bad; the outcome depends on the kinds of animals involved, and their requirements.

*Birds of the Northern Forest comprises Part III of the present volume.

Not all changes are brought about by man, however. I suppose you could say that the introduction of the Old World elm pestilence was chargeable to ocean transport, but once here, its spread has been entirely natural, through the agency of the elm bark beetles. Although this disease is the horror of arborists and shade-tree conservationists, and has caused savage scarring of the face of the entire region, it has altered some bird distributions for the better. As I pointed out in *Birds of the Northern Forest*, three-toed woodpeckers of both species, normally rather sedentary birds of the boreal zone, have begun to move south each winter in considerable numbers, feeding on the infected elms. There is some evidence (admittedly not a great deal just yet, but we can expect more) that the new abundance of dead-elm nesting sites is encouraging a modest recovery of the red-headed woodpecker and the eastern bluebird.

Even one human lifetime can see remarkable changes in the birdlife of an area. I have talked to men who remembered wild turkey hunting and commercial wildfowling in southern Ontario. What a vastly different country it must have been! Even in my own time, although Cory's least bittern has disappeared from the Toronto lakefront, we have gained the cardinal in great numbers, and to a lesser extent the tufted titmouse and the mockingbird. Pileated woodpeckers have much improved their position over the same period. But birds of prey are diminishing, due to the massive use of chemical pesticides in forestry and agriculture. And there are other kinds of change. Thirty years ago, when Ronald Bremner, Donald Macdonald, Robert Ritchie and I would invite the amusement and scorn of our schoolmates by going *birding* (of all things) at every available opportunity, such an activity was highly suspect. Today, birdwatching is commonplace, and utterly respectable. There are several reasons for this. There is little doubt that an interest in our living environment is one of the measures of a maturing society. At the same time as this interest spread from a small group of experts, Roger Tory Peterson's revolutionary *Field Guide* made it possible for anyone to learn to identify the birds. The new enthusiasts have more time and more money with which to indulge what has become a highly civilized hobby.

Travel has become one of the most popular aspects of recreation and, once he is "hooked," the birder likes to see new species for his list, in new places. He now has a greater opportunity to do so. The hobby of amateur photography is mushrooming; of all subjects, nature is among the most popular — especially birds. Now also, there is every sort of additional "enrichment" for the birdwatcher; an amazing volume of lectures, periodicals, books, prints, sound recordings, films, and broadcasts about birds attract audiences that were undreamed of in my boyhood. Organized bird tours go to such places as Africa, India, Antarctica, and the Galapagos Islands. Almost every city and larger town has its bird club and most of them produce regular journals or other reports. There are international, national, provincial and regional organizations. If you want to learn about birds today, there is no difficulty.

An interesting result of all this is that, of the life sciences, none has profited so greatly from amateur participation as ornithology. People of every level of experience who keep notes of what they see, when, and under what conditions and circumstances, are contributing enormously to the general fund of information. So do those who photograph birds, or band them, or record their voices. Ornithology is the beneficiary.

There is no doubt that the most important result of the explosive growth in birdwatching has been widespread concern – and action – for birds' welfare. Legal protection began only a little over fifty years ago, with the Migratory Bird Treaty (1916) with the United States, and broader, public interest has been even more recent. Today, most birds are protected as a matter of course in civilized countries, and by and large the laws are observed. The loss of bird habitat to unplanned land use has taken longer to gain general appreciation, but there are signs that even that is coming.

This metamorphosis in society's attitude to birds has its parallel in the individual. The man with a casual interest in birds around the garden soon develops a positive desire to keep them there – by feeding, watering, planting for nesting sites, and so on. This is usually followed by at least a germ of curiosity about the names and the ways of the backyard birds, and the quite natural urge to attach a label to some unfamiliar migrant that may turn up in spring or fall. Once that curiosity is satisfied – and further whetted – by the acquisition of a field identification book, the process is near completion. Most people who reach this stage soon appreciate the needs of birds and the environments that sustain them, and actively want to help maintain both. It is a very short and easy step from birds to resources in the broadest sense; birds have given the initial impetus to some of the world's most distinguished conservationists.

As I have pointed out many times in other places, "conservation" is a sorely misunderstood word. There was a time when conservation was virtually synonymous with prohibition; it meant blanket holding-the-line, rigid maintenance of the status quo. But nature is never static; it is dynamic, and changeable. So, somewhat later, conservation came to imply some measure of manipulation or management: the *use* of renewable natural resources with enough forethought to ensure a sustained yield from them. Now, it has become something different still. Conservation (it is time for a new word) involves the whole quality of our lives in an environmental sense. It is human ecology.

Like any bird, man is a living, sensate being, with certain fundamental needs related to all of the other life that surrounds him. We must have trees to provide the oxygen we breathe. We must have soil, water, and a multitude of various organisms to produce our food. But there are human needs above and beyond food, water, air, and shelter, because man is a more complex animal than most. We have needs of the mind and of the spirit. But we cannot satisfy our belly or psyche within a habitat that does not include other living things.

The quality of human life is in peril in a technological, urban age. Conditions in our cities – most especially the stresses resulting from over-crowding – mean that conservation now goes far beyond the special province of the agronomists, the hydrologists, and the biologists. Human ecology must become the concern of architects, urban designers, regional planners, sociologists, anthropologists, artists, medical people, teachers, politicians, and all others who touch upon our daily existence. We are *alive*, and to remain properly so, we must have an environment that includes contact with the natural world from which we sprang, and of which we remain an inseparable part. Conservation is just as much about people as it is about birds.

More than five hundred species of birds have been recorded in Canada, and any selection of species for even one region of the country must be arbitrary. Since it is impossible to be exhaustive in a presentation of this kind, Fenwick Lansdowne and I have chosen what we consider to be a representative sample – but only a sample – of the birds to be found in the mixed and hardwood regions of the east. (Birds recognize no artificial, political boundaries, and all are common in the U.S.) Volume I* contains eighteen waterfowl and shorebirds, ten birds of prey, five woodpeckers, five swallows, four flycatchers, and ten others. Volume II* will include a selection of the smaller songbirds, from jays to sparrows.

All the birds in this book occur in the east, but a good two-thirds of them are almost country-wide in distribution. Some, such as the rough-winged swallow and the pied-billed grebe, nest over most of the continent. Others – barn owl, common gallinule, common tern, bank swallow – occur in the Old World as well. None is rare; the red-bellied woodpecker, for example, is very limited in range in Canada, but it is common to the south.

The birds are presented in systematic order – grebes to swallows – according to what is generally agreed to be their evolutionary sequence. Perching birds are thought to have evolved more recently than waterbirds

13

*Birds of the Northern Forest comprises Part III of the present volume.

such as loons and grebes. (Birds are such perishable, soft-boned creatures, however, that the fossil record of ornithology is regrettably slim.) The order and the nomenclature are those of the *1957 Check-list of North American Birds* published by the American Ornithologists' Union. Length and (where necessary) wingspread for each species appear in a foot-note.

These are portraits of individual birds that once were living, painted from skins lent to Fenwick Lansdowne by museums. Since both the date and place of capture will be of interest to some readers, these are provided in an appendix. The geographic origin of some skins may not coincide with the stated area of this book, but that is no more than a reflection of the widespread distribution of some species.

In many species of birds, the sexes are distinctly different in pattern and colour. In others, they are to all intents and purposes identical. In still others, the sexes are distinguishable in the field, but there is sufficient similarity between the two that identification of the species is not in doubt. This has guided the artist throughout. For example, although male and female black ducks do not have precisely the same colouring, it was not considered necessary to illustrate them both. The "family" resemblance is enough.

The text is not arranged formally under standard sub-headings for each species (description, field marks, distribution, habits, nest, eggs, etc.). This information is available from a great many sources in a wide and rich literature. W. Earl Godfrey's *The Birds of Canada* (National Museum of Canada, 1966) is recommended for reference purposes. A limited bibliography suggests additional reading and source material. Since there is nothing more tedious in a popular book than a constant barrage of formal attributions and foot-notes, these have been dispensed with. But my indebtedness to the literature is quite evident throughout; every naturalist is as dependent on his library as a bird is on its feeding territory.

The purpose of the following text is obviously not to present a definitive treatment of eastern birds. It is, however, an attempt to provide a number of selected glimpses into a world that is not ours, but one that we can freely enter anywhere, any time. The aim has been to illuminate to some extent the *fact* of birds in their beauty and diversity, and to illustrate some of the simple pleasures and more lasting intellectual challenges that are so readily available to us in their world. But more than that, I have occasionally called attention to the plight of some troubled species. The birds are important to Fenwick Lansdowne and me, and a plea for their preservation is implicit throughout.

The more you travel and the more intensively you pursue a preoccupation, the more people there are to whom you become indebted. But I am always most conscious of those whose roots are in common with mine and whose lives and interests are interwoven with my own. Especially valued, over many years in the Great Lakes region, has been the inspiration and warm companionship provided by James L. Baillie, H. J. M. Barnett, Lucius F. Barnett, Fred Bodsworth, William H. Carrick, John Crosby, William W. H. Gunn, Eric Nasmith, Donald Pace, Roger Tory Peterson, Jack Satterly, Richard M. Saunders, T. M. Shortt, William W. Smith, Earl V. Stark, Robert W. Trowern, and my wife, Peggy, none of whom bears any responsibility for errors of commission or omission between these covers, but all of whom are indelibly identified with unforgettable moments and deeply satisfying years among the birds. Neither are any textual inadequacies chargeable to those who contributed most, in a variety of ways, to the existence of this volume: William R. Banting, Sylvia L. Danter, M. F. Feheley, Leslie Hannon, John G. McClelland, and Anne Tait.

This was written with my father's memory ever in mind. He knew nothing about birds, but he knew a lot about encouragement.

John A. Livingston

Indispensable to any painter of birds is access to a wide selection of skins; for years my source has been the Royal Ontario Museum, and about half the following paintings were done from birds in its collection. James L. Baillie, of the Department of Birds, once again has given much time and attention to choosing the best examples.

With two exceptions, the remaining skins used were lent by the kindness of Dr. S. Dillon Ripley, Secretary of the Smithsonian Institution, who, when my other arrangements became impractical, freely made available the collection of the United States National Museum. Gorman M. Bond, Research Assistant to Dr. Ripley, kindly undertook the selecting and shipping of the birds.

The figures of the Virginia rail and the female pileated woodpecker were taken from skins in the possession of the Provincial Museum of British Columbia, for the use of which I thank Dr. G. Clifford Carl.

I owe a particular debt of gratitude to another person, Peter Cook, on whose good taste and advice I have frequently relied. In other, technical, ways, not readily apparent to the viewer of these paintings, his help has been considerable.

J. Fenwick Lansdowne

plate 1 — the sketch

PIED-BILLED GREBE
Podilymbus podiceps

plate 1 ## PIED-BILLED GREBE *Podilymbus podiceps*

IN the declining years of the 19th century and the first decade or so of this, the commercial trade in bird feathers and skins was still in full swing. Major victims of the professional hunters were egrets and herons, roseate spoonbills, trumpeter swans—and grebes. It is difficult, perhaps, to see now just what contribution a grebe could possibly make to the fashion salons of the time, but apparently their breasts were in demand by milliners—presumably for the softness and density of the feathering. All that ended, of course, with the Migratory Bird Treaty of 1916; since then, apart from a widespread habitat loss, grebes have led a reasonably secure existence.

Unnatural mass mortality by commercial hunting and marsh drainage is one thing; natural hazards are another. I well remember walking around Grenadier Pond in Toronto one very cold winter day. The pond was frozen except, strangely enough, for one very small pool, no more than two feet in diameter. As I watched it curiously, up in the middle popped a pied-billed grebe. Perhaps the bird's activity had helped to keep the hole open, but its chance of survival seemed slim as it could not become airborne. Like a loon, the grebe is so well adapted for swimming that it has lost much of its aerial prowess. Once in the air it is safe enough, but its wings are short, and it needs a rather long stretch of water for takeoff.

But, in nature, everything seems to even up. If grebes have limitations for flight, they are marvellously adapted to the water. Notice especially this bird's grotesque feet. The toes of loons, ducks, and geese have webs between them; those of grebes are not webbed, but they have become extraordinarily flat. Each toe has, in fact, become a finlike lobe. In motion, the foot as a whole acts like a frogman's flipper: it widens to its fullest extent on the powerful thrusting stroke, and slims down on the return stroke to lower water resistance. Underwater, the grebe uses only its feet for propulsion, and is quite speedy enough to dine well on small fishes, crustaceans, and aquatic insects.

In the nesting season, this is the shyest of our grebes. If its pond is not large enough to allow a good open sheet of water, it will nearly always hide from an observer, behind some clump or sprig of vegetation. If you approach, it will without any apparent effort gradually submerge until only its head is showing. Move even closer, and with an abrupt little "duck-dive" it will somersault beneath the surface and dart away underwater. Sometimes you will have a difficult time finding it when it surfaces; often you will not see it again. This performance gave rise to one of the bird's nicknames, "helldiver," because it appeared to go straight down and never return. Some grebes can dive to depths of twenty-three metres.

Most of our grebes are sociable, gregarious animals that breed in colonies. The pied-bill is the exception. In winter you will see numbers on southern and sub-tropical ponds, living together amicably enough, and they flock on their northward migration, but once they arrive on their breeding grounds they tend to become very jealous of their nesting territories. The nest is built on floating marsh vegetation. The "loudly" striped young birds commonly ride on the parents' backs, both on the surface and below.

This species occurs throughout our hemisphere. In Canada it breeds on fresh water, chiefly east of the Rockies, with a rather small pocket in southern British Columbia. The best identification mark is the peculiar, chickenlike bill.

Length 13 inches. Wingspread 2 feet.   Female, Favourable Lake Mine, Ontario, June 13.
Omemee, Ontario, June 1.

plate 2 — the sketch

GREAT BLUE HERON
Ardea herodias

plate 2

GREAT BLUE HERON *Ardea herodias*

Braking and lurching to a mid-air stall, wide, deeply-cambered wings beating frantically, long stick-like legs awkwardly flailing for support, a great blue heron in the process of landing is anything but graceful. But there is a reason for this cumbersome attempt at helicoptering. The heron's legs are its livelihood, and if one should be damaged in alighting in a tall tree, the consequences could be serious. It may look amusing to us, but it is a life-or-death matter for the heron.

This is our largest heron, a good four feet tall. In rural parts of the country it is often called "crane," but the two families are not allied. Herons are characterized by long, strong, tapered beaks mounted on even longer, highly flexible necks. They usually fly with their heads tucked back on their shoulder; cranes keep their necks outstretched. The great blue is an expert still-fisherman; it will stand on a bank or in shallow water without a single movement for agonizing periods of time, never flinching. Then, ever so slowly, the neck is gradually extended, often at an odd angle, bringing the formidable beak into striking position. Almost imperceptibly, the great head is lowered. Suddenly, with a movement your eye can scarcely follow, a horny javelin flashes beneath the surface, to reappear momentarily with a fish, a frog, or some other aquatic animal. (Insects, mice, small birds and other items are also common in the great blue's diet.) The prey is swallowed with more or less ease, depending on its size; the heron delicately takes a sip or two of water, and settles down again to its vigil.

This is the most numerous of its family in Canada. It breeds on the west coast, and east of the Rockies in a fairly shallow band to the Maritimes, its range coinciding with the most heavily settled portions of the country. It has a wide range of habitats—rivers, lakeshores, marshes, mudflats, ponds, streams—watery places of all kinds, whether fresh or salt. All it needs is a supply of aquatic prey. But even though its requirements are elastic in this respect, the great blue heron is rigidly bound to its special need of mature trees for nesting purposes, in appropriate seclusion. Privacy is becoming one of the rarest commodities of our time, and the herons are beginning to pay the price. Colonies are fewer and fewer.

This is a large, relatively slow-moving bird that has always been a fetching target for the trigger-happy. It is protected by law, but statutory guardianship is of limited value off the beaten track. Even quite innocent and well-meaning intrusion into its colonies by photographers and others can cause the birds to desert their nests.

Most Canadian great blue herons are migratory, but a few manage to survive the winter. When they return in spring, the male takes up a territory around last year's nest. Although the birds are highly competitive about precise breeding sites within their colony, and defend the immediate vicinity of the nest, they are more communal in their feeding habits. Some may own preferred fishing areas in which they discourage other great blue herons, but this is more likely in the non-breeding season. It is quite unusual to find a pair of these herons nesting solitarily; at that time they prefer the company of their own kind. In colonies which include other species of herons, which is frequently the case, the great blues will usually be found in the tallest trees.

The usual clutch of eggs is four. New nestlings in their fuzzy down are not easily described; perhaps a bottle-brush provides the most apt simile.

Length 46 inches. Wingspread 5¹/₂-6 feet.   Male, Willowdale, Ontario, April 4.

plate 3 — the sketch

GREEN HERON

Butorides virescens

plate 3

GREEN HERON *Butorides virescens*

CANADA's next-to-smallest heron is credited with one of the more remarkable accomplishments in the bird world. It is known to have attracted prey by offering bait. Harvey B. Lovell, of the University of Louisville, was watching a green heron fishing in Florida. He threw the bird a piece of bread which it picked up and placed in the water, allowing it to slowly float away. When it drifted almost out of reach, the heron recovered it and placed it close by again. Soon the bird caught a fish which had come to nibble on the bread. Lovell threw it another piece – this time a good distance back on the land. The bird quickly retrieved it and placed it in the water as bait. When some coots came by, the heron gathered in his bait and drove them away, and then placed it back in the water when they had passed.

In his account in *The Wilson Bulletin*, Lovell says: "A clear indication that the green heron knew what he was doing was furnished by the following incident. While he was standing by some floating bread, several small fish broke the surface of the water several feet to his left. The heron immediately became excited, picked up his bread and moved it to almost the exact spot where the fish had appeared." Here you have a member of a family that is not exactly renowned for sagacity evidently capable of learning something quite sophisticated. Was this an example of the abstract recognition of cause and effect, or was it only a fortunate accident? It is impossible to dismiss it as the latter.

The green heron's normal fishing technique, though less dramatic, is by no means pedestrian. It usually perches on small branches close to the water and deftly snatches up small prey as it comes along. Occasionally it will jump in – or even plunge, kingfisher-fashion. This diving can be important when the need arises. Alexander Sprunt IV, of the National Audubon Society, once saw a green heron dive into the water to avoid a hawk that was in swift pursuit.

When it is alarmed, the green heron flicks its tail nervously and will often erect a shaggy, ragged crest. If approached, it will "freeze" in one of a variety of unlikely postures, hoping that protective coloration and absolute immobility will allow it to remain unnoticed. If pressed too closely, it will burst into the air, legs dangling, crest erect, neck extended at a crazy angle, voicing a hoarse *quow*! as it goes. In more leisurely flight it looks blackish, much like a crow, but with shorter wings and a longer bill. For a heron, this one is surprisingly manoeuvrable in the air, and makes its way among tangles and thickets with ease. Its aerobatics are especially interesting in courtship flight, when both sexes clap their wings sharply beneath their bodies.

Unlike most herons, this species is not particularly sociable. It is usually a solitary nester, although limited groups are found occasionally. Outside the breeding season, any gregariousness that may have been achieved in a colony is promptly lost. This bird is every bit the self-sufficient individual – a character implicit in Fenwick Lansdowne's portrait.

Green herons are scattered widely over this hemisphere, but in Canada they breed only in southern Ontario, extreme southern Quebec and New Brunswick. Like all our herons, they are forced to be migratory.

Length 18 inches. Wingspread 2 feet.   Female, Long Point, Norfolk Co., Ontario, May 4.

plate 4 — the sketch

BLACK-CROWNED NIGHT HERON

Nycticorax nycticorax

plate 4

BLACK-CROWNED NIGHT HERON *Nycticorax nycticorax*

THE several members of the heron tribe in Canada are all worthy of our attention, but this one has a special appeal. The others are mostly daytime feeders, and more or less conspicuous. The night heron's unusual appearance, its reclusive nature by day and its mysterious wanderings at night combine with its strange guttural voice to give it a most intriguing personality.

Most herons are more or less social, at least at times, but this one is especially gregarious. It roosts and nests in crowded colonies, in somewhat fetid conditions, although individuals will stake out and maintain their own favourite fishing grounds. The birds rest motionless and silent in the dense cover of trees during the day, waiting until dusk to venture forth for their night-long hunting. It is at late twilight that you will most enjoy watching them, as their sturdy, thickset bodies move on broad wings in silhouette, with an occasional deep-throated *quock*! to announce their passing. They work in shallow water, chiefly on coarse fish, crayfish, frogs and various insects, but they will turn to small mammals such as mice and voles if the opportunity arises. Usually they concentrate on still-fishing, but they will sometimes stalk their prey, and they are able to do some swimming. Food items are usually modest in size, but I have seen one bird with an immense catfish which took him more than an hour to swallow.

This unusually interesting species has the distinction of having been involved in what would seem to be the very first scientific experiments in bird banding in America. In 1902, P. Bartsch made up some special bands which he put on the legs of black-crowned night herons taken in colonies near Washington, D.C. The bands carried serial numbers, the year of the experiment, and the instruction to return them to the Smithsonian Institution. He banded twenty-three birds, of which one was recovered not far away in Maryland. Bartsch carried on in subsequent years, and one of his birds turned up in Cuba, another in Toronto. Thus a research activity was launched that has had immeasurable influence on our knowledge of the seasonal movements of birds, their routes, their longevity, and many other kinds of information that could be gathered in no other way.

Few herons are so compatible with human settlement as the black-crowned night heron. Although it is no more immune to overt disturbance than any other heron, it seems able to tolerate close contact with man, persisting to this day within the borders of large cities. Here, however, it runs the risk of contamination through its food by the various and virulent effluents of the affluent society. Insecticidal residues and other toxic substances in the water, together with industrial and municipal wastes, are making its fishing grounds ever less attractive and productive.

Nesting colonies are characteristically jammed, active, and noisy. Courting and mated birds seem to recognize each other by their head plumes alone, not by coloration. Vigorous fights over territorial invasion sometimes develop between neighbours; contesting birds advance upon each other in a threatening low crouch from which they attempt to seize the opponent's bill, head, or wing. This is accompanied by a multitude of indescribable noises, most of them throaty and squawking. The nest is built of coarse sticks and twigs, with a finer lining. Little if any attempt is made at sanitation; the person of delicate sensitivity should keep his distance from a black-crowned night heron colony.

This species is readily identified by its stocky build, its rather short and heavy bill, and its generally grey colour. Young birds are speckled brown. In flight, night herons look especially chunky and neckless. This is virtually a cosmopolitan bird, and it nests in almost every imaginable wooded situation, but its colonies in Canada are spotty. Major centres are the central and southeastern prairies, the lower Great Lakes and the St. Lawrence valley. Farther south, you find the related and somewhat similar yellow-crowned night heron, but it rarely ventures as far north as Canada.

Length 25 inches. Wingspread 3³/₄ feet.   Male, Islington, York Co., Ontario, Sept. 16.

plate 5 — the sketch

LEAST BITTERN
Ixobrychus exilis

plate 5   LEAST BITTERN *Ixobrychus exilis*

Our most secretive and tiniest heron, no bigger than a dove, is also by far the most difficult to find and observe. It is the least likely to fly, preferring to run and creep through the marsh cattails. It seems nowhere common, but it is probably a good deal more numerous than most of us can prove by personal experience. Once found, however, this little bird is worth all your patience and, if you keep perfectly still, sometimes you may be able to watch it for extended periods.

There is much less difficulty in hearing one. The bird has a very wide, varied vocabulary. One of the more recognizable notes is a dovelike *coo* which it makes in springtime. In addition, there are other calls which, if you are not careful, you might credit to some of the least bittern's neighbours – gallinules or coots, pied-billed grebes, or even frogs.

This bird behaves much more like a rail than a heron, stalking about among dense sedges, grasses, and bulrushes, always staying very close to the ground. If you disturb it, it will vanish in a trice – on foot. Sometimes, if you are lucky, it will jump into the air and fly weakly for a short distance, revealing yellowish-buff patches on warm chestnut wings.

There is a rare colour phase of the least bittern, in which the pale areas are replaced by reddish chestnut. At one time this was thought to be a distinct species, and it went by the name of Cory's least bittern (*Ixobrychus neoxena*). This was one of the more important birds of my boyhood, as its world centre of abundance happened to be in the marshes around Ashbridge's Bay in Toronto. I never saw one alive, but there was always the possibility, in those magic times when something new happened every day, that just one more early-morning visit to the marshes would pay off.

There *was* one, however, with which I had close association. This was a mounted Cory's – old and badly eroded – that teetered in an ancient glass case in the high school I attended. This was a significant bird, and it deserved more appropriate quarters; in

the course of time James Baillie, of the Royal Ontario Museum, persuaded my biology teacher to donate it to the R.O.M.'s distinguished collection. Regrettably, our headmaster learned of the arrangement and immediately vetoed it. After all these years, I have no idea where that rare specimen eventually came to rest; perhaps it has served to inspire subsequent generations of schoolboys.

That "Cory's" least bittern has been down-graded from a full species to a colour phase is, however, no indication of its diminishing importance. Colour phases and their role in evolution are of great interest; they are well known in animals such as screech owls and grey squirrels. The mysterious chestnut bird should still be watched for, wherever there are least bitterns. Some may remain at Lake Okeechobee, Florida, or in the Long Point marshes of Lake Erie. But it will not be seen again at Ashbridge's Bay, which has long since become the site of a sewage filtration plant.

Although this bird is habitually terrestrial, it is an agile climber, and nearly always builds its nest above ground level. The nest is a structure of very little substance, but it is strong enough to hold the four or five greenish-white eggs which both parents incubate. This is not a colonial heron; nests are usually solitary. Near the nest, the birds are more likely to attempt to conceal themselves by "freezing" than by running or flying. It has been reported that the birds have such faith in their unmoving posture that they can be approached and picked up in the hand. Even downy young will freeze; this is clearly an innate behaviour pattern that they have not had time to learn.

Least bitterns are completely dependent on the availability of fresh-water marshes. As wetlands are being drained and filled everywhere, especially in the more southern parts of the country, the future of the bird seems to be limited to whatever areas of natural habitat we eventually see fit to leave it. It lives chiefly in southern Ontario (where marshes are disappearing fastest), with small outposts in southern Manitoba and southern New Brunswick.

Length 13 inches. Wingspread 1¹/₂ feet.   Male, Hamilton, Ontario, June 1.

plate 6 – the sketch

AMERICAN BITTERN

Botaurus lentiginosus

plate 6

AMERICAN BITTERN *Botaurus lentiginosus*

THE bittern never perches in trees. It is almost always on the ground, and very rarely leaves the cover of dense marsh vegetation. It is most noteworthy for its dedicated practice of the art of self-concealment by "freezing." The bird is marked and coloured astonishingly like the dead reeds and cattails of its surroundings, and when it chooses to strike a motionless posture it can be almost impossible to see. It usually takes a rigid stance with its bill held stiffly in the air, its feathers tightly compressed as though in an attempt to become a tuft of grass. It remains immobile, staring at you glassily over its bill; some observers have seen it sway perceptibly, as though in rhythm with the movement of the vegetation. If you move around it slowly, it will also move, in order to keep facing you. Lester Snyder and Shelley Logier, of the Royal Ontario Museum, once repeatedly circled a bittern in this way, to a point where the bird got itself so turned and twisted around that it ended careened on its side and partially under water! Such is the bittern's unshakable faith in camouflage.

The big "thunder-pumper" or "stake-driver" has a wide range in Canada, from central British Columbia and Great Slave Lake to James Bay and Newfoundland, southward wherever there are suitable wet fields, bogs, and marshes. The nicknames derive from the bird's voice. Its deep, booming call, especially in spring, consists of three or four syllables, preceded (at close range) by sharp clicks of the bill. The sound is delivered by means of the bird swallowing air; it consists simply of well-regulated "burps." It carries well, although at a distance its low frequency and muffled quality sometimes make the source difficult to pinpoint.

This is another solitary-nesting heron. Two or more nests close together have been thought to be evidence of polygamy rather than of social nesting. Females appear to look after the young by themselves. The nest is a sort of platform made of marsh vegetation a mere four or five inches above the level of the water. If you approach the nest and the freezing posture doesn't work, the bittern explodes out of the vegetation in front of you, flaps hurriedly on wide, brown wings to another part of the marsh, and heavily plops in again.

The long, strong bill is an efficient instrument for snatching up marsh animals such as mice, small birds, fishes, crayfish and frogs. It can also be a weapon of defence. Robie W. Tufts has a splendid account of this in *The Birds of Nova Scotia*. "On one occasion I banded and released a juvenile in a field near a cattail swamp where cattle were pastured. Drawn by curiosity, a large steer that had been watching the operation at fairly close quarters drew near with head lowered, sniffing audibly, as though to investigate. Meanwhile, the bird, instead of beating a hasty retreat to cover, as it could well have done, stood its ground, and with head drawn in close to its body, glared menacingly at the steer. Finally, and with a suggestion of timidity, the steer's nose came within inches of the poised bird. Suddenly the sharp beak shot out and upward, stabbing the animal viciously on the tender part of the nostril; whereupon, with a loud snort, the steer turned and went galloping across the field. The bird, after gaining its composure, strode off slowly in a dignified manner and soon disappeared."

There are bitterns of the genus *Botaurus* on four continents; they are very similar, and some authorities consider them all one species. Our bird seems to be an inveterate wanderer on migration; there are more than forty records of its occurrence in the United Kingdom.

Length 27 inches. Wingspread 3¹/₄ feet.   Male, C. Henrietta Maria, Kenora Dist., Ontario, July 5.

plate 7 – the sketch

BLACK DUCK
Anas rubripes

plate 7 ## BLACK DUCK *Anas rubripes*

THIS sturdy, splendid duck is the second most important migratory waterfowl in Canada; it is to the east what the mallard is to the west. Swift, sagacious, implacably wild, it is one of the hardiest of its family. Cold weather does not bother the big "black mallard," as New Englanders call it. It frequently arrives for spring nesting while ice still covers many of its ponds and streams, and egg-laying and even incubation may be under way before the snow disappears.

Ducks are jealous of their nesting territories, and wild aerial chases are frequent sights in late April. Sometimes these pursuits degenerate into common fights, with drakes driving off other drakes and even pursuing other pairs. For nesting, the birds like good cover, usually the shelter of low bushes or tall grass. The female chooses the site and makes a shallow cup out of available materials. The first egg is laid in about nine or ten days, and the full clutch of about nine eggs is complete ten days later. Now, incubation begins, and the drake leaves the area to join other new bachelors on a nearby pond.

Ducklings become "imprinted" on the first moving thing they see and hear, soon after hatching. Generally this object is their mother, and the bond between parent and young keeps the brood together, and thus safer, than if each individual were wandering about on its own. That is why bunches of small ducklings always walk and swim in such close-knit, tight formation behind the duck. The young waste no time in learning to fend for themselves, and almost immediately begin a diligent search for small invertebrates, and other food. Animal protein is essential to strong early growth. The birds will fly when they are eight or nine weeks old. As soon as they are effectively airborne, they part company with their mothers, gathering in large groups.

In July and August the black ducks begin to move from small ponds to larger lakes and marshes, and from there they push on to the Atlantic shore; gradually great migrant and wintering flocks build up along the coast. Courtship and pair formation against the following spring have taken place by this time (ducks, noted for their concupiscence, make it a short off-season), and pairs remain together over the winter. Much wishful-thinking anthropomorphic rubbish has been promulgated about birds possessed of such fidelity that they mate for life and remain celibate after the disappearance of one of the pair, but a few facts help maintain the attractive notion. There are at least two recorded instances in which a black duck, whose partner was shot by gunners, refused to leave its mate.

The black duck is a dabbler, that is, it feeds at the surface of a pond by immersing its head in the water and tipping its bottom into the air. This group also includes mallards, pintail, wigeon, shovelers, and the various teal. They are characterized by a broad, spatulate bill which is equipped with sieves along its sides, making it possible for the bird to sift and strain water for tiny bits of food. These ducks are so closely related that they frequently hybridize: especially blacks, mallards, and pintail.

On the Atlantic coast during winter the black ducks eat snails, periwinkles, mussels and other shellfish. When they arrive on the fresh-water breeding grounds in our latitudes, they switch their diet to the seeds of sedges, rushes, and such plants. They are found in summer south from Ungava and eastern Manitoba, with occasional nesting in Saskatchewan and Alberta. Unlike the cosmopolitan mallard, this species is strictly North American. Many shooters claim it is the most challenging game waterfowl in the world.

Length 23 inches. Wingspread 3 feet.   Male, Nettichi River, James Bay, Ontario, July 19.

plate 8 — the sketch

WOOD DUCK

Aix sponsa

plate 8

WOOD DUCK *Aix sponsa*

ENWICK Lansdowne's brilliant portrait spares me the task of even attempting to describe the male wood duck – surely the most gorgeous waterfowl in the world. The flamboyance of the drake is approached only by the male mandarin duck of east Asia. Although the latter is quite dissimilar in colour and pattern, the females of the two are nearly indistinguishable. They are both perching ducks, which nest in trees.

Audubon knew this bird as the "summer duck," and his Romantic prose outdoes even *his* luxuriant style when he describes it. On the earthbound, factual side he stated that the female bird transports the downy ducklings in her bill from the nesting hole to the water. There seems little evidence of this. Apparently the small birds just tumble out and fall lightly to the ground beneath. Sharp little claws on their toes no doubt enable them to clamber out of the nesting hollow in the first place.

The hole itself is sometimes the former home of a large woodpecker, such as a pileated, or even a flicker. Wood ducks seem to be able to compress themselves remarkably to enter openings that would seem to be far too small for them. Most often, however, the nest is in a natural cavity in a tree, up to fifty feet from the ground. It does not need to be over the water or even very near it; the birds are perfectly prepared to make the chicks undertake a substantial overland hike to their first swim.

Wood ducks are readily attracted to artificial nesting sites. One of the easiest to construct is simply an old nail keg with an entrance hole about four inches in diameter, set on a pole over the water. Wood chips or sawdust should be placed inside, and a hole cut in the bottom for drainage. Putting it over the water discourages predators of various kinds.

In Illinois, students conducted an investigation of 820 unsuccessful nestings of wood ducks over a seventeen-year period. They discovered that the losses were chargeable 51% of the time to fox squirrels, 37% raccoons, 10% snakes, and 2% opossums. In Canada, raccoons are the most common offenders. A nesting box on a pole in the water is the best defence. But predation is the natural thing, and we should not concern ourselves about it unduly. The economy of nature simply could not cope with the survival of a dozen new wood ducks each year from every mated pair.

At one time this bird was very abundant in eastern North America. But it is a somewhat tame and unwary creature, and gunners brought such pressure to bear that it soon became extremely difficult to see a wood duck anywhere. It was placed on the protected list for a time, and began to recoup somewhat. It is by no means out of the woods yet, however, and the irony of the situation is that if it were permitted to, it could probably become one of our most common and most familiar water birds.

Richard Pough wrote in 1951: "Unfortunately, the two millions or so of our citizens who hunt ducks have not been willing to exempt from hunting even this one rather small species so that the 150 million of us who do not hunt can have it around in abundance where we can enjoy its beauty." Nothing much has changed in the meantime, save the numbers of people. In 1967, Ontario shooters were still permitted to kill four wood ducks per day, with a possession limit of eight, inconceivable though it may seem to many of us that anyone could wittingly destroy one.

In Canada the wood duck occurs in southern B.C., central Saskatchewan, south-central Manitoba, southern Ontario, extreme southern Quebec, and, in a limited way, in the Maritimes.

Length 18 inches. Wingspread 2¹/₄ feet.   Male, Mud Lake, Scott Tp., Ontario Co., Ontario, October 6.
Female, Ashbridges Bay, Toronto, Ontario, October 16.

plate 9 — the sketch

TURKEY VULTURE

Cathartes aura

plate 9

TURKEY VULTURE *Cathartes aura*

THE name of the bird clearly has nothing whatever to do with its family relationships; "turkey" is merely for the bare red head of the adult. This is the only vulture that occurs in Canada on a regular basis; the black vulture of the south turns up only on very rare occasions. Happily, this great bird seems to be extending its range in our country; it has moved into all the provinces from Ontario westward.

The vulture shows conspicuous adaptations for its way of life. The head is not feathered, for sanitary reasons; feeding on carrion can be a messy job. The feet are small and relatively weak for a bird of this proportion, for, as Roger Tory Peterson has aptly put it, "its prey cannot escape." It finds its food by quartering the landscape in graceful, effortless, soaring flight, which is made possible by especially well-developed tendons and ligaments in the wings. A notable reduction in breast muscles (they aren't needed for soaring) is evident in the bird's heavy, ponderous flapping as it leaves the ground. This species shows a conspicuous dihedral in soaring flight, and tends to rock gently from side to side as it takes advantage of thermal columns and updrafts from cliffsides and other sources.

It has long been disputed whether vultures find their food by eyesight or by a highly developed sense of smell. As long ago as the 1830s, John James Audubon was busy conducting experiments (exposing one carcass, covering another) which indicated to his satisfaction that the vulture uses only its eyes. Later experiments did not seem to be conclusive, with results going both ways. The controversy continues to this day. In areas where vultures are more common, however, such as tropical Africa, eyesight would *seem* to be the key.

Vultures are usually in attendance within minutes of a big cat's daytime kill, often before the victim is dead. They get their clue by seeing the descent of other vultures. Rare is the carcass that remains uneaten long enough for putrefaction to provide any evidence of its presence. Possibly, sensory development varies between species of vultures, or groups of species.

The turkey vulture builds no formal nest. It lays its two eggs directly on the ground in a hillside cave or crevice, under a stump or hollow log, or on a cliff ledge. Young birds are in the "nest" for at least two months before they take to the air. Delicacy prevents my describing the odoriferous feeding of the chicks at this stage; that is best left to one's imagination. As in all large birds, the young spend much time in wing-exercising as they grow larger, with strenuous flapping, and stretching. An interesting sidelight on this is the report that a young vulture kept in a cage until three months of age, in such close confinement that it could not exercise its wings, was unable to fly when released.

Although their food habits are repugnant to people, vultures obviously play a very important role in the economy of nature, especially in warmer parts of the world. Without the activities of this "sanitation squad," equatorial regions would be much less pleasant places than they are. In many areas they cluster in streets and backyards, as tolerant of human approach as domestic pigeons. There are vultures of various kinds, including the condors, throughout our hemisphere; the closest relative of our species is the very similar yellow-headed vulture of Central and South America. Old World vultures, which are not related to our birds, inhabit southern Europe, Africa, and Asia.

Length 29 inches. Wingspread 5³/₄-6 feet. Female, Salmon R. near Beaver L., Lennox and Addington Cos., Ontario, November 20.

plate 10 — the sketch

SHARP-SHINNED HAWK
Accipiter striatus

plate 10 ## SHARP-SHINNED HAWK *Accipiter striatus*

OF our three accipiters, the bird-eating true hawks, this is the smallest. It is no larger than a mourning dove, and thus the birds it eats are generally those of the size of sparrows or warblers, although it will not hesitate to attack larger targets upon occasion. It does not restrict itself to birds, however, and will take small mammals and large insects from time to time.

In all hawks, the females are perceptibly larger than the males. This can result in some confusion between this species and the quite similar Cooper's hawk. A large female sharp-shin may be almost the same size as a small male Cooper's, in which case you can differentiate between them by the shape of the tip of the tail, which is square or notched in the sharp-shin, rounded in the Cooper's.

As hunters, these birds are the last word in cool efficiency. They are very fast, very strong, and highly manoeuvrable, making their swift and silent way through dense woodlands and tangled shrubbery with no apparent effort – places that other birds of prey would never attempt. The typical accipiter flight pattern consists of several quick flaps of the wings followed by a short sail, then more flapping, then sail again. This characteristic locomotion, together with their shortish, rounded wings and long tails, separates the accipiters from all other birds of prey.

As a group, these hawks have been among the most violently persecuted of our birds. All birds of prey are disliked by some people, but the accipiters, because of their food habits, have long been subject to massive, senseless attack. Sharp-shinned hawks are spectacular migrants, and on their autumnal flights southward they are relatively easy prey to those who would destroy them. Formerly, before enlightened legislation prevented it, there used to be great hawk shoots at key migration points such as

Cape May, New Jersey. In *Birds Over America*, Roger Tory Peterson tells of having seen, in 1935, some 800 sharp-shins attempt to cross the firing lines. "Each time a 'sharpy' sailed over the treetops it was met by a pattern of lead. Some folded up silently; others, with head wounds, flopped to the ground, chattering shrilly. By noon 254 birds lay on the pavement." But those were the old days, and such organized kills are things of the past. Although uninformed or indifferent individual hunters still take their toll today, it is much less severe.

One of the finest places to watch the fall migration of sharp-shinned hawks is Point Pelee National Park, in extreme south-western Ontario. Here, great flights of birds proceeding south-westerly along the north shore of Lake Erie are funnelled down the point and out across the end of the lake. I have counted more than 1,000 sharp-shins there in a single day. One morning, when there was an especially heavy flight of songbirds *and* hawks at the tip of the peninsula, one sharp-shin was in such relentless pursuit of a yellow warbler as it shot round a red cedar that it could not change course in time to avoid running straight into James Baillie, who was standing beside me. But accipiters are rarely unable to control their movements; they are among the most agile of predatory birds.

This is essentially a wilderness species, inhabiting the forest country from coast to coast. It does not like human company, and usually avoids settled areas. Occasionally one will take up residence near a winter bird-feeding station, which can pose a delicate question of policy. But we must always remember that predation is an essential factor in the economics of nature, and that the culling of surpluses is inescapable and necessary. There are a lot more chickadees and juncos than there are sharp-shinned hawks.

Length 12 inches. Wingspread 2 feet.   Female, Kingsville, Essex Co., Ontario, September 18.

plate 11 — the sketch

RED-SHOULDERED HAWK

Buteo lineatus

plate 11   RED-SHOULDERED HAWK *Buteo lineatus*

THE word "hawk" for members of the genus *Buteo* is a misnomer. The true hawks are the sharp-shin, the Cooper's, and the goshawk — the bird-eaters. The red-shoulder and its relatives are soarers that catch their prey by dropping on it from above, not by pursuit. It follows that they kill very few birds, simply because most buteos are not sufficiently nimble to catch them. So they eat mostly small mammals, reptiles and amphibians, and large insects. They will also eat crustaceans, and I have seen a red-shouldered hawk catch an unwary panfish by plopping into the water on top of it from a low overhanging branch.

This is a comparatively inactive creature for a bird of prey, and (especially in the south) an unsuspicious one. It spends most of the day sitting around and reviewing the situation from a tree or telephone pole, waiting for its prey to come by. It does not invest as much time soaring about on the active hunt as some of its close relatives do. Far from being a shy bird, it may well have profited from settlement of the eastern part of the continent; the change from forest to open fields for hunting and scattered woodlots for roosting and nesting seems to suit it perfectly.

The most noteworthy thing about all the buteos is their effortless, soaring flight. Like the vultures, they have broad, slotted wings that allow them to take the maximum advantage of updrafts. Thermal columns (streams of warm air rising from the ground) are especially useful to the soarers, who will swing round and round, climbing an invisible spiral staircase higher and higher, without ever a wingbeat. Other updrafts are the result of the topography of the country below. Cliffs and escarpments, and even large buildings, will cause prevailing winds to rush upward with enough force to support the circling birds. It is no accident that migrating birds of prey tend to be especially noticeable in places like Toronto's Scarborough Bluffs or Pennsylvania's Hawk Mountain.

When it is in flight, which is the time most of us see a hawk, this bird is clearly identifiable as a buteo by its soaring posture, long, broad wings, and wide tail. It is more slender than the related and commoner red-tailed hawk, and it shows a palish patch near the end of each wing. The broad-winged hawk is chunkier and smaller.

Pairs are said to remain together from year to year, often re-using the same nest each spring. They will give it a minimal clean-up and restoration, sometimes adding bits of new green foliage to the old sticks. Audubon said that his birds did not necessarily nest in exactly the same spot from year to year, but that they did return to the same copse or woodlot. The average number of eggs is three. Both sexes incubate, and care for the young birds. At this season the bird is exceptionally vocal. Its loud, piercing scream is readily imitated by blue jays.

There are five recognized races, or subspecies, of the red-shouldered hawk, of which the most attractive in my opinion is the pale, sandy-coloured bird of south Florida. In Canada, the red-shoulder is not widely dispersed; it is found only in southern Ontario and the south-western extremity of Quebec, and very occasionally in New Brunswick.

Length 21 inches. Wingspread 3¹/₂ feet.   Female, Hadlyme, Connecticut, January 7.

plate 12 — the sketch

BROAD-WINGED HAWK
Buteo platypterus

plate 12

BROAD-WINGED HAWK *Buteo platypterus*

Our smallest buteo is also undoubtedly the commonest, although its breeding distribution and habits are such that it may not be as frequently seen by most of us as some of its more familiar open-country relatives. This is a nesting bird of the dense woodlands; although it does occur in the west – east of the Rocky Mountains – its centre of abundance is the vast deciduous forest of the southern halves of Manitoba and Ontario, southern Quebec, and New Brunswick.

This is not a conspicuous bird at nesting time. It likes the leafy, covert surroundings of its woods; there is so much of that kind of country in eastern Canada that breeding pairs are hard to find. Broad-wings subsist during the summer on the mice, shrews, and other small mammals of the forest floor, and take good numbers of reptiles and amphibians, as well as insects. Its habitat being what it is, it follows that this is a somewhat more sprightly species than some of its close relatives, and no doubt it catches a number of small birds.

But if it is infrequently seen in spring and summer, in the autumn the broad-winged hawk is one of the most notable of Canadian birds. It appears in immense flocks during its southward migration. The only eastern buteo that leaves the country altogether in winter, its numbers begin to build up in early September for a flight which will take the birds to Central and South America. By the second to third week in September, the migration is in full stream. The hawks move out of the great eastern forests in a generally south-westerly direction until they reach the barrier of the eastern Great Lakes.

Buteos do not usually like to fly over extensive stretches of water; there are not enough consistent updrafts to accommodate their soaring flight. So, as they reach Lake Ontario, they turn west, following the lakeshore and the numerous bluffs, escarpments and other updraft-producing topographical features they need, towards the Niagara Peninsula. Very large flights are seen along the north shore of Lake Ontario from Cobourg westward. But it is when the masses of birds flow southwest along Lake Erie that the migration becomes truly spectacular. From Long Point westward, especially at a place called Hawk Cliff, near Port Stanley, Ontario, on a good day it is sometimes possible to see thousands upon thousands of broad-wings and substantial numbers of other species as well. On one fantastic day, seventy thousand birds were counted! The best dates, according to Earl Godfrey in *The Birds of Canada*, are from September 18 to 23. These are average dates, of course; because so much depends upon the weather, we can never be precisely sure when the flight will reach its peak.

In *Canadian Audubon* magazine, Olin Sewall Pettingill Jr. described the meteorological background. "In the fall, hawks tend to migrate south in greatest numbers on the second days after cold fronts when there are *steady* northwest to west winds and ample sunlight to produce thermals. . . To see hawks migrating in any appreciable numbers you must study weather maps and predictions so as to be present at places where the birds are known to pass when these wind and sunlight conditions prevail."

William W. H. Gunn, whose contribution to our knowledge of the influence of weather on bird migration has been the basis of much of the foregoing, is now plotting bird movements by means of radar (*see* ring-billed gull, *Plate 25*). The combination of a radarscope and a weather map is making fall hawk-watching much more predictable – and thus more people can enjoy it.

The broad-wing is identified by its small size (for a buteo), stocky build, and, in the adult, broad black-and-white bars on the tail. Young birds, which are sometimes numerous in the Florida Keys in winter, lack the distinctive tail pattern, but are pale under the wing, which has a dark border.

Length 15 inches. Wingspread 3 feet.   Male, Cedar Swamp, Coldstream, Ontario, April 29.

plate 13 — the sketch

MARSH HAWK

Circus cyaneus

plate 13 MARSH HAWK *Circus cyaneus*

At a distance, the long-tailed marsh hawk looks superficially like a turkey vulture, with its long wings held in a typical V-shaped dihedral pattern, gently rocking back and forth, and doing a great deal of gliding. But there the resemblance ends; they are not related, even though some of their habits are similar. The best field mark for the marsh hawk is its shape, combined with a white rump patch.

In Britain, this fine bird of prey is known as the hen harrier. The harriers are a world-wide group of specialized hawks whose way of life is quite unlike those of their relatives. This is the only North American species. Harriers hunt by patiently quartering a marsh or grassy field at a very low elevation, watching for small mammals upon which they quickly pounce with long, slim legs. They catch snakes and amphibians too, and, occasionally, small ground birds such as rails, but marsh hawks aren't sufficiently swift or dexterous on the hunt to be significant bird-catchers. Sometimes they even run into trouble with mammals. Robert Trowern has told me of a marsh hawk which was repulsed and driven off by a large European hare in defence of her litter.

This hawk commonly eats carrion, a habit which has brought it a full measure of trouble. People are woefully prone to make instant judgements based on the slimmest circumstantial evidence. The harrier often eats game birds, for example, that may have died of wounds or of some other cause. The incautious (or prejudiced) observer rushes to the conclusion that these were the hawk's own victims, and promptly shoots it. A very great number of marsh hawks have been killed over the years by gunners under the mistaken impression that the birds compete with them for game. Except under the most unusual and rare circumstances, they do not. Another unfortunate result of scavenging can be the transference of pesticidal residues from the eaten to the eater. This is happening in our generation among peregrine falcons, bald eagles, and ospreys, all of which are seriously declining in numbers, as the result of ingesting toxic chemicals with their food. I believe that poisoning of its food resources is also affecting the marsh hawk.

Very few birds of prey habitually nest on the ground; the marsh hawk is an exception. The nest is well hidden. In the breeding season, the courting marsh hawks put on an extravagant aerial performance, described in *The Life of Birds* by Joel C. Welty. "(The male) plunges directly earthward from a great height, turning somersaults and uttering shrill cries during his descent. At other times, he impresses the female by performing an up and down roller-coaster flight, rising only a few metres above the ground and looping the loop and screeching on each downward plunge." The aerobatics of marsh hawks are not limited to courtship flights. In what might be termed "practice sessions," adult birds drop or pass prey items to the young in mid-air. For such a dogged hunter, the marsh hawk is a miraculous flier, when it cares to be.

This widespread species breeds from Alaska to the Maritimes, wherever there are suitable open marshes, prairies, and long-grass meadows. The male marsh hawk is blue-grey; the much larger female is brown, as are the young.

Length 20¹/₂ inches. Wingspread 3³/₄ feet.   Male, St. George, Utah, November 1.

plate 14 — the sketch

SPARROW HAWK

Falco sparverius

plate 14

SPARROW HAWK *Falco sparverius*

THIS species is another victim of the uniquely North American custom of calling all diurnal birds of prey "hawks." The sharp-shinned hawk (*plate 10*) is a true hawk; this bird is a falcon – our smallest. It is known as a falcon by its pointed wings, long tail, and strong, rapid wing-beats. At close range the falcons are also characterized by a singular tooth-and-notch arrangement in the bill.

Its colloquial name to the contrary, the sparrow hawk lives for the most part on large insects. Many people would like to see its name changed to "grasshopper falcon." An even preferable vernacular name might be "American kestrel," for clearly this bird is the opposite number of the very similar kestrels of the Old World. In addition to insects, its diet consists of the very smallest mammals, reptiles and amphibians, with some little birds thrown in. The size of the falcon (about that of a blue jay) limits its feathered prey to the small end of the scale.

This is easily our most common and best-known falcon. Unlike the others, which are essentially wilderness species, the little kestrel seems to have adapted itself admirably to man and human development. It has made itself completely at home around farms, villages and suburban residential areas, and even within cities. It seems that wherever there is a telephone pole or a television antenna from which the bird can survey its hunting grounds, it is perfectly content. Such look-out perches are very important. The bird will quietly and systematically survey its feeding territory, then launch itself swiftly into the air in pursuit of a delectable passing locust. At other times, especially over grassy areas, it will hover in mid-air as it checks the prey possibilities below.

Nesting is usually in holes in trees, sometimes in appropriate crevices in man-made structures. The birds will also come to artificial nesting boxes, but an old woodpecker digging is probably used most often. The average clutch of eggs is four. The young grow rapidly, and weigh as much as the adults in about three weeks. There is nothing like the high protein diet of a bird of prey to promote fast and healthy development in the early stages.

Since it is so common in so many parts of the country, it is not surprising that the sparrow hawk is often kept in captivity for purposes of falconry. Obviously, it is not capable of delivering anything significant in the way of game, but it can provide the beginner with a certain amount of interest and pleasure, and, presumably, experience. This may or may not be a positive thing. There is not much falconry practised in Canada, but in those places where there are nuclei of devotees they seem to attract a good deal of publicity, much of which is no doubt well deserved. But the publicity in turn attracts numbers of would-be new participants. The fear of many conservationists is that birds of prey falling into the hands of novices are not likely to survive the experience. Many young people attempt to emulate their heroes without going to them for proper guidance, and the danger is that a lot of people can go through a lot of captive birds in the course of a year. We have no birds of prey to spare.

The sparrow hawk breeds from coast to coast in southern Canada in summer, and is migratory. Some winter in the southernmost parts of the country, but much greater numbers spend the off-season in the south, most especially in Florida. In the Lake Okeechobee-Kissimmee Prairie country and in the Keys, Alexander Sprunt Jr. conducted random counts and "found them to occur at the rate of one a mile over a span of 13 miles." Over one 47-mile stretch of the upper Keys, my wife and I once counted 77 sparrow hawks: about one every three-quarters of a mile.

Length 10¼ inches. Wingspread 2 feet.   Male, Islington, York Co., Ontario, January 26.

plate 15 — the sketch

RUFFED GROUSE
Bonasa umbellus

plate 15   RUFFED GROUSE *Bonasa umbellus*

THE ruffed grouse must be *the* game bird of broad-leafed and mixed forests in southern Canada, in terms of both numbers and popularity. A dashing, spirited, but wary fowl, it tests the skill and accuracy of gunner and photographer alike. Generally one's acquaintance with it is limited to a shattering split-second when the bird erupts like a land mine from the dead leaves of the forest floor, and immediately disappears with a loud whir of wing feathers. Then, absolute silence . . . and small likelihood of your seeing that bird again that day.

There are two distinct colour phases of the ruffed grouse, as there are in screech owls: a grey phase and a red phase. According to Earl Godfrey in *The Birds of Canada*, "the grey phase is commoner in interior western Canada, and both phases are more or less common in eastern Canada, but in extreme south-western British Columbia reddish-brown is predominant." The difference in colour is most obvious on the birds' tails.

Ruffed grouse prefer deciduous or mixed woodlands, although in summer they are more likely to be found in hardwoods, in winter, in conifers. There is little doubt that the bird is the beneficiary of clearing and fire, as is the white-tailed deer. Both prefer the new, lush, second-growth to a pure stand of mature forest. Since the grouse moves around very little in the course of a year, its home base must have enough variety in the way of vegetation to keep it going both winter and summer. Mixed forests are essential to its survival.

Despite its fame as a game bird, the ruffed grouse's greatest distinction is its unique spring mating performance. The birds are promiscuous, which means that individuals meet, mate, and go their separate ways. No pairs are formed. But it is the manner of the sexes' meeting which is so intriguing. The solitary male selects a prominent log or stump in the forest, where he takes an elevated position. He raises his wings and, slowly at first, then more and more rapidly, beats them against the air in a way that produces the effect of a muffled, swiftly accelerating drum-roll. The sound carries for a good distance through the forest, advertising the male's presence and preparedness. Receptive females within hearing range are attracted into his territory by the drumming, just as many female toads and frogs "home" on the singing of the males.

The female looks after the duties of nesting and incubation by herself, and usually builds at the foot of a stump or tree. But parental chores are not as onerous as they are in many families of birds; the precocial young are ready to forage for themselves within a day of hatching. The brood sticks together, however, for better protection against barred owls, foxes, and other potential enemies.

The grouse family is circumpolar in the northern hemisphere. Except for those that live in the most extreme climates, they are mostly sedentary, and do not migrate to any appreciable extent. For this reason they have had to develop adaptations to existence in cold weather. Ptarmigan, for example, have fully feathered feet and toes, which act as well-insulated snowshoes. A ruffed grouse's extremities are not feathered, but for the wintertime it grows thin, horny, pectinations along the sides of its toes. They do nothing for warmth, but they help in a locomotive sense as snowshoes. All species are densely feathered on the body, and all are extremely well camouflaged.

The ruffed grouse is found from the Yukon to Labrador and southward, in suitable habitat. It is subject to more or less regular cycles in abundance; populations will build to a peak over a period of years, drop off dramatically, and then slowly start building up again. The nature of this periodicity has yet to be completely understood.

Length 18 inches.   *Male, Arden, Kennebec Tp., Frontenac Co., Ontario, November 20.*
Female, De Grassi Pt., Simcoe Co., Ontario, May 24.

plate 16 — the sketch

BOBWHITE
Colinus virginianus

plate 16 BOBWHITE *Colinus virginianus*

No game bird can be better known or more popular in the eastern and southern U.S.A. than this little (7-ounce) quail. Not much in the pot, but apparently highly desirable in the field, it is one of the mainstays of the gunning industry in that part of the world. In Canada, however, it occurs naturally only in the south-westernmost part of Ontario, although (usually unsuccessful) attempts have been made to establish it in other parts of the country, such as southern British Columbia.

At one time the bobwhite was more widely distributed and more common in Ontario than it is now. As the forest lands were cleared, and wide brushy pastures and fallow fields took their place, the birds moved northward. The general planting of corn was a contributing factor. C. H. D. Clarke, of the Ontario Department of Lands and Forests, says that the bobwhite's range in our part of the world reached a maximum in the 1840s, but it is now limited to a handful of counties along the north shore of Lake Erie. The best place to see the birds in Canada today is between London, Ontario, and Lake St. Clair, where vast stretches of cornfields help them to maintain themselves during the difficult Canadian winter. Bobwhite are still reasonably dependable in that area.

No doubt the gradual shrinkage in the bobwhite's Canadian range following the initial invasion was the result of "clean farming." When farmland is meticulously manicured, there is no room for this quail. It must have sufficient brambly, rough, tangly places for cover and enough other ground vegetation to forage in. Clean farming also involves the removal of old or half-dead orchard trees and rotten fenceposts; this has contributed in great measure to the decline of other birds, such as the red-headed woodpecker and the eastern bluebird.

The bobwhite is easily identified by its diminutive size and its head pattern. In the adult male, the head markings are very conspicuous in black and white. Females and young birds are coloured in brown and buff. This is a gregarious animal which lives in groups or coveys, but there is a natural, self-imposed limit to the size of the flock. Coveys with a membership of up to about thirty are the maximum. Richard Pough says, "Each group makes its headquarters and roosts at night in good cover, ranging out to feed along brushy travel lanes for 300 to 400 yards and scattering in all directions when flushed. No covey allows others to trespass, nor does any covey accept additional members once the quota of 25 to 30 has been reached." There is only foraging space for so many birds in any one suitable area.

Bobwhite leave the coveys and form pairs for spring breeding. There is a very interesting pattern to their egg-laying. The female is said to lay her daily egg somewhat later each day, up to the point when it is occurring in the evening. Then, she will skip a day, and resume laying in the morning, until the clutch is complete. Both parents incubate the fifteen or so eggs for about three and a-half weeks. The young are precocial, able to move about and feed upon hatching. They are also born with the ability to voice the famous *bobwhite!* call of their species. This accomplishment is innate, not acquired, as experiments with young birds have demonstrated.

Length 10 inches. Male, Ruscomb, Essex Co., Ontario, November 10.

plate 17 — the sketch

KING RAIL
Rallus elegans

plate 17 KING RAIL *Rallus elegans*

JOHN James Audubon discovered and named this fine big rail, which put him "one up" on his contemporary Alexander Wilson, who with other early naturalists of the time thought it to be the adult of the clapper rail, a related salt-marsh species. The king rail is a bird of the fresh-water marshland; to all intents and purposes the birds are opposite numbers in the two habitats.

The rails constitute a world-wide and cosmopolitan family; they are found on all continents (except Antarctica) and many oceanic islands. The expression "thin as a rail" no doubt came from the birds' remarkable ability to slink through narrow, seemingly impenetrable openings in their densely vegetated habitat. Our rails are all birds of marshlands, wet meadows, and such places. They are always secretive, sticking to the ground, rarely flying. That they are perfectly able to fly is obvious from their migratory travels, but fortunate is the observer who has ever actually seen any rail fly a significant distance. They swim efficiently, although this feat is rarely seen either.

The reluctance of these birds to reveal themselves was vividly illustrated in my first sight of a king rail in Toronto. The bird was on a little island in an artificial waterfowl pond in High Park, in the west end of the city. It was surlily skulking beneath a dense willow bush, the branches of which drooped well out over the water. At first, it was quite impossible to see, but then someone noticed its reflection in the still water, which was quite identifiable. We watched the bird at length, but only through its image. The steadfastly hiding rail hadn't though of *that!*

Difficult though it was to observe on that occasion, the king rail is not as a rule quite so retiring as many of its relatives. Given the right opportunity and a share of luck, you can sometimes see this species out in the open. But don't count on it. Its voice is always a good give-away: a sort of deep *bup-bup-bup*, with clicking variations on the basic theme. Like so many marsh birds, most rails are quite vocal.

The king rail is limited in distribution in Canada, and has occurred as a breeding bird only in a narrow belt along the north shores of Lakes Erie and Ontario from Lake St. Clair to Toronto. It is much more common in the eastern half of the United States, wintering in the south-east and along the shores of the Gulf of Mexico.

Length 17 inches.   Male, Louisiana, April 17.

plate 18 — the sketch

VIRGINIA RAIL

Rallus limicola

plate 18 ## VIRGINIA RAIL *Rallus limicola*

*T*HIS bird looks to all intents and purposes like a miniature king rail, but it is much more common in Canada than its larger relative. In situations where size comparison is impossible, its grey cheeks readily identify the Virginia rail.

You will hear rails far more often than you will actually see one. The voice of this species sounds to me somewhat like that of a wood frog: a sort of metallic *ka-dick, ka-dick, or ka-duck, ka-duck*. Like all of its relatives, however, it has a wide repertoire, and many and irregular are the rail sounds you can hear in any large marsh after summer nightfall. On these occasions, it is accepted practice to lob small stones or sticks into the marsh. The rails, startled, will often respond with an identifiable cluck or other call, sending the birders home content. Lister Sinclair, with whom I have spent many such evenings, claims to be undisputed champion at scoring direct hits on the heads of rails in utter darkness. This must be what happens, he says, because he never hears anything further from them. Sinclair's most frequent victim is the elusive yellow rail.

Despite its name, the Virginia rail occurs all across southern Canada, except for mountainous and arid regions. Almost any sort of fresh-water marsh situation seems to suit it, including even brackish areas of light salinity. It winters from southern British Columbia through to the southern states and Central America. In view of its conspicuously weak and unimpressive flight on those rare occasions when it flushes, it is hard to comprehend how the bird could manage such long migratory journeys. Unquestionably it is a more efficient bird aloft than its summer behaviour would indicate.

The nest is built of woven marsh vegetation just a few inches above the water, and may contain eight or ten eggs. Downy young rails are black, which has sometimes led to erroneous reports of the black rail in Canada – a bird which, except on extraordinary occasions, does not occur in this country. Young Virginia rails are very active immediately after hatching, and can swim and dive, as well as run among the reeds. This is one of several species that occasionally, but not as a matter of practice, lay eggs in the nests of other birds.

Length 9¹/₂ inches.   Duncan, British Columbia, January 26.

plate 19 — the sketch

SORA

Porzana carolina

plate 19 SORA *Porzana carolina*

THE little sora's is the characteristic voice of marshes and other wetlands everywhere in Canada from the Mackenzie southward, except for western British Columbia and the northern part of Newfoundland. Its unmistakable descending whinny and querulous springtime whistle *ker-wee?* (Peterson) are among the first bird calls the beginner learns and retains with some confidence. This ubiquitous species is by far the most abundant of our rails. It is an adaptable bird, and seems to be able to find a living for itself in the most unpromising habitat circumstances. The merest little slough or tiny pond surrounded by green vegetation will attract and support a pair of soras. Large marshes are filled with them.

The sora's nest is constructed of grasses and leaves, cuplike, and fastened to the stems of taller marsh plants. Both sexes incubate the dozen or so eggs (a record of 18 exists) which are stacked in layers. The young are active swimmers at birth. One observer watched a young sora actually hatching: it rolled out of the egg, tumbled over the side of the nest, and swam away. At this stage, the young bird is a very peculiar sight. It is a roly-poly bunch of fuzzy black feathers accented by a brilliant patch of orange at the throat, and a yellow bill with a swollen red base.

During the spring and summer, soras live to a great extent on insects and other small marsh animals. In fall they turn vegetarian, and concentrate on the seeds of aquatic plants such as wild rice. On this high-calorie fare they fatten rapidly, building strength and stamina for their long trip southward, which may take them to the Gulf states and California, or to northern and central South America.

Our only other short-billed rail is the yellow rail, which is a bird of considerable mystery in Canada. It nests north to James Bay and the Mackenzie in shallow, short-grass marshes, and to the south has bred no more than thiry to forty miles north of Toronto, but its nest is rarely found. This bird, which is even smaller than a sora (7 inches), seems about as willing to flush as a mouse would be. The only sure way to see one is to catch it. It's best to try this at night. It has been accomplished (in my presence, exactly once) by getting a "fix" on a calling bird with two or more flashlights and then moving in on it. One night at the Holland Marsh, north of Toronto, my friend Jim Baillie caught one with a stab that would have done credit to a professional shortstop. I had heard them many times over the years, but that was only the second yellow rail I had ever seen. The yellow rail can be induced to reveal itself through its voice. You resort to the simple expedient of rapping two pebbles together in a special rhythm: *click-click; click-click-click.* As often as not, the bird will respond.

Soras require no such strategems. They are usually quite vocal, and if the observer waits long enough and patiently enough, they can be readily watched at twilight, whether morning or evening, as they carefully make their way around the edges of open water in search of their invertebrate food.

Length 8³/₄ inches.   Male, Toronto, Ontario, May 13.

plate 20 – the sketch

COMMON GALLINULE
Gallinula chloropus

plate 20   # COMMON GALLINULE *Gallinula chloropus*

THE old name for this species was "Florida gallinule," which was inappropriate on at least two counts. First, the bird is cosmopolitan, and on this continent breeds northward into southern Ontario and extreme south-western Quebec. Second, *the* gallinule of Florida, which only rarely comes much farther north, is the purple gallinule, smaller and brilliantly coloured. Its range extends from the Gulf states to South America; occasional wanderers have turned up in Canada.

This is the Old World moorhen, one of the more widely distributed of birds, which occurs on all continents except Australia (where it is replaced by a relative) and, of course, Antarctica. Despite its somewhat chicken-like appearance and its occasionally ducklike behaviour, it is a member of the rail family that has taken more to the open water and, indeed, more to the drier land, than most of its marsh-dwelling relatives.

The common gallinule is identified by its dark body with white on the sides and under the tail, and by its red bill and frontal shield. Notice that its feet, like those of the rails, are not webbed or lobed. It swims perfectly well nonetheless, with a characteristic forward bob of the head at each stroke of the foot.

Few fresh-water marshes within its range are without the common gallinule, which seems to prefer areas that are broken with bits of open water. It will often make use of grassy or reedy ponds that are surprisingly small. The bird seems to be very good at looking after itself, and is not as fussy as some of its kin. It will make itself at home even within cities, if parks, golf courses, or other such areas provide even the least bit of appropriate habitat. In Europe I have noticed that this species is much more tame and fearless than it is in North America. Here, although it will live in close proximity with man, it is still shy. In Old World parks you will often see moorhens walking about on the grass like so many domestic pigeons.

Its long toes serve the gallinule well when it makes its way about a marsh. As it walks on the floating vegetation, from lily pad to lily pad, it reminds you of the more extreme jacanas of the tropics. When it is not picking its way along on foot, finding bits of vegetation and small animal life, the gallinule tips up like a dabbling duck, white bottom in the air.

The shallow nest is a flat affair made of marsh plants, sometimes partly floating, sometimes more firmly secured to the reeds and mud. Occasionally the bird has a delightful way of decorating its nest with bright objects such as pieces of flowers and bits of paper. During courtship, the male makes the best possible use of his limited adornments, displaying his brilliant red bill and flashing the snowy feathers beneath his tail. This species is known to go in for a form of symbolic nest-moulding during its courtship performance, in the course of which it may build a number of "dummy" nests. Some of these structures may be used as stand-by platforms at a later date, when the young hatch.

Ten or a dozen eggs are laid. The newly hatched chicks are covered with fluffy black down; they have red bills and a most peculiar, semi-naked, red "tonsure" on the top of the head. They swim immediately but are cared for by the hen for about a month, at which point she is preparing for her second brood of the year, and it is time for them to go their separate ways. By this time the young birds resemble the adults, but are duller and paler.

Gallinules are notoriously noisy birds. This is especially irritating in view of the fact that they are often so difficult to see. Many of their notes are quite chicken-like, and a large spring pond with every gallinule in full throat often sounds like a henyard. Other notes include a peculiar sort of "laughter," and sundry croaks and chuckles.

Length 13¹/₂ inches. Wingspread 1³/₄ feet.   Male, S. Toronto, Ontario, July 6.

plate 21 — the sketch

AMERICAN COOT

Fulica americana

plate 21 AMERICAN COOT *Fulica americana*

*A*LTHOUGH coots look superficially very like gallinules (or moorhens), notice especially the difference in their toes. A gallinule has long, slim toes like those of typical rails; a coot has extraordinary swollen lobes which remind you of the foot of the unrelated grebe. On the grebe, though the entire toe is lobed; with the coot, it is a *series* of independent lobes. The net effect is the same, however — better propulsion in the water. The white frontal shield is a good field mark; the gallinule's is red.

The coot is even more ducklike than the gallinule, when it is on the water. It swims and dives constantly; unlike most of the rail family it is very gregarious: it even consorts with flocking ducks to a great extent in the non-breeding season. In both structure and behaviour, it is the most aquatic of its family. Like a loon or a grebe, it has difficulty getting off the water in a hurry, and has to taxi long distances before it can become airborne. Often when you disturb a large flock of coots, they will scurry and splash their way across the water in a pseudo-take-off which never actually materializes; the birds just settle down again in another part of the lake or pond.

Coots are highly sociable at all seasons, but they are also notably aggressive and quarrelsome. Especially at breeding time, ponds and lakes are filled with the noise of their splashing, squawking, ill-tempered disputes. Here, the large sharplyclawed toes come into play as they lock in what William Whitehead so accurately described as "foot-to-foot combat." The sounds they make at these times are almost indescribable, but Richard Pough has summarized the descriptions as "croaks, toots, grunts, cackles, coughs, quacks, coos, whistles, squawks, chuckles, clucks, wails and froglike plunks and grating sounds." Which seems to pretty well cover it.

Safety in numbers seems to be the coot's policy in the winter, when very great flocks gather on lakes and other open water. At the approach of a potential enemy such as an eagle, hundreds of coots have been seen to jam together in a solid, compressed mass of slate-grey feathers, much in the way in which a large, loose flock of starlings will often "ball" at the sight of a hawk.

Coots are confirmed migrants, but do not as a rule travel in large flocks, as so many other birds do. H. Albert Hochbaum, of the Delta Waterfowl Research Station in Manitoba, says that coots travel singly, but that these individual birds make up large aggregations that apparently fly within hearing distance of each other. Sometimes they do it the hard way. In *The Migrations of Birds*, Jean Dorst reports upon a remarkable observation made by A. G. Prill, who "found American coots moving northward overland *(on foot!)* in the driest zones of an immense swampy area in Oregon during May, 1929. At least 8,000 birds marched past one spot in a morning, and Prill estimated that 10,000 or more crossed the area in four days." Other birds migrate on foot (the flightless Emperor penguin of the Antarctic has no choice in the matter); we are told that the wild turkey used to do so in the eastern part of this continent.

There are coots of one kind and another on six continents. Ours has a rather scattered breeding range in Canada, with its centre of abundance on the Prairies, but coots are found here and there in most southern parts of the country, from British Columbia to New Brunswick.

Length 15 inches. Wingspread 2¹/₄ feet.   Male, Toronto East, Ontario, May 20.

plate 22 — the sketch

KILLDEER

Charadrius vociferus

plate 22   ## KILLDEER *Charadrius vociferus*

THE most prevalent and familiar plover in Canada earned its vernacular name from one of its call-notes, and its specific name *vociferus* from the manner in which it delivers those calls. From British Columbia to the western Maritimes, all of southern Canada resounds to the shrill voice of the killdeer in spring and summer. Save possibly the robin, no native species is more conspicuous or more widely known.

There can be few if any indigenous birds (excepting, perhaps, the horned lark) that have been such obvious beneficiaries of the settlement of North America. Pastures, airports, cultivated fields, and flat waste areas of all kinds have provided optimum habitat for the adaptable killdeer, which must have increased substantially since Europeans arrived on this continent. It is unlike most shorebirds; it does not need water or watery places for nesting, and it can move to and make use of every scrape and scar the bulldozer and the earth-mover leave in their wake. Roadsides and railroad beds are used, and, occasionally, even parking lots.

The only thing a killdeer needs is a flat, open view. There is no nest as such; the merest hollow in the ground will do, with a few bits of grass for lining. The four eggs are buffy with dark markings. They are magnificently camouflaged and, in a sense, there is no real need for a nest; the colour of the eggs is their best concealment. It is interesting that if you do happen to spot them, and for any reason disarrange them in the nest, the adult killdeer will place them back in the right position again, with their narrow ends all pointing together. Presumably it is easier for her to cover them that way; they take up less room. Also, it is probable that there is less heat loss this way, or that it is greatly slowed down.

The adult killdeer itself is well camouflaged, despite the fact that it can be conspicuous when it chooses. If it remains perfectly still, the disruptive pattern of its markings (as opposed to the cryptic camouflage of the eggs) breaks up its outline, and the bird becomes just another scattering of small pebbles and their shadows. But when it is alarmed, all caution vanishes, and the excited bird uses voice and plumage, feathers and posture, in what appear to be frantic attempts to "distract" you from its nest.

The killdeer is world famous in this respect; it is the classic example cited in all reference to the distraction displays of birds. One must be careful, however, not to impute the wrong kind of motivation to the bird. It seems that this electrifying performance is the result of conflicting urges on the part of the killdeer: the urge to escape and the urge to protect its brood. The two tend to cancel each other out, with the result that the bird flutters about awkwardly and noisily, giving every appearance of being injured (the "broken-wing act"), and thus easily available prey. This act has the *effect* of distracting the attention of a predator from the nest or chicks to the adult bird – but it always stays well out of range. This mechanism, if we can call it that, certainly gets results, but we should not allow ourselves to think that the bird does it *consciously*.

Many birds do this type of displaying, most of them shorebirds, of which the avocet is possibly the most striking. But in my experience, the most unusual species to put on this act was a short-eared owl in the Galapagos Islands. With Roger Perry, I was photographing one of its young on the ground, when the adult owl launched a very elaborate "broken-wing" performance. When that failed to distract us from the young bird, the old owl sailed over and cracked me on the head. That worked.

The killdeer is an early arrival in spring, and late to leave in the fall. It is a hardy bird and a strong flier, and has turned up from time to time in Europe.

Length 10 inches. Wingspread 20 inches.   *Female, Massett, Q.C.I., April 23*

plate 23 — the sketch

AMERICAN WOODCOCK
Philohela minor

plate 23

AMERICAN WOODCOCK *Philohela minor*

You might say that the woodcock looks like a parody – or at least a grossly overdrawn and biased illustration – of adaptation and specialization to a narrow way of life. Certainly it has gone a long way for a sandpiper in committing itself to a limited field of activity: a life spent almost entirely on the ground in search of earthworms. But it must be said that no bird catches them more efficiently, and that where suitable habitat is available, the woodcock is a highly successful species.

This is not an obvious bird in the sense that a killdeer or a kingfisher is, and chances are that most people will never see one. But it is by no means rare, and if it is difficult to find at other times of the year, the sounds it emits in the springtime in its evening courtship display are easily identifiable. The woodcock inhabits alder swamps and other dense, moist thickets where the soil is soft and rich and the cover abundant. On the ground, its cryptic camouflage makes it almost impossible to see, but the ardour of springtime gives it away every time.

The male takes up station to sing in a small opening in an alder swale or other wet second growth. The sound he delivers falls somewhere between the nasal *beent!* of a common nighthawk and a human "raspberry" (the only man who can imitate it is Richard M. Saunders of the University of Toronto). After giving several of these notes, the bird takes to the air, circling a good distance upward, and then he slips, swoops and spirals downward, twittering gently as he descends. This elaborate and engaging performance continues all night long, if the moon is full, and only stops completely if the night is utterly dark. It serves to notify females, who are on adjacent territories of their own, that it

is time for mating. Firm pairs are not formed, and the birds may mate with various neighbours. Nesting and incubation are left to the females.

Structurally, the woodcock is perfectly designed for its specialty. If you are going to make a career of standing around with your bill deep in the ground, it pays to have a good range of eyesight. The bird's very large eyes are so placed in the skull that it has a greater range of binocular vision to the rear (where it needs it most) than it has to the front. The bill is long and slender, with a flexible tip; it can probe down to about three inches in soft soil in its never-ceasing pursuit of earthworms. A very short neck and diminutive legs have obvious value in keeping everything close to the ground.

Its diet of earthworms has alarmed many people who are interested in woodcocks. Earthworms and certain other invertebrates can store in their bodies substantial quantities of toxic pesticides, without being killed. A concentrated dose of the poison is then passed on to the bird that eats the worm. (The insidious chain from DDT to elm leaf to earthworm to robin has been well documented.) It is feared that woodcock on their wintering grounds in the southern United States may in this way pick up more pesticidal residues than is good for them – as a species. The same may be true in the eastern part of their Canadian range, where so much aerial spraying for spruce budworm control has been carried out in the last decade. Studies of this question are in progress and, happily, research efforts are being intensified all the time.

The woodcock's range in Canada extends from south-eastern Manitoba across southern Ontario and extreme southern Quebec, through to the Maritimes and the lower tip of Newfoundland.

Length 11 inches. Wingspread 18 inches. Male, Coboconk, Ontario, October 18.

plate 24 — the sketch

SPOTTED SANDPIPER

Actitis macularia

plate 24 SPOTTED SANDPIPER *Actitis macularia*

Wherever there is water in Canada, southward from the northern Yukon, Labrador and Newfoundland, you will find the spotted sandpiper — the most wide-ranging and commonest of its family. It seems that no pond, stream, lake, or river is without its complement of these beguiling little birds, whose thin whistles are heard from coastal tide pools to spruce-rimmed tarns of the far north. This is invariably the first sandpiper with which the new birdwatcher will become familiar, and it is one of the easiest to identify.

The conspicuous dark spots on breast and belly are seen only on adult birds in summer. Young, and winter adults, are clear white below. But the "spotty" is immediately recognizable in any plummage by its voice, its tilting, teetering behaviour on the ground, and its unusual flight. The voice is a thin, plaintively whistled *peep* or *pee-wee*, or a series of these. Whether standing or walking, the bird constantly tilts its rear end up and down in an amusing nervous action, the reason for which is not understood. This habit is so deeply ingrained in the species that young hatchlings begin to do it almost immediately. I have seen downy little chicks out of the egg only a matter of hours, tipping and bobbing every bit as much as the adults.

The flight is especially distinctive. When the bird is flushed (and you will often get very close to one before seeing it), it will give a few alarmed calls and then flutter away along the shore with bowed, stiffly vibrating wings held apparently below the horizontal; it soon comes to rest again and resumes its fidgety teetering. Although it seems a weak flier, it travels as far as central South America.

A number of observers have reported on the surprising underwater behaviour of this small sandpiper. Henry Marion Hall was one of these. In *A Gathering of Shorebirds* he says, "While fishing in the Housatonic River in Connecticut I once came upon a spotted sandpiper with a brood of chicks about one-third grown. I tried to catch one of the lively sprites but it dived from the margin of the stream and swam away underwater, using its small wings vigorously."

George M. Sutton wrote in *The Auk* of a similar experience with a grown bird. "When the bird first flushed, its wings were fully spread, and it was headed for the open water of the lake. Upon seeing me towering above it, however, it turned its course abruptly downward, and without the slightest hesitation flew straight into the water. With wings fully outspread and legs kicking, it made its way rather slowly along the sandy bottom, until it was about eight feet out, in water three feet deep. I pursued the bird, thinking at the time, strangely enough, that it was wounded. When I reached it, it tried to go farther but apparently could not. Bubbles of air came from its mouth, and air bubbles were plainly seen clinging to the plumage of its back. At the time it was captured its mouth, eyes and wings were all open, under water, and it remained at the bottom seemingly without difficulty. As it lay in my hands above water it seemed tired for a second or two, and then, without warning shook itself a little, leaped into the air, and with loud, clear whistles, circled off a few inches above the water to a distant point of land."

Spotted sandpipers rarely nest far from water. The nest is an informal matter — just a scrape or shallow depression in the ground, thinly lined with grass. It may be in the open, or under a stump or shrub. Four eggs are normally laid; they are buffish, with dark blotches and spots.

Length 7¹/₂ inches. Wingspread 13¹/₂ inches.   Female, Laird, Algoma Dist., Ontario, June 13.

plate 25 — the sketch

RING-BILLED GULL

Larus delawarensis

plate 25

RING-BILLED GULL *Larus delawarensis*

Iɴ the first half of the 19th century, John James Audubon was under the impression that this was the commonest gull in North America. Although it may have been so at that time, this species is quite sensitive to disturbance, and many of the eastern colonies have been deserted in the intervening years. (But there are degrees of disturbance, and the birds' sensitivity could scarcely be blamed for the loss of a valued Montreal gull colony to the building of Expo 67.) However, nearly all the gulls seem to be prospering nowadays, for reasons not really understood, and despite its eviction from many favoured places in the east, the ring-bill has held its own, or even increased, elsewhere.

Gulls are very adaptable birds. Both this species and the California gull of the Prairies have learned to take advantage of agriculture. Great noisy flocks follow the farmers' ploughs and harrows, picking up insects and their larvae as they are exposed. And they are quick to take advantage of garbage dumps. This flexible opportunism of gulls so far as human activities are concerned has posed one of the great bird problems of our time – the increasing incidence of bird strikes on jet aircraft. A bird sucked into the intake of a jet engine can cause severe damage; birds fly at relatively low altitudes, and jet aircraft are especially vulnerable at takeoff and landing. Airports have attracted great numbers of gulls, right across the country, as airstrips are splendid places for sunning and loafing. Also, in the past, it has always seemed that the open spaces between runways and around airports were prime sites for the establishment of garbage dumps, or even for cultivation, both of which attract gulls by the thousands. The entire ecology of airports is now under study, so that the environment may be made less attractive to birds and thus somewhat safer for jets – and people.

The problem of birds at airports has led to other fascinating studies. William Gunn has been working intensively for several years on the detection of bird movements, including migration, by radar, so that when a major flight of birds is detected, aircraft traffic can be detoured appropriately. Not only air safety, but also ornithology is the beneficiary of such research programmes; radar and other technological devices are adding immeasurably to our knowledge of the ways of birds.

A strangely patchy breeding distribution in Canada is recorded for the ring-billed gull. It nests across much of the Prairies, in southern Ontario, the north shore of the Gulf of St. Lawrence, and in isolated spots in Labrador, Newfoundland, and elsewhere. We often are inclined to think of gulls as sea-birds, but they are coastal birds at best, never pelagic, and many of them, such as this species, breed in the middle of vast continents.

Although so many of our ring-bills live inland, good numbers are still coastal, and have a remarkable special adaptation for living in a salt water environment. Gulls and sea-birds have little or no access to fresh water in these places, so they are forced to drink sea water. But a bird's kidneys are even less efficient than those of a mammal in coping with salt water; a gull would have to excrete more than two litres of urine to deal with the salt in one litre of sea water, which would be a losing – and dehydrating – proposition. So, there has evolved an auxiliary system of salt disposal – a gland in the head which processes the bird's blood and gets rid of sodium chloride, which drips from the bill in highly concentrated solution. This gland exists in penguins, cormorants, gannets and others, as well as in gulls.

All gulls are consummate fliers; their motion in the air is graced with lightness, buoyancy, and manoeuvrability. They do a great deal of soaring and gliding, but such is their control that ring-billed gulls are expert flycatchers. Major insect hatches in farming country are frequently accompanied by wheeling, darting flocks of elegant ring-bills; it is one of the most attractive aerial performances of any of our birds.

Length 18½ inches. Wingspread 4 feet. Male, Little Lake, Barrie, Ontario, June 23.

plate 26 — the sketch

COMMON TERN
Sterna hirundo

plate 26

COMMON TERN *Sterna hirundo*

THE grace and elegance of the common tern in flight are misleading; it appears a delicate, shimmering wisp of a bird, yet it sustains long-distance flights that demand unparalleled endurance – from central Canada as far as Mexico, the Falkland Islands, and the Straits of Magellan. In the Old World, it nests from Britain to Siberia and winters south to southern Africa, New Guinea, and the Solomons. One vagrant even made it to Fremantle, Western Australia, six months after having been banded as a chick in Sweden.

When we think about the amazing distances some of them travel, we might expect birds to get lost more often than they actually do. Much research has gone into the methods of orientation used by migrants, and common terns have frequently been subjects of experimentation. Jean Dorst tells of common terns released in Connecticut and Maine which "headed immediately south-east if the sun was visible, but not if it was hidden behind heavy clouds. This orientation can probably be attributed to the fact that terns on the east coast of the U.S.A. tend to fly south-east or east when they are lost or released over land. This may be an inherited tendency, for the birds are apparently aware that by flying in this direction they will eventually reach the coast. It is hard to account for all these facts on the basis of simple, visual landmarks. A real sense of orientation seems to exist, one linked with natural phenomena of which man remains unaware."

Migrating terns travel in large flocks, and it has been found that the inhabitants of a colony tend to stick together throughout the year. The young birds move south together in their first fall flight, and this association appears to continue through their lives. The same is true to a great extent of mated pairs, over three-quarters of which remained paired in the following season, in one breeding colony studied.

Tern colonies are notoriously frantic, helter-skelter, noisy places. The degree of nest-building seems to vary with the individual bird; some are attractive cups of dry grass, others are non-existent, with the two to four olive-brownish spotted eggs laid directly on bare rock. The eggs are so well camouflaged that they are surprisingly inconspicuous; the visitor must walk through a tern colony with great care. Adult birds will flutter and plunge about your head, dive-bombing angrily and making an ear-splitting racket. Although they threaten you fiercely, I have yet to be touched by a common tern, whereas the very closely related arctic tern has no qualms about striking your head sharply with its bill. It can be surprisingly painful.

Most colonies of common terns are situated on low, flat, rocky islands in both fresh water and salt. They will also use pebbly spits and other low-elevation places as long as they are sufficiently above high water and protected from mainland predators. The birds have lost so many nesting sites in our time that when they occupy a new one it is noteworthy. That this happens at least occasionally, even with today's general scarification of the landscape, was illustrated recently. Dredging and filling associated with the "development" of Toronto Island resulted in the creation of a long, low bed of sand and gravel fill. Almost as soon as this new, artificial habitat appeared, the terns moved in – the first nesting of this species ever recorded in the Toronto area. Such is the readiness of wild birds to take advantage of whatever crumbs we see fit (even inadvertently) to throw them.

Length 15 inches. Wingspread 2¹/₂ feet.   Male, Favourable Lake Mine, Ontario, July 21.

plate 27 — the sketch

MOURNING DOVE
Zenaidura macroura

plate 27   MOURNING DOVE *Zenaidura macroura*

With the exception of the introduced Old World rock dove (domestic pigeon), the mourning dove is the most numerous and widely ranging of its family in North America. It nests from coast to coast in Canada, but only in a rather slim belt in the southernmost part of the country. That this coincides nicely with the bulk of human settlement may be more than sheer accident. The mourning dove is one of the comparatively few forms of native wildlife to which human occupation of the continent could well have been a positive advantage.

Ideal mourning dove habitat is open, sparse meadows and pastures for feeding, with woodlots and hedges for cover and nesting. Agricultural development has created an abundance of such country. Ironically, some soil-mining on our part does not bother the bird; it rather likes its grassland to have lots of bare spots. Weed seeds are staples, and we have managed to produce plenty of *them.* Also, mile after mile of wide cornfields have added to the availability of winter food and cover, and in southernmost Ontario good numbers of the birds manage to over-winter. They are not reluctant to live in city parks; their fearlessness and willingness to take up permanent residence at such close quarters with man has undoubtedly built up their numbers in the last few human generations.

A dove's nest is a somewhat unattractive and insubstantial construction of small twigs, nearly always on a horizontal branch well above our eye level. It is built solely by the female, with materials provided by the male. Two pure white eggs are incubated by both parents for about two weeks. The new hatchlings, like those of all pigeons and doves, are fed for the first little while on "milk." This highly nutritious substance, which is provided by both parents, is strikingly similar to the milk of mammals, protein-rich and high in fats. It is produced by an upsurge in the production of cells in the lining of the crop, which are then shed in great quantities and fed to the young in a form that resembles curds. For the first few days this is the only food the nestlings take; then they graduate to regurgitated masses of small weed seeds and the more familiar pigeon mast. The young are brooded almost continuously until they are surprisingly large.

In a quantitative sense the mourning dove is an extremely important game bird in the southern United States; the annual kill runs into millions. The bird is a swift, whistling flier, and no doubt tests a gunner's speed and control, but I have often wondered at the rewards involved in shooting a four ounce bird. After cleaning, it would hardly seem worth the effort; I suspect that substantially fewer may reach the table than are annually shot down. An open season on mourning doves was declared one year in Ontario, but such was the public outcry that it was not continued. In the northern parts of their range, mourning dove populations have a difficult enough time getting through the winter without having to endure a prior decimation in an autumn shooting season.

The bird's name derives from its voice: a mournful, repetitious cooing that has a strange ventriloquistic quality. In appearance it is superficially like (though much smaller and duller) the extinct passenger pigeon, which paid with its existence for the greed and ignorance of the second half of the 19th century. Paradoxically, settlement destroyed the one species and helped the other.

Length 12 inches.   Male, Christchurch Parish, South Carolina, May 11.

plate 28 — the sketch

YELLOW-BILLED CUCKOO

Coccyzus americanus

plate 28 YELLOW-BILLED CUCKOO *Coccyzus americanus*

THAT such a strikingly handsome bird as this should be so infuriatingly secretive and shy is one of the crosses the birdwatcher must learn to bear. Occasionally you will glimpse one in flight, in which case the large white tips on the tail feathers combined with a reddish flash on the wings will identify it. But make sure you recognize it quickly; it will immediately dart into the most impenetrable thicket, where it will skulk immobile for an eternity, crouching round-shouldered in the deepest shadow. A rare glimpse at close quarters will reveal the yellow lower mandible, though viewing at that range is difficult with cuckoos.

The world-wide family of cuckoos is a very large one, comprising some 130 species, and including such North American birds as roadrunners and anis. The best-known member of the family seems to be the European cuckoo, whose voice is one of the few bird songs that nearly everybody recognizes. This and certain other Old World cuckoos are parasitic: they lay their eggs in the nests of other birds, banking on the maternal instincts of the foster-mother to see the young cuckoo on the wing. This practice has become so specialized that in some areas the eggs of the cuckoos have come to resemble those of their favourite victims. Even more remarkable is the fact that more than one "clan" of cuckoos can co-exist in the same locality, each "clan" producing eggs resembling those of its usual host. New World cuckoos are not parasitic as a rule, although there are occasional instances of it in this species. It has even been known to lay in the nest of its cousin, the black-billed cuckoo, which is also known to have returned the compliment.

This is a more southern bird than the black-billed, and its range in Canada is correspondingly restricted: the extreme southern portion of British Columbia, southern Ontario, and the bottom tip of New Brunswick. Cuckoos appear to vary a great deal in numbers from year to year and, in spring migration in the east, one year one species will predominate, the next year, the other. But that is a local condition; the black-billed cuckoo ranges much more widely in Canada as a breeding bird.

Cuckoos are known wanderers, and often seem to be caught up in autumn storms. They are not the strongest fliers in the world, preferring to feed in dense shrubbery near the ground, and rarely moving any distance; perhaps their chances of being carried by weather systems are greater than those of the more aerial birds. This species has been recorded in the Maritimes and Newfoundland, and has even turned up in Europe.

Young cuckoos are fantastic creatures; like newly hatched pelicans and cormorants, they seem to advertise their reptilian ancestry more blatantly than most birds. Lester Snyder and Shelley Logier found a yellow-billed cuckoo's nest at Long Point, Ontario. "The young were quite active when disturbed. They scrambled about the bush, using the wings and bill for climbing. One young which was brought to our camp demonstrated a remarkable reptile-like behaviour. When it was placed on the table and one reached to pick it up, it erected its somewhat horny plumage and emitted a buzzing hiss like the sound of bees escaping from a tunnel in dry grass. This performance was certainly unbirdlike in all respects." C. E. Bendire described the newly hatched young as "repulsive, black, and greasy-looking creatures, nearly naked, and the sprouting quills only add to their general ugliness." From such modest beginnings comes one of our most elegant birds.

Length 12¹/₄ inches.   Male, Southport, North Carolina, May 11.

plate 29 — the sketch

BLACK-BILLED CUCKOO
Coccyzus erythropthalmus

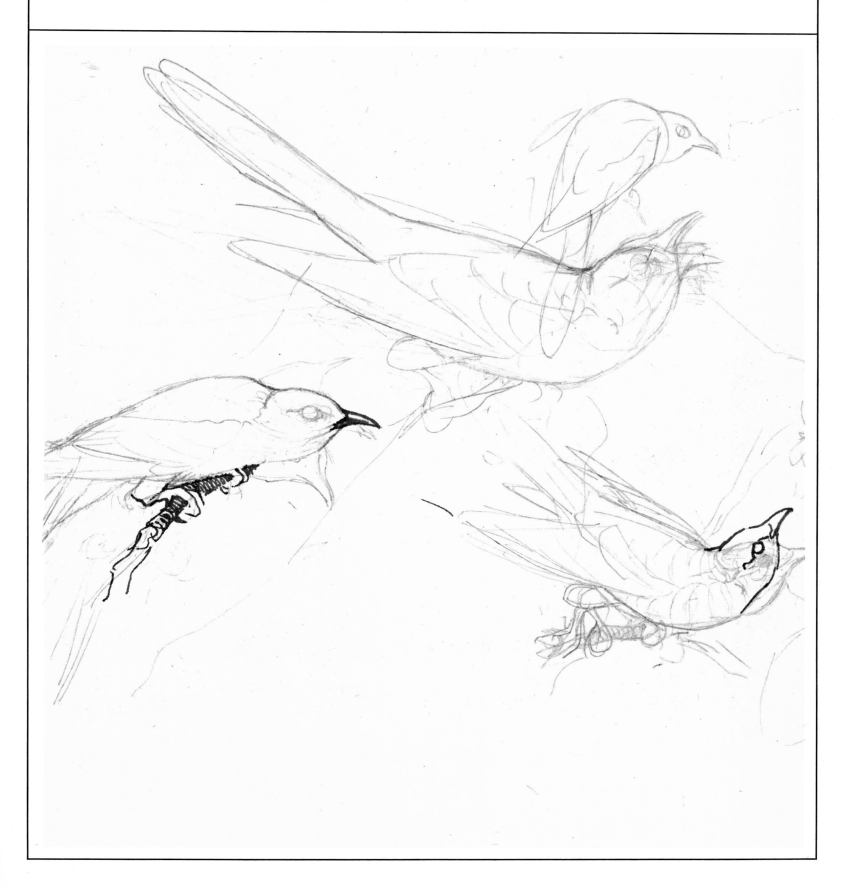

plate 29

BLACK-BILLED CUCKOO *Coccyzus erythropthalmus*

*A*CROSS forested southern Canada east of the Rocky Mountains to the Maritimes, the black-billed cuckoo is the most familiar representative of its family. It is especially noticeable in years of forest tent caterpillar infestation; this and the yellow-billed are among the very few birds that will eat these seemingly unpalatable creatures. They also devour other kinds of hairy caterpillars with evident relish, including the colonial web net builders of wild cherry trees. The stiff spines of their victims do not seem to bother the birds, even though their stomachs are frequently lined with "fur" as the result.

In its furtive, stealthy behaviour this species is essentially like the yellow-bill. The only person I know who can consistently spot a hiding cuckoo is my wife Peggy, who has never satisfactorily explained her technique. The bird sits tight in a dense bush, where its browns and olives blend astonishingly with the shrubbery around it. Sometimes, if it is convinced that you cannot see it, it will allow an unexpectedly close approach. But, once you pass the invisible tolerance line, it will slip sinuously away to another hiding place. The best evidence of its presence, as with the other species, is its voice. In this bird, it consists of a very long string of low notes on the same pitch, delivered in groups in rhythmic sequence. The call of the yellow-bill is more hollow and woody, beginning with a series of clucks that gradually become more drawn-out and slower, dropping off at the end. It sometimes sounds for all the world like a pied-billed grebe.

In *The Birds of Minnesota,* Thomas S. Roberts reported on the peculiar nest-feeding behaviour of this species. "When the old bird returns, the food, which is very likely to be *live* caterpillars, is concealed in the throat. As a nestling raises its head with open mouth and rapidly vibrating wings, the parent thrusts its bill deeply into the open maw and the young bird grasps securely the smooth bill of the old bird, in which action it is greatly aided by several soft papillae or disks in the roof of the mouth. Then, with a slow, pumping motion, the squirming caterpillars are transferred with some difficulty from one mouth to another. The process is a slow one, the birds being attached a minute or more and the transfer aided, apparently, by a sucking effort on the part of the nestling." No doubt the spots in the mouth of the young bird also act as targets or "releasers" for feeding activity by the parent.

Nestling cuckoos look amazingly like prickly little lizards. They are covered with stiff spines, which are the sheaths of feathers forming inside. These sheaths break open almost simultaneously in just a matter of hours, and the bird removes them with its bill. In half a day the bird is transformed from a kind of reptilian urchin into a proper young cuckoo (minus the long tail, which takes a little while longer).

Migrating black-billed cuckoos fly as far south as Colombia, Ecuador, and northern Peru. Sometimes they are recorded in Europe.

Length 11³/₄ inches.   Male, Southport, North Carolina, May 16.

plate 30 — the sketch

BARN OWL

Tyto alba

plate 30

BARN OWL *Tyto alba*

THE "monkey-faced owl" has been the very model for spine-tingling folklore over many centuries. In its appearance, voice, nocturnal habits and most especially its choice of nesting sites (abandoned buildings, belfreys, lofts, ruins, etc.) it does all the things that you *expect* an owl to do. And it does them all surpassingly well. In Canada, it is restricted as a breeding bird to the extreme south-western corner of British Columbia and southern Ontario from Niagara Falls westward. Barn owls of several sorts are found all over the world, but this is the only representative of its family in North America.

Barn owls are quite different from other owls in anatomy and general appearance. The long legs and skinny toes (they look that way because they are more lightly feathered than those of other owls), the small eyes and peculiar shape of the face are all good field marks for this species. Seen in flight from below, the bird appears to be pure white, and even for an owl, the head looks extraordinarily large.

Owls have remarkable eyesight, but they also have incredibly acute hearing. Experiments with this species have shown that the bird's directional hearing enables it to find a prey target accurately by ear alone, in total darkness. It is said to hear most efficiently at frequencies above 9,000 cycles per second. The squeak of a mouse elicits an immediate reaction, as I have found by imitating the sound at night and drawing a barn owl to within a foot or two of my car window.

This bird is very traditional in its nesting sites, using the same place year after year. It does not build a conventional nest, but the debris of many seasons gradually accumulates, producing a kind of soft covering for the floor of a disused attic, church tower, or other suitable location. For many years barn owls nested (hopefully, they do yet) in a silo near Queenston, Ontario. A long ladder allowed access to the nest; the floor surrounding it was littered to a depth of several inches with felt-like pellets of regurgitated indigestible material, and the bones and feathers of small prey species.

The eggs are pure white, and there may be between five and ten or more. Unlike birds such as ducks, which do not begin incubation until the entire clutch of eggs is laid, owls start to incubate with the first. The result is that the young birds vary dramatically in age and size. In years when food supply is ample, all or most of them survive. When the squeeze is on in terms of food, frequently the younger, smaller birds die of starvation or are actually eaten by older and stronger siblings. Barn owls dispose of a great many mice; half-grown young have been observed being fed as many as ten prey items per night. The old birds are kept busy while the young are growing, which can be at almost any time of the year. Barn owls have no defined nesting season.

Since this owl is so adaptable and flexible in the sites it will use for nesting, it is perhaps surprising that it has not dispersed more generally in Canada. An interesting speculation has been made that its spread through New York State in the past few decades was due at least in part to the arrival of electricity, and most especially, of electric refrigeration. As all the old ice-houses fell into disuse, the barn owls moved in!

The most remarkable concentration of barn owls in my experience (even including the numbers in the Florida Keys in winter) is in Guayaquil, port city of Ecuador. Here, the banks of the Guayas River seethe with rats; statuary and other projections on downtown buildings are homes for barn owls, which make a prosperous living from the squalid conditions below.

Length 18 inches.   Male, Corpus Christi, Texas, February 2.

plate 31 – the sketch

SCREECH OWL

Otus asio

plate 31 # SCREECH OWL *Otus asio*

SEVERAL species of owls have "horns," or tufts of feathers, on their heads, but the others are much larger than the little screech owl. It can only be confused with the rare flammulated owl of southern British Columbia, but that bird has dark, not yellow, eyes. The name of the bird is quite absurd; there *are* owls that screech, scream, and shriek, but not this one. Its voice is a low, quavering whistle with a strange tremulous quality; oddly enough, it is easily imitated.

The most singular thing about this small, attractive owl is that it comes in two colour phases. Adult birds may be either grey or reddish: this coloration is permanent, yet it has nothing whatever to do with age, sex, or any other consideration. Both colours may occur in one brood, and mated pairs may be the same or different colours. In my experience the red phase seems to be more common to the south, where the two colours are found about equally. In Canada, the grey phase predominates. The red bird does not occur at all in British Columbia, but there is a darker, brownish subspecies there.

No other Canadian owl habitually and commonly takes up residence in cities. The screech owl must have trees for nesting, usually large ones with natural cavities or old woodpecker holes, and a little bit of open ground to hunt in, but otherwise its requirements are few. I well remember a pair of nesting screech owls in an old oak tree on the University of Toronto campus. One of the birds was so aggressive to passers-by that Professor Richard Saunders, who had to pass that tree on the way to his lectures took to carrying an umbrella with which to protect himself.

The food habits of screech owls, like those of all birds of prey, vary with the seasonal abundance of their victims. This is a small bird that takes proportionately small prey. It is always on the lookout for frogs and mice, of course, but in season it will catch great numbers of moths, June bugs, grasshoppers, crickets, and such small fry. In winter, when times are somewhat harder, the sedentary owls must work a little more strenuously, and they often turn to bird-eating. But there are lots of house sparrows to keep them going in the cities, and the owls' effect on the native bird population must be minimal.

Generally the only glimpse you get of a screech owl at home is of its little face and "ears" framed in the opening of its nesting hole in a tree. Even when you cannot see the bird, if you know the hole is inhabited, sometimes a few sharp raps on the bark will prompt it to peer out at you. If the bird is caught away from home, it will sit motionless as close to the trunk as possible, relying on its excellent camouflage. If it thinks it is being observed, it will perceptibly shrink in girth and stretch in height, stiffly erecting its head tufts in an apparent attempt to become a part of the tree itself.

In North America, screech owls range from Alaska to Mexico; in Canada, they nest regularly only in south-western British Columbia, the south-eastern Prairies, and southern Ontario.

*Length 10 inches.   Male, Ellendale, Delaware, March 24.
Male, Dagsboro, Delaware, January 18.*

plate 32 — the sketch

BARRED OWL

Strix varia

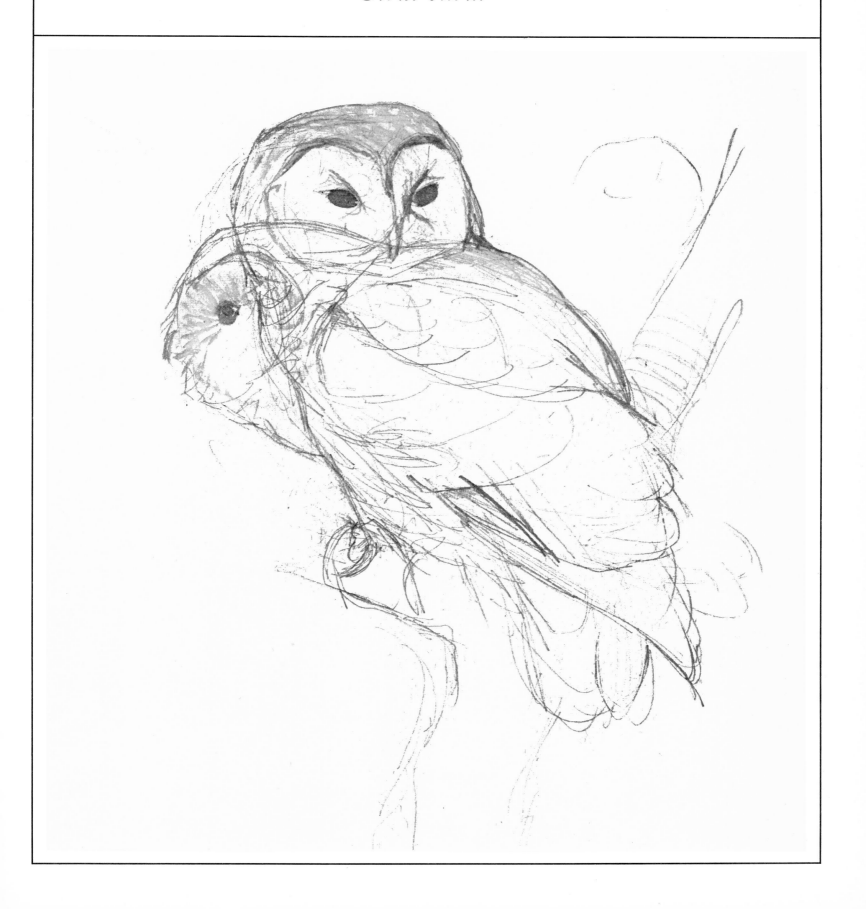

plate 32

BARRED OWL *Strix varia*

Its round, tuftless head and dark eyes distinguish this large fluffy owl from all others except the scarce spotted owl of south-western British Columbia, a much darker bird with no stripes on the lower part of its body. The barred is a fairly common owl, as owls go, throughout the forested parts of southern Canada, from central British Columbia to the Maritimes. This is the northern limit of its range, which extends through the United States to Central America.

This is a woodland species that only occasionally ventures into the cities. It prefers dense stands of deciduous forest and, for such a large bird, makes its way among the trees with remarkable finesse. It has a mild and gentle disposition for a big owl, and rarely tackles such formidable prey as does the great horned owl. It limits itself to things the size of frogs or lizards, with mice the major part of its diet, but it is sprightly enough to pick up grouse chicks occasionally. At night I have seen one hawking in mid-air at moths attracted to a floodlight. Sometimes it catches and eats lesser owls.

The usual voice of the barred owl is distinctive, and easy to imitate. It consists of a series of hollow hoots in a certain rhythm: *Who cooks for you? Who cooks for you-all?* The bird will often call in the daytime (at a distance it sounds like a dog barking),

and if you respond, sometimes it will come up to you. Around the nest, the birds give a variety of other deep-throated notes.

Nesting is usually in a hollow tree, but the bird has also been known to use the abandoned nests of hawks or crows, as a great horned owl does. Once Fred K. Truslow, the distinguished bird photographer, showed me a barred owl's nest on the ground in Florida's Everglades National Park, but that is exceptional. Birds have been known to return to the same nest, or to the immediate vicinity, for as long as twenty to twenty-five years, according to Alexander Sprunt, Jr.

Since barred owls can often be approached quite closely, they are frequent victims of the traditional prejudice which for so long has surrounded all birds of prey. A boy with a .22 rifle finds a big owl a fetching target, and not enough parents yet recognize the positive, beneficial influence of predatory animals in the wildlife community. The barred owl is an especially inoffensive animal, weakly equipped for killing, which does no harm whatever and a great deal of good. It is legally protected now in most parts of the continent, which it richly deserves, but many still fall before the weapons of the uninformed and the indifferent. We remain a frontier people in many ways.

Length 20 inches.   Male, West Point, New York, January 28.

plate 33 — the sketch

SAW-WHET OWL

Aegolius acadicus

plate 33   SAW-WHET OWL *Aegolius acadicus*

THE exceptional tameness of this little owl is well known. It can readily be approached, touched, and even caught in the hand. I have done so on many occasions. Before a general "clean-up" of Toronto's lakeshore took place several years ago, numbers of saw-whets used to rest in dense willow jungles during their fall migration. Many were banded, but many more were killed or injured by unthinking children. Some of these disabled birds were caught and cared for by local birdwatchers.

One such bird in particular which I took home with me shed some interesting light on owls in general. This one had suffered a broken leg and a damaged wing, both of which healed in due course, and eventually the bird was as good as new. I lived at that time in an unusually dark and almost windowless apartment; the owl had the free run of it. As night came on, it would perch on a select lampshade in the hall. Then, as everyone went to bed and began turning out lights, it would follow from room to room until the last bulb was extinguished. At this point, the trouble would start. In complete darkness, with no light source at all, the bird would panic, fluttering about in the hall until someone would get up and turn on its lamp. There it would perch contentedly all night long. Of course owls can see no better in complete darkness than we can; their famed eyesight is a matter of being able to make do with the absolute minimum of illumination.

My bird did very well on a diet of liver and chicken heads; after a day or so of forced feeding it ate readily. It did so well, in fact, that when the time came for its release it was quite unwilling to leave. I repeatedly turned it loose from the back porch, but each time it would slip back through the kitchen door before it shut. Only after I threatened it with a broom did it finally take its leave. The children of the house missed it, and would mournfully gaze at its favourite perch, an empty quart soda bottle on top of the refrigerator, which remained for some time as a souvenir. (The bird's lampshade had long since been dealt with.)

The name of this bird derives from one of the noises it is reported to make, which has been likened to the sound of a saw being filed. My own experience with its voice is limited to one occasion. Fenwick Lansdowne and I once heard a saw-whet in Ontario's Muskoka country, which gave an interminable series of soft metallic *pings* somewhat like the sound of water dripping.

The saw-whet owl is found in deep woodlands from coast to coast in southern Canada. Its range somewhat overlaps that of the more northern and quite similar boreal owl. The latter bird is larger (about 10 inches), with a yellow bill and a dark border around its facial discs. Both nest in holes in trees, the saw-whet usually in the abandoned diggings of flickers and other woodpeckers. Like those of other owls, the five or six eggs of the saw-whet are white.

When they are not nesting, these attractive little birds like to roost in dense shrubby tangles, or in evergreens. Usually they move as close to the centre as possible, often surprisingly near the ground. They are easy to miss; I can remember passing and repassing some small conifer a number of times in the course of a day, only to eventually spot the bird, which had undoubtedly been there all the time.

Small owls are frequently preyed upon by larger owls, and this must be the fate of a good many saw-whets (and may account for their willingness to take their chances close to the ground). Bird banders in Toronto who had ringed several of these birds in migration once found one of their saw-whet bands only a day or two later in the regurgitated pellet of a long-eared owl.

Length 8 inches.   Male, Princess Anne, Maryland, December 17.

plate 34 — the sketch

WHIP-POOR-WILL
Caprimulgus vociferus

plate 34 WHIP-POOR-WILL *Caprimulgus vociferus*

IN south-eastern woodlands, few summer sounds are more commonplace than the voice of this species, and yet there are not many familiar birds that are less frequently seen. Commencing at twilight, and continuing late into the night, the male whip-poor-will endlessly repeats the monotonous and far-carrying song from which it gets its name. The bird may call scores or even hundreds of times without stopping. E. H. Forbush has reported upon the rare patience of John Burroughs, who "made a count which so far as I know exceeds all others. He records that he heard a bird 'lay upon the back of poor Will' 1,088 blows with only a barely perceptible pause here and there, as if to take breath."

Caprimulgus means "goatsucker." A fantastic folk-tale persisted for many generations to the effect that birds of this family descended upon flocks of goats at nightfall to drink their milk. It is not difficult to deduce how the legend was born: the crepuscular and nocturnal habits of this strange, swift, silent-flying bird were peculiar enough, and its enormous mouth seemed made to order for sucking milk. But, in fact, the birds live entirely on invertebrates.

The whip-poor-will is superlatively adapted to its way of life. The bill is quite small, but the open mouth is immense; like a kind of flying funnel, it takes in hapless low-flying moths. Bristles about its gape presumably widen the scope of the trap. On the wing, the bird is surprisingly deft and manoeuvrable, thanks to its long wings and tail. Its dense, soft feathers are very like those of an owl; the result is soundlessness aloft and superb camouflage when the bird is at rest. The legs and feet are small, short, and quite weak, to the point that goatsuckers cannot perch across a twig as other birds do. They must rest horizontally along a branch large enough to accommodate the entire body. Very often they rest directly on the ground.

No nest is built. The two eggs, which may be white, or spotted and blotched, are laid on the ground in the dry leaf litter of the forest floor. Winsor Marrett Tyler, in A. C. Bent's *Life Histories*, gives an appealing description of the downy nestlings. "The little whip-poor-will chick, hatching out from an invisible egg, finds itself lying on the ground, with dead leaves all about. The dead leaves look like the chick, and the chick looks like the dead leaves; no one can tell them apart; practically the chick *is* a dead leaf, and, although hatched, it is still invisible, just as it was when hidden in the egg."

The food of the whip-poor-will consists mostly of those flying insects that are abroad at night – moths, mosquitoes, and others, also crickets and grasshoppers. The bird has been seen to forage awkwardly on the ground, but this behaviour must be exceptional, in view of its anatomical limitations.

Although it is anything but rare, the whip-poor-will is not as abundant as it once was in the region. Its need for dry, well-drained hardwood forests has resulted in its gradual decline, concurrent with that of its essential habitat. C. H. D. Clarke has pointed out that the bird cannot tolerate the presence of large grazing animals in its woods, and as cattle have been turned into so many of our farm woodlots, a very great deal of otherwise perfectly suitable whip-poor-will environment has been at least temporarily destroyed.

Length 9³/₄ inches.   Highland Falls, New York, May 31.

plate 35 — the sketch

COMMON NIGHTHAWK

Chordeiles minor

plate 35 COMMON NIGHTHAWK *Chordeiles minor*

Far from being a hawk, this bird is a goatsucker or nightjar, a relative of the whip-poor-will. But, unlike most other members of its family, is just as likely to be seen in the daytime as at night. The nighthawk is another of the small band of birds that seem to have been helped by human settlement of this continent. Unlike the whip-poor-will, which needs for its nesting woodlands with a carpet of dry leaves, this species likes flat, open, rocky or gravelly places. The pebbled roofs of modern buildings have created a wealth of nighthawk habitat — probably much more than was available to them before our time. As the result, every city and town in Canada from coast to coast (except for Newfoundland) has its full complement of noisy, conspicuous nighthawks.

The birds are especially evident during migration, when large loose flocks move during the daytime and early evening. One of the greatest congregations I have ever seen was on a late-August day in Regina, Saskatchewan, when a vast number of birds flowed like a flat plume of smoke across the prairie sky. (As I write this, in Toronto on Labour Day weekend, my son Peter has just come in to report a flock of at least 100 nighthawks circling overhead just before dusk, right on schedule.)

Nighthawks customarily fly and feed at much greater altitudes than whip-poor-wills, which do their hunting close to the ground. They live entirely on flying insects, which they pursue with darting, erratic, but highly controlled aerobatics. Examination of nighthawk stomachs has been revealing: some contained as many as fifty different species of insects. One bird has eaten 2,175 flying ants. Another contained 34 May beetles (June bugs), a substantial load for a bird of its size.

In season, the nighthawk is a notably vociferous creature. Its call, a loud, somewhat grating and nasal *beent*! is one of the most familiar sounds of summer evenings in the city (yet surprisingly few people seem to be aware of its source). Another sound, this one mechanical rather than vocal, is produced by the male bird in the course of his courtship performance. He plummets swiftly earthward, then swings aloft again very abruptly; the air rushing against his feathers produces the avian version of a sonic boom. In the early 19th century, Alexander Wilson, pioneer American bird student, guessed that the sound was made "by the sudden expansion of his capacious mouth." After more careful observation, his contemporary and sometime competitor, John James Audubon, came to the right conclusion, calling the sound a "concussion."

The nighthawk is readily identified in flight by the striking white patches on its long, pointed wings. At rest, the wingtips are longer than the tail (the whip-poor-will's are shorter). Should there still be any doubt, choice of habitat is nearly always diagnostic.

In the American Southwest there is another species of nighthawk which is somewhat smaller and flies very close to the ground. Since all these birds are completely dependent on flying insects, in our latitudes they must migrate. The nighthawk winters throughout most of South America.

But not all goatsuckers migrate. The related poor-will of the far west has been discovered to answer the winter food problem as some mammals do — by hibernating. Thus far, it is the only bird in the world known to have undertaken such an unbirdlike inactivity. It seems that cool weather, as it cuts down on the insect supply, reduces the bird to a kind of torpidity which is the accepted rule among reptiles and amphibians. From medium to deep torpor one might suppose that it is a relatively short step to hibernation, but it is a giant leap for a bird. All the goatsuckers are extremely well feathered and insulated, however, as was demonstrated by a female nighthawk that was able to hold the temperature of her eggs to a constant 46°C even though the gravel roof around her soared to a blistering 61°C (142°F).

Length 10 inches.   Male, 85 mile, Cariboo, British Columbia, July 4.

plate 36 — the sketch

CHIMNEY SWIFT

Chaetura pelagica

plate 36 ## CHIMNEY SWIFT *Chaetura pelagica*

*A*LTHOUGH an overwhelming majority of birds can fly to at least some extent, and most of them well, few can match the almost total commitment of the swifts to the air. Except for the need to deposit their eggs on something of substance, they are wholly emancipated from the terrestrial world. Feeding, drinking, even mating, are accomplished on the wing. Swifts are characterized by their tiny bills and feet, enormous mouths, cigar-shaped and apparently tailless bodies, and their stiffly tapered, often bowed wings. But they are especially and immediately recognizable by their flight, the fastest in the bird world – erratic, volatile, darting. The wings often give the appearance (but only the appearance) of beating alternately. This jagged pattern of flight, with wings set stiffly and much planing between series of beats, is diagnostic of the swifts.

Before pioneer days in North America, chimney swifts nested in hollow trees, and no doubt many still do, although I have never seen a nest of this species in anything but a man-made structure. Just as flat roofs have been so beneficial to the nighthawk, and farming to the killdeer and mourning dove, so the advent of chimneys opened up new and ideal possibilities for the swifts. But in addition to the millions of chimneys now available to them, swifts have used such other structures as empty wells and cisterns, out-buildings, silos, and barns. It is difficult to imagine that before the arrival of white men the chimney swift could possibly have been as numerous as it is today.

The nest is placed on the inside wall of a chimney, or hollow tree. It consists of small twigs glued together in the form of a half-cup which is cemented to the vertical surface. (The swift cannot take off from the ground, and it must collect nesting material while hovering on the wing.) The "glue" is the product of substances secreted by the bird's salivary glands, and is remarkably strong. Bird's nest soup is the end result of an even more highly refined practice among the cave swiftlets of the Far East, which build the entire nest of saliva. The "farthest out" swift nesting procedure I have seen is that of the palm swift of equatorial Africa, which glues its two eggs *on end* to a tiny patch of material cemented to a wildly swinging palm frond. If swifts could work out some method of incubating their eggs on the wing, no doubt they would soon be doing it.

Chimney swifts are solitary, not colonial, nesters, but in migration they are notably gregarious. Colossal flocks move together, roosting in suitable chimneys and such places, including trees, en route. John James Audubon tells of a giant hollow sycamore in which he estimated 9,000 swifts were roosting. Congregations between 5,000 and 10,000 have been reported in large chimneys. The greatest flock of birds I have ever seen consisted of swifts; in the Rift Valley of Kenya, Roger Tory Peterson and I could not begin to estimate the number of a great horde we watched one sundown – it could have been 100,000 birds, or even more. In this hemisphere, chimney swifts winter in the Amazon Basin – how many of them, no one knows.

This is the only swift in eastern North America; there are three others in the west, and about eighty species in the world.

Length 5¹/₂ inches.   Male, Overpeck Creek, New Jersey, June 5.

plate 37 — the sketch

RUBY-THROATED HUMMINGBIRD
Archilochus colubris

plate 37 RUBY-THROATED HUMMINGBIRD *Archilochus colubris*

THE smallest of all the higher vertebrates is a bird – the tiny bee hummingbird of Cuba – a mere 2¹/₄ inches long. The larger (for a hummingbird) ruby-throat is the only member of its family in eastern Canada, although others occur in the west. There are more than three hundred species of hummingbirds, all of them in the Americas, the majority in equatorial regions.

These are the only birds which habitually hover in mid-air, with a buzzy, insect-like wingbeat so rapid that the precise nature of it is impossible to see. We knew little about hummingbird flight before the arrival of high-speed photography, especially that done by Crawford H. Greenewalt, who likens a hummingbird to a helicopter in its technique. "To be sure, the wings go backward and forward, more like the oars of a boat than the circular whirl of the helicopter rotor. The effect, however, is much the same. If a helicopter hovers, the rotor is in a plane parallel to the earth's surface – so are the wings of a hummingbird. As the helicopter moves forward or backward, the rotor tilts in the appropriate direction – so do the wings of a hummingbird. The helicopter can rise directly from a given spot without a runway for take-off – so can a hummingbird."

Greenewalt's magnificent photographs brought to the world for the first time the almost unreal and unbelievable brilliance and beauty of this family of birds. Most of their blazing colours are the result of structural effects rather than pigmentation. The rather scaly feathers produce their iridescence from the play of light on their surfaces. The only true pigments in hummingbirds are black and rufous; all the rest of their gorgeous colours are mechanical. The result, in the words of Professor Jacques Berlioz, is "a brilliancy and a variety of tints unrivalled in any other group of birds."

As you might anticipate from their flamboyant appearance and volatile nature, male ruby-throated hummingbirds are confirmed philanderers, moving from partner to partner in the course of the breeding season. The female builds a nest by herself, and when she is ready to mate she does so, in a somewhat undiscriminating way, with the first male who comes along. He then departs in the search for other females, taking no part in the rearing of the brood. The nest is a delicate cup about 1¹/₂ inches wide, decorated with lichens and bound together by spider silk, firmly anchored across a suitably small branch. The two bean-sized eggs are white. Young birds are fed by regurgitation, on a fare that consists chiefly of flower nectar and diminutive insects. Feeding involves the most memorable sword-swallowing act ever chronicled. The parent stands over the young bird, and jams her long, sharp bill directly downward – and seemingly endlessly – into the young one's open gape. Demands for food are insatiable, and the old bird must work hard to satisfy them.

The fast-moving, almost perpetually airborne hummingbird uses up a great deal of energy. Hummingbirds have the highest metabolic rate of all vertebrates, even including that fiery mammalian furnace, the shrew. At sundown, when further foraging is impossible, the bird's metabolic processes must slow down and move at a more moderate rate for it to get through the night without starving. The bird thus slips into a semi-torpid condition which might, if extended for a period, lead towards true hibernation.

Length 3¹/₂ inches. Male, Halifax, North Carolina, June 11. Female, Eastville, Va., June 18.

plate 38 — the sketch

BELTED KINGFISHER
Megaceryle alcyon

plate 38

BELTED KINGFISHER *Megaceryle alcyon*

KINGFISHERS are a cosmopolitan group of over eighty species, of which we have only one in Canada. Most kingfishers do not actually eat fish, and many live a long way from water of any kind. But all are highly predatory, and take insects, reptiles, and even small birds and mammals. The belted kingfisher is an inveterate fisherman, however, a special line of work which some authorities suggest may have developed after, not before, the group as a whole evolved. In other words, the spearlike bill may have been "pre-adapted" for fishing while the belted kingfisher was still chasing lizards and locusts like its relatives.

Except for its habit of plunging into the water after small fishes, the kingfisher is in no way an aquatic animal. Rather it behaves very much like its kin, the mot-mots, bee-eaters, and rollers, all of which perch motionless, flycatcher-like, on a branch or stub, waiting for some prey item (usually an invertebrate) to come by. It is easy to speculate that for the kingfishers, fishing is a recent development.

Kingfishers are solitary birds, with each pair demanding and defending a good stretch of riverside or lakeshore. They have favourite perches where they regularly sit to survey the water and its contents. They do not stick strictly to fish, however, and willingly take small crustaceans and insects, and some small mammals. The nest is situated at the end of a burrow about four or five feet long (sometimes as much as ten), which is dug into a vertical bank by the birds. The same tunnel may be used, and extended, year after year. Six or seven eggs are laid, and like those of so many hole-nesters, they are white. The young are in the nest for about a month.

On their first hunting excursions young kingfishers are awkward and clumsy; it takes time for them to reach a degree of proficiency. That the parents at least occasionally lend a helping hand in the learning process is clear in one report: an adult bird caught a fish, subdued it with a few whacks without actually killing it, then dropped it back into the water for one of the young birds to practice on.

The general rule among birds is that in those species where the sexes have different plumages, the male is the more colourful. The kingfisher is unconventional; it is the female who has the extra, chestnut "belt" from which the bird gets its name. In Canada, in addition to the kingfisher, only the phalaropes have this peculiarity, but in their case the male takes over all the duties of incubation. L. L. Snyder has evidence that this switch in kingfisher colour is accompanied by certain changes in the behavioural norm. He once saw "a mid-April courtship flight of a pair of belted kingfishers during which the female was the pursuer and the male the pursued."

Kingfishers are hardy birds; they arrive early in the spring and linger as long as they are able in the fall. Occasionally they over-winter in the most southerly parts of Canada, but most seem to move south to Florida, where they are particularly abundant. Along the Tamiami Trail in January there seems to be a kingfisher every few hundred feet — such proximity to their own species the birds would never tolerate at nesting time. Kingfishers breed from coast to coast, north as far as the Yukon, James Bay, and central Labrador.

Length 13 inches.   Female, Pierce, Idaho, July 1.

plate 39 — the sketch

YELLOW-SHAFTED FLICKER
Colaptes auratus

plate 39

YELLOW-SHAFTED FLICKER *Colaptes auratus*

THE flicker is our only woodpecker which (in the manner of the European green woodpecker) feeds much of the time on the ground. Other species do it very occasionally, but usually only in periods of acute food shortage. Flickers regularly probe our lawns and garden borders for ants and other small insects, although they are just as proficient at digging in trees as any other woodpeckers. Not many animals eat ants; the suggestion has been made that since the flicker habitually does, it proves that the bird has no sense of taste. On the other hand, zoo-keepers know that when the ant supply is low, South American giant ant-eaters can be induced to eat substitute food – even hamburger – so long as it is coated with formic acid. Surely it is possible, then, that flickers *can* taste, and that they *like* ants – and formic acid. They have unusually large salivary glands, which may have a function in neutralizing the acid.

Although they do so much foraging on the ground, flickers nest in trees like any other woodpeckers. Both sexes work at excavating a hole in a tree (usually a dead one) as high as 60 to 90 feet from the ground, although often much lower. Robie W. Tufts tells an interesting story about nesting. He put out a hollow stump as a nesting box for the birds, and placed sawdust in the bottom. Much to his surprise, as soon as they arrived in spring, "they began immediately to remove the sawdust, a beakful at a time, working in alternate shifts for the better part of two days." They then pecked off chunks of the log itself and let them fall to the bottom. That was, apparently, more to their taste.

The normal clutch is six to eight white eggs. Fourteen have been recorded, but that many could possibly be the product of two females. This is not to suggest, however, that flickers are incapable of laying unusual numbers of eggs. In one famous experiment, a flicker's eggs were removed from the nest as fast as they were laid, with the exception

that one was always left as a "nest egg." In its attempt to cope with the daily loss of its labours, the bird laid 71 eggs in 73 days.

Another notable exercise involving flickers had to do with the ways in which the sexes recognize each other. Male flickers differ from females externally by the presence of a black "moustache" mark which the female lacks. The female of a pair was trapped, and artificial moustaches were stuck to her cheeks. When she was released, her mate immediately attacked her, taking her for an intruding strange male. When the moustaches were removed, he accepted her back immediately. Both sexes have a conspicuous white rump patch, which is especially prominent in flight. This is a more general recognition mark, narrowing the bird down to the species flicker; once that is determined, the facial markings identify the sex.

In southern British Columbia and the mountains of Alberta, this species is replaced by the very closely related red-shafted flicker, which also reaches into extreme south-western Saskatchewan. Hybrids between the two are common where their ranges overlap and, as you would expect, they appear orange. I have twice seen "orange-shafted flickers" at Rondeau Provincial Park on the north shore of Lake Erie, although the red-shafted does not normally occur in the east at all. Hybrids can be extremely variable in colour and pattern. In some, the colour in wings and tail is orange; in others, yellow and red feathers alternate, giving the *effect* of orange. The moustache marks of male hybrids may be either black or red – or they may even have one of each.

Yellow-shafted flickers are migratory, and although a few remain in southern parts during the winter, most spend the off-season in the central and southern United States. Except for the areas occupied by the red-shafted species, they are found in Canada from coast to coast, north to treeline.

Length 13 inches.   Male, Chester, South Carolina, October 1.

plate 40 — the sketch

PILEATED WOODPECKER

Dryocopus pileatus

plate 40 PILEATED WOODPECKER *Dryocopus pileatus*

THERE is no mistaking this dashing bird, which is almost as big as a crow — by a wide margin the largest woodpecker in Canada. Few birds are more arresting in appearance; the word "pileated" derives from the Latin *pileus*, a conical felt hat or cap. It is a memorable occasion every time you see one and, happily, we seem to see more of them in recent years than we used to. When I began to be interested in birds in the early 1930s, pileated woodpeckers were extremely scarce in the Toronto region, and it was several years before I saw my first. Today the bird is reasonably numerous in parks right in the middle of a city that has become substantially larger since then.

The changing fortunes of this species are probably related both to habitat alteration and to human protection. Like its great cousin of the south, the precariously surviving ivory-billed woodpecker, the pileated must have mature forest with enough dead big trees to accommodate it. The cutting of the original woodland, and attendant fire, reduced pileated numbers drastically. Now, much hardwood is again approaching the mature stage, and the birds have taken advantage of it.

They have also been quick to take advantage of protection. Before and after the turn of the century, pileated woodpeckers were frequent victims of gunners who were after trophies in that taxidermy-conscious time. They called them "woodcock" in those days and you will see far too many of these striking birds in old glass cases from musty Victorian parlours. But that is also a thing of the past and, with changing human attitudes, the birds have made the best of the opportunities offered them.

This is a strange species. Usually it is wary, furtive – singularly unapproachable and difficult to observe. Other times, especially in the winter, it can be almost unbelievably tame. One day I walked in Ottawa's beautiful Gatineau Park with a woman whose interests theretofore had been almost wholly confined to the theatre, and to whom I tried to reveal the world of birds. Naturally I hoped that something of even moderate interest would turn up. Suddenly, a magnificent pair of pileated woodpeckers appeared from nowhere, settled on a tree immediately in front of us, and repeatedly circled its trunk only a few feet from us. If only we could always provide a novice with such a dramatic introduction to wild nature!

If you cannot always see pileated woodpeckers, at least in the spring you can always listen for them. They are mostly silent at other seasons, but at breeding time their loud and resonant flickerlike calls ring through the forest, accompanied by resounding drum-rolls produced by their hammering on a hollow trunk or limb. The birds are not at all fussy about the tree they select for nesting, except that it be large and usually dead, but they show a fondness for beech, in my experience.

The entrance to the nesting cavity, which is excavated by both sexes, is usually well sheltered by the dense canopy of the forest. It is often square or oval in shape, unlike the round hole of a flicker, and proportionately larger. But pileated woodpeckers are most easily detected by the evidence of their search for food. Great rectangular or oblong excavations are cut vertically in rotten trees as the birds pursue their search for ant colonies. Often the diggings are just a few inches above ground level, other times, much higher. But the size of the chips lying on the forest floor, or on the snow, leaves no doubt about the identity of the carpenter.

Length 17 inches. *Male, South Carrollton, Kentucky, October 25.*
Female, Victoria, British Columbia, October 18.

plate 41 — the sketch

RED-BELLIED WOODPECKER
Centurus carolinus

plate 41

RED-BELLIED WOODPECKER *Centurus carolinus*

THIS is an extremely local bird in Canada, breeding regularly only in south-western Ontario's Middlesex County, but it is typical of the great Carolinian hardwood forest, which has only limited representation in the area. It is also seen more or less regularly in the woodlands of Point Pelee National Park and Rondeau Provincial Park.

Although I had made some acquaintance with this attractive bird in the southern U.S., my first experience with it in Canada was an especially notable one. It had been learned from some source along the birders' grapevine that a farmer near Melbourne, Ontario, had found red-bellied woodpeckers nesting in his woodlot, and a carload of Toronto enthusiasts went to have a look. We arrived at the farmhouse, knocked on the door, and were told that the man we were looking for was out ploughing. In a field, we discovered a tractor busily snorting away, and perched somewhat incongruously on top was a very large man with binoculars slung round his neck and Peterson's *Field Guide* sticking from the pocket of dusty blue overalls. No more ploughing was done that day, as the jovial Dougal Murray showed us his woodpeckers. That was a good many years ago, and we all remember with affection our first introduction to a new (to us) Canadian nesting bird and the beginning of a long friendship. Skilled bird students pop up in some unexpected places.

This is the only Canadian woodpecker that combines a zebra-barred back with red on the head. Don't invest much time trying to see the red on the belly; it is there, in both sexes, but not readily discernible in the field. The bird has a churring call-note quite like that of the red-headed woodpecker, which often inhabits the same type of deciduous forest. It is quite noisy when feeding.

Unlike most woodpeckers, this species eats a good deal of vegetable food. Depending upon the season and the availability of forage, half of its diet may be made up of beech and acorn mast, berries and domestic fruit. It frequently stores food items such as acorns, nuts and insects for future use by jamming them into a crack in a post or tree trunk. In various parts of its range it is not above raiding corn cribs and orange groves. It often becomes quite tame and approachable.

Where they occur in winter, red-bellied woodpeckers come to feeding trays readily for suet, seeds, and dried fruit. They do not appear to migrate to any extent.

Length 9¹/₂ inches. Male, Alexandra, Virginia, February 8.

plate 42 — the sketch

RED-HEADED WOODPECKER
Melanerpes erythrocephalus

plate 42 # RED-HEADED WOODPECKER *Melanerpes erythrocephalus*

SEVERAL of our woodpeckers are often wrongly identified as "red-headed" because they show some patch of red, but this one is the genuine article. It is undeniably one of the most handsome of North American birds. At rest, it is striking enough, but in flight, as it bares unexpectedly large snow-white wing patches in contrast with its blue-black body and blazing head, it is the most conspicuous bird we have.

Would that we had more of them. The red-head's fortunes have been intimately related to human activities, and it follows that they have been mixed. This is not a bird of the very deepest forest, so it is possible that in pioneer times it was not especially abundant. Then, with the clearing of the land, it became a relatively common bird at the edges of fields, in open forests and untidy orchards. A bit later, two new factors sent its numbers into a sharp decline. The first was the advent of "clean farming," which involved the taking out of dead or dying orchard trees, the removal of deadwood from farm woodlots, the replacement of old, rotten fenceposts, and the general tidying up of the land. The hole-nesting birds were in immediate trouble.

The widespread clean-up was one problem; another was new and formidable competition for the few sites that remained. The European starling, introduced to this continent at New York City in 1890, also nests in holes. It spread with astonishing speed. The red-headed woodpecker is a strong and vigorous bird, but in most places it was no match for the incredibly adaptable and successful starling. The foreign intruder also routed the similarly vulnerable eastern bluebird.

A new and completely unanticipated hazard appeared with the automobile. The red-headed woodpecker has the unfortunate habit of perching on fence-posts, then taking off in a low dip across the road. A great many are killed by passing cars – a mortality factor that no one could have guessed at two generations ago.

Now, however, I think that the bird's chances may be improving slightly – at least for the moment. Nothing ever seems to happen in nature without someone deriving some good from it somehow, and perhaps now it is the turn of this singularly hard-pressed woodpecker. In the last several years, the imported fungus infection called Dutch elm disease has taken a terrible toll of trees in eastern Canada. Its spread has been largely unchecked for perfectly understandable economic reasons. The disease is transmitted by bark beetles which transfer it from dead wood to living trees. Dead elms are thus reservoirs of the infection, and should be removed. But they are very costly to remove, and a great many more remain standing than have been taken care of in "sanitation" campaigns. These standing dead elms are beginning, in my view, to contribute to a modest recovery of the red-headed woodpecker (and, just possibly, of the eastern bluebird).

Dead wood provides both nesting sites and a supply of wood-boring insects and other animal food. But the red-head is not limited to the diet afforded by dead trees. It readily eats fruits, berries, and nuts. It also engages with surprising success in the unwoodpecker-like practice of flycatching – chasing and snapping up winged insects in mid-air. It is also occasionally alleged to take the eggs and young of other birds, and has even been known to attack a mouse. It is a remarkably versatile and flexible bird, if only we will give it a chance in the form of breeding sites.

Length 9³/₄ inches. Male, Colorado.

plate 43 — the sketch

DOWNY WOODPECKER
Dendrocopos pubescens

plate 43 # DOWNY WOODPECKER *Dendrocopos pubescens*

Our smallest woodpecker is also one of the most generally and intimately known. It readily visits backyard feeding stations in winter, and nests in pretty well all parts of the country north to the limit of trees. The similar but larger hairy woodpecker breeds over much the same area. The simplest way to distinguish the two is by their bills: the hairy's bill is large, almost as long as its head; the downy's is very short and stubby, much smaller than the length of its head. As is so often the case, our birds of the genus *Dendrocopos* have their Old World counterparts in the three species of European spotted woodpeckers. Others occur in Africa and Asia. There is a wonderful and varied proliferation of woodpeckers in the world – more than two hundred species of them. They range in size from tiny birds less than four inches long to striking giants almost as large as a raven. Many of them have at least some red about the head, but as we have seen, there is only one redheaded woodpecker.

Woodpeckers are finely specialized for their unique way of life. Since most of them live on the insects that infest the rotting bark of diseased and dead trees, they have developed appropriate structural adaptations. Usually insects have to be dug out, so the bill is long, strong, and chisel-like. It is mounted on an unusually large and heavy skull, and driven by a flexible and slender but very strong neck. The tongue of a woodpecker is extraordinarily long; it can be extended deep into an insect gallery. Its tip is often armed with spear-points, barbs, or bristles, as with the sapsuckers, depending upon the specialty of that particular species.

Since most of the time they are working vertically, parallel to the tree trunk, woodpeckers prop themselves against it by means of unusually stiff tail feathers. Strong feet hold the bird firmly to the bark as it chips away. The feet are built for clinging, and not many woodpeckers go in for proper perching on twigs or branches. The little downy is an exception to this rule; it commonly forages in smaller bushes and shrubs, and frequently perches crosswise in the manner typical of songbirds, but one that is uncharacteristic of woodpeckers.

Most of our woodpeckers do not migrate to any great extent, but populations seem to shift southward in the autumn, withdrawing from the more extreme regions of their range. We have downy woodpeckers with us all year long, but they may or may not be the same individuals in both summer and winter. In the most southern areas, they are probably sedentary, year-round residents. Downy woodpeckers are especially noticeable in the spring, when their courtship involves much noisy chasing about, high-pitched chattering, and rapid drumming on some suitable sounding-board.

The nest is dug by both sexes in a branch or trunk that is often softened by disease and insects to allow easy access, although they will sometimes dig successfully in sound wood. An average of five eggs is laid in the chips at the bottom of the cavity; they make no conventional nest. Both parents take care of the young birds, which emerge from the nesting hole and climb about on the trees before they can actually fly.

Length 6 inches. *Male, Louisville, Georgia, December 27.*
Female, Fort Thompson, Florida, February 28.

plate 44 — the sketch

EASTERN KINGBIRD

Tyrannus tyrannus

plate 44

EASTERN KINGBIRD *Tyrannus tyrannus*

EW summer birds are as noisily conspicuous as this one. Intemperate, belligerent, a kingbird can hardly escape the notice of anyone with or without an interest in birds. Far from being shy and self-obliterating, as so many birds are, it seems to call attention to itself in every conceivable way.

Many of the larger flycatchers are pugnacious animals, but the kingbird in particular does not hesitate to assault any large bird that comes into its area. As Earl Godfrey has put it, "A crow, hawk, heron or other large bird passing nearby is immediately and ignominiously driven off by the fury and agility of the kingbird's attack." Kingbirds have been known to fly at vultures, people, and — on at least one occasion — a low-flying small aircraft.

The tyrant flycatchers are a New World family, mostly tropical, comprising some 365 species, of which 22 are on the Canadian list. Many of them have strident voices; none could be called a "singer." To feed, a flycatcher typically perches on some eminence that commands a good unobstructed view of the area. When a flying insect is sighted, the bird launches itself in a fluttering swoop, snaps up the morsel, and sails back to its perch. The kingbird is especially distinguished for the arrogant, cavalier way in which it does it. Calling loudly whether perched or flying, grandly fanning its white-tipped black tail, the vociferous bird defiantly presides over his feeding territory.

Concealed in the black feathers of its crown the kingbird has a brilliant orange-red patch which is said to be displayed in moments of high agitation. When you consider that this species appears to be in a chronic state of agitation, it is surprising that the crown patch is so infrequently seen. There are reports of its being used in display between competing males, and for the intimidation of potential enemies, but I have only rarely and fleetingly seen it in the field.

The kingbird is flexible in its choice of nesting sites. Usually the bulky, well lined nest is built from ten to twenty feet up in a tree (normally in the open), or in shrubs adjoining watercourses. William Smith showed me one nest which was in the top of a stump in a quiet bay, scarcely a foot above the surrounding water. The usual four eggs are considered by some people to be the most beautiful in all the world of birds — creamy white, spotted with a variety of combinations of different colors.

Kingbirds are like all flycatchers in their absolute dependence on hatches of flying insects for their livelihood. Their seasonal activities are therefore governed by the temperature, and they are forced to be conscientious migrants. Although they are very jealous of territorial prerogatives at nesting time, they are notably gregarious during migration. One of the best places to see masses of kingbirds, whether in spring or fall, is Point Pelee National Park. The tip of the point is often alive with dozens of kingbirds — sometimes hundreds — all moving about with their stiff, "tip-of-the-wings" flight, all calling shrilly. On some occasions in the spring, the northward-moving birds are unfortunate enough to encounter a sharp drop in temperature, which eliminates all flying insects for a day or two. Then, it is possible to see kingbirds foraging on the sandy beaches or in the grass for alternative invertebrates. They will also take wild fruits when pressed.

Length 8¹/₂ inches.   Male, St. Paul, Minnesota, June 21.

plate 45 — the sketch

GREAT CRESTED FLYCATCHER
Myiarchus crinitus

plate 45 GREAT CRESTED FLYCATCHER *Myiarchus crinitus*

THIS showy flycatcher provides much of the colour – for eye and ear – in our southern woodlands. It is a good-sized bird for one of its family, with a full-throated, harsh, and carrying voice. Few people can have failed to hear its ringing *weep!* even though they may not have known the source. When the bird is glimpsed as it flourishes after an insect in the dense canopy of the forest, its cinnamon-rufous tail is the best field mark.

There are several other quite similar members of the genus *Myiarchus*, three in the United States and more in Central and South America (there is even one in the far-off Galapagos archipelago), but Canada has only this one. All are much the same in general appearance and behaviour. This proliferation of the genus reflects the wide spectrum of food possibilities that is available in the warmer regions. The closer you move to the equator, the greater the amount and variety of insect life, and the wider the opportunities for specialization and thus radiation among closely-related and presumably recently evolved birds.

The crested flycatcher nests in holes, and its environment being what it is, it frequently uses the abandoned cavities of woodpeckers. Natural holes are used as well, and occasionally the birds will condescend to nest in an artificial box. The nest itself is very interesting, often resembling a kind of trash-heap more than it does a bird's nest. Some surprising materials and objects somehow find their way into the crested flycatcher's home. A. C. Bent has listed some of them: leaves, animal hair, chicken and other poultry feathers, bark fibres from trees, hemp, rootlets, pieces of cord string, strands from ropes, large quantities of grass and pine needles, a few small twigs, feathers of grouse, owls, and hawks, a rabbit's tail, woodchuck fur, seed pods, bits of bark, cloth, and paper, pieces of onion skin, cellophane, paraffined or oiled paper, bits of eggshells, and pieces of horse manure.

But of all the improbable things that are found in the nests of crested flycatchers, the one that has puzzled ornithologists the most is the occasional presence of cast-off snakeskin. This raises a difficult question. What in the world could be its function? No one really knows, but since there is some similarity between dry snakeskin and some of the other favoured materials – onion skin, wax paper, cellophane, and so on – the bird would seem to be attracted by the texture and perhaps the shininess and even the noisiness of the material. But as Lester Snyder says in *Ontario Birds*, "We cannot attribute a purpose in respect to such habits of birds, and often, as in the present instance, it is not always possible to perceive that the species derives any special benefit from certain fixed habits." In other words, there doesn't always have to be a reason for everything.

In Canada, the great crested flycatcher breeds in suitable leafy forests from south-eastern Saskatchewan through southern Ontario to the lower half of New Brunswick, straggling into Nova Scotia.

Length 9 inches.   Male, La Raya, Rio Cauca, Bolivar, Colombia, January 22.

plate 46 — the sketch

EASTERN PHOEBE

Sayornis phoebe

plate 46 ## EASTERN PHOEBE *Sayornis phoebe*

WE all have our pet "gripes," and one of mine has always been the name of this bird. To my ear, the bird does not say the word *phoebe* nearly as clearly as, for example, the black-capped chickadee does, or, for that matter, the eastern wood pewee. This can be misleading to beginners, but tradition and usage are such that we seem to be stuck with it. The phoebe's voice is harsh and raspy; the chickadee and pewee whistle the two-syllable song.

The phoebe is dignified historically as the very first species of bird to be banded or ringed in North America. The imaginative experiment was conducted by the great John James Audubon, when he lived at Mill Grove, in Pennsylvania. He attached light threads to the legs of nestling phoebes (just to complicate the issue, he called them "peewees"), but found that they invariably removed them. "I renewed them, however, until I found the little fellows habituated to them; and at last, when they were about to leave the nest, I fixed a light silver thread to the leg of each, loose enough not to hurt the part, but so fashioned that no effort of theirs could remove it." Next spring, when the birds returned to the area, Audubon "had the pleasure of finding two of them had the little ring on the leg."

Audubon did not have to wait long for the birds to return, as phoebes are among the very first migrants to turn up after the winter — much the earliest of the flycatchers. At that time of year, when there may or may not be a sufficient supply of midges and other flying insects, phoebes frequently resort to vegetable food. I have seen them eating the white berries of poison ivy in such circumstances.

Phoebes have a special affinity for water, and also for man-made structures. The happy combination of the two in the form of small bridges is the most usual place in which to find a mud-and-greenstuff cup nest which is securely fastened to a beam or trestle. Other structures are used, such as cottages, barns, and out-buildings, where ledges and eaves offer shelter. Before there were such things to nest on, the birds liked to use rocky ledges with some overhang above them, but such sites were hard to come by.

The phoebe is a plain little bird, but an appealing one. There are several superficially similar small flycatchers; the phoebe is separated from the others instantly by its habit of flirting its tail up and down. You could not really call it "wagging" because it is usually in a more or less vertical plane, but it is an absolutely diagnostic feature. This bird has no other conspicuous field characteristics; the others have various combinations of eye-rings and wing-bars, both of which the adult phoebe lacks. The phoebe's bill is black — a useful mark at close range. At a distance, the entire large head appears black, in contrast to the dusky look of the back.

The eastern phoebe ranges in Canada from New Brunswick west and north to the Mackenzie, east of the Rocky Mountains. The related Say's phoebe, a somewhat more handsome, pale bird with a black tail and rusty-cinnamon underparts, is a westerner that does not often venture farther east than the Saskatchewan-Manitoba border, although wanderers have turned up in Ontario and Quebec.

Length 7 inches.   Male, Overpeck Creek, New Jersey, September 11.

plate 47 — the sketch

EASTERN WOOD PEWEE

Contopus virens

plate 47

EASTERN WOOD PEWEE *Contopus virens*

SOME of our smaller flycatchers can be quite bewildering in the field, especially the very smallest ones, the members of the genus *Empidonax*. They are all more or less greenish in colour, with wing-bars and eye-rings. The wood pewee, on the other hand, is an essentially grey bird, with wing-bars but *no* eye-ring. The wing-bars and the pale lower mandible separate it from the slightly larger phoebe. But the two are rarely seen together. The phoebe is a very early migrant, arriving in early to mid-April, while the more sluggish pewee is not expected until about the third week in May. The phoebe frequents human buildings; the pewee prefers the shady retreat of hardwood forests.

Many birds are already well along with nesting by the time the pewees come on the scene. You are not likely to see them arrive; the first clue to their presence is generally the slow, plaintive *pee-a-wee* that seems to float down lazily and reluctantly from the green canopy above. There is a reason for the pewee's late arrival in spring. It is not so likely to eat vegetable food as the phoebe is; since it is almost entirely dependent on insects, its slow progress northward is a form of insurance against a late spring and possible thin times on the way to its breeding grounds.

The pewee hunts as most flycatchers do, by waiting on a favourite perch until a desirable insect flies by. Unlike the phoebe and kingbird, however, which hunt in the open, the pewee chooses a dead branch or twig somewhere up in the broad-leaved foliage, and works from there. It darts out with a quick flutter, takes up an insect with its sturdy, flattened bill (sometimes aided by the stiff bristles which surround its mouth) – often with an audible sharp *snap*. It may take more than one victim before swinging round and back to its perch again. Most of these prey items are very small flies and bees, but A. Dawes Dubois saw an adult pewee return to the nest "with a good-sized butterfly, a red admiral, which the young bird swallowed, wings and all."

The surprisingly small nest of the wood pewee is saddled across a horizontal branch, decorated with lichens. Generally it is from twenty to forty feet up. Usually, there are three eggs; they are creamy-white with an arrangement of variously coloured blotches and spots around the larger end. Incubation takes slightly under two weeks, and the young birds soon appear to be much too large for a nest that was none too roomy for the sitting adult in the first place. Young songbirds grow rapidly; the pewees are ready to leave the nest in about fifteen to eighteen days.

It is a short summer. The wood pewees nested some time in June, and a few weeks later they are ready for fall migration. They leave earlier than most, but they are leisurely little birds, and they have a long way to go. Flying by night, they make their way to Central and South America.

The eastern wood pewee nests from south-eastern Manitoba through southern Ontario and Quebec to the Maritimes. Its counterpart in the rest of the country is the western wood pewee, which breeds from the southern part of the Yukon and the Mackenzie through the entire western area to south-central Manitoba. The two species (surely they cannot have been separate species for very long) are almost indistinguishable in the field except for their voices. The western wood pewee has a harsh and nasal song in contrast to the clear, whistled notes of the eastern bird.

Length 6½ inches.   Male, Glenwood, Illinois, May 26.

plate 48 — the sketch

TREE SWALLOW
Iridoprocne bicolor

plate 48 ## TREE SWALLOW *Iridoprocne bicolor*

THE brilliant metallic-blue lustre of the male tree swallow is one of the great pleasures of early springtime. On the average, the birds arrive soon after the middle of April. That is an early date for an insectivorous bird, a gamble on an early hatch of small flying insects sufficient to carry them through. But it is not all left to chance. The more northern populations of tree swallows are in part vegetarian. They are known to be fond of bayberries, which can sustain them in weather that discourages tiny invertebrates. But tree swallows of the south are not so versatile; they are totally insectivorous, which means that in cold snaps and resulting insect famine they are more vulnerable than their northern counterparts.

I have seen tree swallows darting about the stiff, naked branches of a flooded wood while there was still much ice and snow, and only patches of open water. What they were feeding on was not evident. These are tough birds, however, and when the very first tentative, warming rays of sunshine release hordes of midges, their summer has begun.

In the days before settlement, tree swallows nested – as most of them still do – in holes in trees, preferably near water. But many of them have now taken to artificial nesting boxes, where they are available. Eastern bluebirds prefer boxes of the same size and type, and this has occasionally led to trouble.

In A. C. Bent's *Life Histories*, F. Seymour Hersey gives an account of a dispute between the two species. Bluebirds were already occupying a nesting box in his garden, when a pair of tree swallows arrived and gave signs that they wanted that box.

Mr. Hersey promptly put up two more boxes, but the swallows ignored them and persisted in attempting to evict the bluebirds (which already had eggs). This they finally accomplished, and the bluebirds moved into one of the new boxes, leaving the tree swallows in occupation of the first. Then a second pair of tree swallows appeared, and drove the unfortunate bluebirds away for good.

The fortunes of this kind of competition can go either way, however. William H. Carrick, the renowned naturalist-cameraman, witnessed a similar encounter when he was living in Uxbridge, Ontario. He had placed out bird boxes, one of which was occupied by a pair of tree swallows. In this instance, bluebirds invaded the box at one of those rare times when both of the tree swallows were absent, threw out the three swallow eggs, and took over. It is doubtful whether this would have been the outcome had one of the swallows been present. It would seem that tree swallows and bluebirds are reasonably evenly matched, but like the red-headed woodpecker, both have suffered grievously from competition with the hole-nesting European starling.

Tree swallows have an interesting and delightful habit of using white feathers, where they are available, for lining their nests. These are in good supply around most chicken-yards, but in areas where they are scarce they seem to be a very desirable commodity, keenly contended for. Once it has got one, a bird will occasionally play with a white feather, catching and releasing it in the air and doing all sorts of complex aerobatics in the process – a charming sight.

Length 6 inches. *Male, Benemah Co. St. Maries, Idaho, April 1.*

plate 49 — the sketch

BANK SWALLOW

Riparia riparia

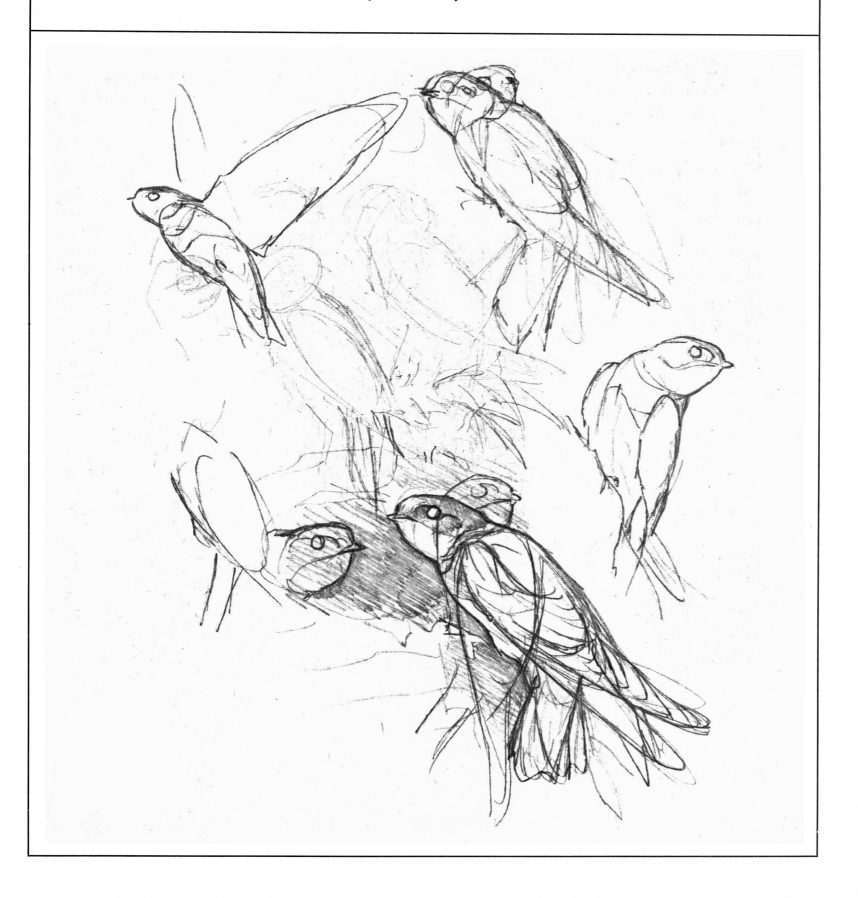

plate 49 ## BANK SWALLOW *Riparia riparia*

Our smallest, most delicate swallow is known as the sand martin in Britain; the two populations are of the same species. Both its colloquial and scientific names accurately describe the bird's best-known characteristic: it nests in burrows dug into the vertical sides of the banks of streams and lakes. You will also find its colonies in the sides of quarries, gravel pits, and other human excavations, including road and railway cuts. It is the only swallow to habitually do this, although it is the regular practice among some kingfishers; mot-mots, bee-eaters, and the like.

It is mysterious how a slight, fragile-looking little bird like a swallow, with its tiny bill and feet, can burrow from two to four feet, or even more, into the earth. Dayton Stoner has described the process in A. C. Bent's *Life Histories*. Both sexes take part in the digging, which is accomplished with much jabbing by the beak, scratching with the feet, and a sort of "shuffling" movement of the wings which apparently helps the bird to get rid of loose dirt.

At the end of the tunnel there is a feather-lined nest in which is laid an average of five white eggs. They are incubated, and the young brooded and fed, by both parents. The young are in the nest for about three weeks before reaching the flight stage, but are said to return to the burrow for the night during the first month. A young bird reared in a tunnel would seemingly have little chance to exercise its wings and none to practice flying – a limitation, one would think, for a bird so aerial as a swallow. Its first aerial venture has to be successful – and usually is. Depending on the location of a colony and the prevailing weather, a second brood may be raised in the course of the summer.

The bank swallow breeds from coast to coast roughly to the limit of trees from the Yukon to Labrador, with the exception of south-western British Columbia and the eastern three-quarters of Newfoundland. It winters in South America; in the Old World, in Africa and southern Asia. For years, people could not explain its sudden disappearance each fall. Its migrations – or, more properly, its absence in winter – led to the legend (from Aristotle and Pliny the Elder onward) that the swallow was a hibernator. Its strange habit of living in colonies in holes tunnelled into the ground must have helped give rise to the legend. No less a pundit than Dr. Samuel Johnson informed us that swifts, swallows, and others "conglobulated" in a ball and spent the winter asleep in the mud at the bottom of frozen ponds. Many people believed that swallows and other birds flew to the moon to spend the winter. (Now that a hibernating bird *(Plate 35) has* been found, however, perhaps we will have to review the literature with more humility.)

It is interesting that the bank swallow exhibits somewhat loose family ties. Although both sexes may look after the eggs and hatchlings, the female is known to leave the brood to the sole attention of the male parent, while she seeks out a different partner for the second brood of the summer. This laxity in the pair bond is unusual among small birds, but it does occur also in the house wren, while hummingbirds *(Plate 37)* reach the height of promiscuity. Young bank swallows are ready to breed when they are less than one year old, that is, at the beginning of the spring following the summer in which they were hatched.

Length 5¹/₄ inches.   Female, Lewiston, Idaho, September 1.

plate 50 — the sketch

ROUGH-WINGED SWALLOW
Stelgidopteryx ruficollis

plate 50

ROUGH-WINGED SWALLOW *Stelgidopteryx ruficollis*

SOME bird names are of considerable value in field recognition; others are not. This is one of the latter. The name is derived from an anatomical peculiarity that is only evident visually under magnification. But if you stroke the outer edge of the outermost flight feather, you will feel a certain roughness which is caused by hundreds of tiny hooks along its edge; their function is not known. Either way, you have to have the bird in the hand.

This is the most southern of our swallows; although it breeds from British Columbia to the south-western corner of Quebec, it is confined to a very narrow band that in some areas is just a few miles north of the border of the U.S. It is much more common and widely distributed to the south of us — all the way to southern Brazil. Identification is a matter of separating it from our only other brown-backed species, the bank swallow. That bird is smaller, has a conspicuous dark breast-band, and a much more erratic, irregular flight. The larger rough-wing has a dull wash on the throat, and flies more directly, with fewer wingbeats.

In the manner of a bank swallow, this species occasionally burrows into sand banks and other exposed surfaces to build its nest. But unlike the bank swallow, it is not colonial, and will nest in any suitable crevice or cranny in a rock face, or even on a human structure of some kind. It is very adaptable in this sense, but its solitary nesting habits no doubt tend to keep its numbers down.

Joseph Grinnell and T. I. Storer in *Animal Life in the Yosemite* described the attractive courtship flight of the rough-winged swallow. "From time to time the males were seen in pursuit of the females and, while so engaged, to make rather striking use of their seemingly plain garb. They would spread the long white feathers at the lower base of the tail until they curled up along either side of the otherwise brownish tail. The effect produced was of white outer tail feathers, such as those of the junco or pipit. Males can by means of this trick be distinguished from the females at a distance of fully fifty yards."

John James Audubon was the discoverer of the rough-winged swallow. He first noticed a flock of the birds when he was living at Bayou Sara, in Louisiana. They looked so much like bank swallows that he nearly overlooked them, but something prompted him to collect four or five of them. He looked at them, "thought them rather large," and popped them in his bag for further examination at leisure. A number of years later, his friend Rev. John Bachman, of Charleston, S.C., sent him four swallows' eggs which he said were laid by birds that looked very much like bank swallows, but which nested in the walls of an unfinished brick house. Bachman said. "It is now believed that there are two species of these birds." Indeed there were, and on his next trip to Charleston, Audubon collected a pair which were the basis for his scientific description.

I have seen this species in November and December in Guatemala, but at that season would have no way of knowing whether the birds were from our part of the world or were local and non-migratory. This points up one of the weaknesses of bird study based on field observation alone. Banding is one of the obvious answers to this problem. But we should never overlook the vital importance of adequate study collections; only a specimen in the hand, in the lack of a banding record, could have answered my Central American question.

Length 5³/₄ inches.   Male, Mississippi, September 27.

plate 51 — the sketch

CLIFF SWALLOW
Petrochelidon pyrrhonota

plate 51   CLIFF SWALLOW *Petrochelidon pyrrhonota*

EW birds are as legendary as this one. Though only one legend surrounds it, that one is enough, for this is the famous swallow of the mission of San Juan Capistrano, in California. Widely publicized for their allegedly unchangeable arrival time at the mission each spring, the birds were even the subject of a popular song I vaguely remember from the thirties. Jim Baillie has the secret. "The swallows always turn up on the same day because no one would dare look for them *before* March 19." The same phenomenon existed at one time in Toronto, where the whimbrels always used to arrive on May 24. They don't any longer – probably because the holiday date has been changed. They now arrive on the Monday *nearest* to May 24 – an extraordinary development which perhaps deserves further study.

Even if the Capistrano myth has been exploded, it in no way detracts from the cliff swallow's fame as a migrant. It nests as far north as Alaska, and winters from Brazil to Argentina. We usually think of a swallow as a slight, darting, buoyantly flying little bird; we rarely think of the enormous challenge it faces twice each year on its migratory journeys.

In the mid-1930s, Frederick C. Lincoln plotted on a map the average spring arrival dates of the cliff swallow. By linking the spots at which birds arrived on certain dates, he came up with isochronal lines which shed much light on the nature of the swallow's migratory progress. On March 10 western migrants are at the top of the Gulf of California; eastern birds are still as far south as Mexico City. By March 30, birds travelling up the west coast have almost reached Vancouver, whereas those in the east are still on the Gulf coast of Texas. By the middle of June both Alaskan and Maritime birds

have reached their final nesting grounds.

Why this slow-down by eastern birds around the Gulf of Mexico? It is a detour that adds at least 2,000 miles to the trip. Why do the birds not fly across rather than around the Gulf? Lincoln reasoned that the cliff swallow is a daytime migrant, and that, unlike many birds, it feeds throughout its journey. As he points out, "Flying along the insect-teeming shores of the Gulf of Mexico, the 2,000 extra miles that are added to its migration route are but a fraction of the distance that these birds actually cover in pursuit of their food." Anyone who has watched a cliff swallow fluttering after insects like a bat will see the point of the argument.

Cliff swallows might more properly be called "eave swallows," because even though many of them still nest on cliffs, many more use the eaves of houses, cottages, barns, and out-buildings. The nest is intriguing from an engineering point of view. It resembles superficially a small flask, or bee-hive, built of little mud or clay pellets which are gathered in appropriately moist locations and cemented together. There is usually a protruding, retort-like neck which is used as entrance and exit, but sometimes the nest is not roofed over, and somewhat resembles that of a barn swallow.

The fate of the nest and its occupants is often predetermined by the materials used, and their quality varies from place to place. Naturally clay is the best and strongest substance. Nests built too hastily or in very damp weather sometimes collapse before they are finished; others dry out, become crumbly, and may be the victims of summer thundershowers. In many parts of its range, the cliff swallow has been gradually edged out by competition from the imported house sparrow, whose liking for farm buildings is well known.

Length 6 inches.   Lac la Hache, British Columbia, May 19.

plate 52 — the sketch

PURPLE MARTIN

Progne subis

plate 52 # PURPLE MARTIN *Progne subis*

*A*LTHOUGH it is by no means the most common, our largest swallow is probably held in more affectionate regard than any other bird — and often by people who scarcely know another species. The reason is the martin's willingness to forsake hollow trees for its colonial nesting and to use man-made bird houses. Often these are "high rise" apartment buildings with twenty or even two hundred compartments. Martins do not appear to mind how ornate these structures become; many I have seen are so baroque that you would expect them to frighten the birds away for good. The boxes are placed on poles up to about twenty feet in the air, and a circular metal squirrel guard is often a good idea.

Martins are unpredictable birds, however, and seem to be choosy about the boxes they will occupy. One house may be overflowing while another nearby is completely ignored; the reason is rarely apparent. Sometimes it will take several years before they will accept a new box, but once they do, they will return year after year.

In Bent's *Life Histories*, Alexander Sprunt Jr. tells a remarkable story of the purple martin's homing instinct. "One of the most striking examples of a returning martin colony I ever heard was related to me by Alston Clapp, of Houston, Texas. While in his yard on one occasion he showed me his colony and said that the year previous he had taken down the house to paint it. Something delayed him, and it was not up when the martins arrived. Attracted by a great chattering one morning, he went out into the garden and saw the birds fluttering and circling about in the air *where the house should have been*, at the exact elevation occupied by it when placed!"

In spring, the martins arrive in our latitudes about the beginning of May. Unfortunately, the introduced house sparrow and starling begin nesting earlier than that, and many of the choicest sites are already occupied when the martins get here. This has had a serious effect on martin populations in many places. Many people who keep bird houses get around the problem by leaving the entrance holes boarded up until the first martins arrive. From that point on, they can generally look after themselves.

Like other swallows, the purple martin lives almost exclusively on flying invertebrates — winged insects, drifting young spiders, and the like, although the bird is also known sometimes to exhibit a great (and inexplicable) fondness for egg-shells. Almost all of its food is caught on the wing, and it drinks while in flight by dipping its bill into the water, as other swallows, and swifts, do. Audubon noted that martins even bathe while on the wing, "when over a large lake or river, giving a sudden motion to the hind part of the body, as it comes into contact with the water, thus dipping themselves into it, and then rising and shaking their body, like a water spaniel, to throw off the water."

Considering that the purple martin has been a familiar dooryard bird since the first white settlements in North America, and that even the Indians were on friendly terms with it, it is unusual that nothing whatever was known of its winter range until quite recently. Each fall, the birds simply disappeared off the face of the earth. The advent of widespread bird-banding cleared up the mystery. In 1936, a bird banded in Minnesota was found in Para, Brazil. It is now thought that almost the entire North American population winters in the Amazon Basin. Since its nearest relatives are all tropical or sub-tropical species, no doubt the purple martin is a northward pioneer of a sort, and its dramatic return to equatorial regions for the winter sheds light on the evolution of traditional migratory behaviour.

Length 8 inches. *Male, May 9.*
Female, Laurel, Maryland, September 13.

Birds of the Eastern Forest : 2

Contents

Author's Foreword

*I*T is well known, though not always acknowledged, that change is the one constant in all of life. We sometimes forget that change made possible all the living things we know. To students of birds, the most profound and dramatic change in the entire history of animals was the development of a reptile's scale into the feather of a bird. No one knows precisely when that happened, but it was something more than 140 million years ago. That is the approximate age of the oldest feather on record, a fossil imprint from the shale beds of Bavaria. It belonged to a strange creature called *Archaeopteryx* ("ancient wing").

Archaeopteryx was no ordinary bird. For one thing, it had teeth. Also, it had clawed fingers on its forelimbs and a long lizard-like tail with twenty vertebrae. But it was indisputably a bird, because by definition a bird is an animal with feathers. The change from *Archaeopteryx* onward has been brilliant and spectacular, but it all started with some little tree-clambering dinosaurs whose scales gradually changed into something much fancier to help sustain their lengthening leaps from branch to branch. In Darwin's words, "from so simple a beginning, endless forms most beautiful and wonderful have been, and are being evolved."

There is no way of knowing how many different kinds of birds evolved. Expert opinion is divided, but a round figure of one million is reasonable. Of these only a small fraction have ever co-existed at any one time. At present there are between eight and nine thousand species of birds in the world; in North America we have about seven hundred and seventy-five. Such an assemblage is unwieldy for the student, and long ago biologists began to sort out animals into groups of obviously related species. Clearly an ostrich is in a different group from a hummingbird or an owl or a thrush. The result is that the list of birds of the world is broken down under twenty-eight major headings called "orders," of which we have nineteen in North America. Of these by far the largest is the order "Passeriformes," which includes more than half the species of birds on earth.

All the birds in this volume are members of the order Passeriformes ("perching birds"). Many other kinds of birds can and do perch (herons, hawks, kingfishers, and many more), but they do not belong to this group. In general the perchers are the smaller birds, the ones we usually call "songbirds" regardless of the quality of their voices. The only members of this order in Volume I were the flycatchers and the swallows.

The perching birds are relatively recent arrivals, in an evolutionary sense. Warblers, vireos, tanagers, blackbirds, and finches are so new, in fact, that it is sometimes difficult to decide just who belongs to what family (the yellow-breasted chat is an excellent example). This problem is especially troublesome in the American tropics, where all of these seem to overlap to at least some extent, and where a number of birds do not seem to have yet "made up their minds" whether they are going to become one thing or another. Change is still very much with us.

Some of our most familiar birds are still in the process of busily subdividing into something else. Most of us know a song sparrow, but *the* song sparrow is impossible to define, as north of Mexico there are over thirty different geographic races, or sub-species, of the bird. Each is potentially a new species. So in looking at the various "kinds" of song sparrows we are actually witnessing new species on the assembly line. We are seeing the process of evolutionary change.

There is no question that of all the changes our planet has seen, none has taken place so quickly as those brought about by technological man. Some have had unexpectedly wide ramifications. In 1967, in the process of writing Volume I*, I mentioned the dangers presented by the transference of the residues of chemical pesticides from prey species to predatory birds. "This is happening in our generation among peregrine falcons, bald eagles, and ospreys, all of which are seriously declining in numbers, as the result of ingesting toxic chemicals with their food." What I was unable to say was *how* it was happening; at that time we did not know. The circumstantial evidence was there, but positive identification of the poisoning mechanism was lacking. How did DDT and other pesticides affect the birds?

Now we know. Almost coincident with the publication of Volume I in the fall of 1968 there came firm clinical proof of the relationship between chlorinated hydrocarbon insecticides and bird reproduction. Experiments conducted with captive sparrow hawks by the U.S. Bureau of Sport Fisheries and Wildlife showed that repeated small doses of the poisons had the effect of altering enzyme balances in the birds' livers. In turn this affected the birds' sex hormones, such as oestrogen. This resulted in changes in the birds' calcium metabolism: their eggs had shells which were so thin or insubstantial that they could not be incubated without breaking, or would not permit the proper development of the embryo. The decline in numbers of the peregrine falcon has been catastrophic; it has been followed by similar trends in the bald eagle and the brown pelican, among others. The kind of change brought about by widespread environmental degradation is the kind we would happily do without.

*Part I of the present work.

Whether "human nature" can change is another matter. It seems to me that if a day ever comes when we cannot enjoy and value and take steps to protect birds for their own sakes, without reference to our own interests, we will be in grave trouble. On a television program in 1969, Lamont Cole, the distinguished ecologist of Cornell University, said to me somewhat sadly that he had "pretty nearly given up trying to promote conservation on the grounds of aesthetics." That is a melancholy thought, and although I am forced to agree, I continue to hope most fervently that it will not always reflect the true state of our civilized condition.

In the last half-dozen years there has developed an acute public awareness of the precarious state of the human environment. It didn't come a moment too soon. Now, perhaps steps will be taken to alleviate the condition of the living world as a whole. I suppose we who value nature can take some comfort from the expectation that as long as people are still around, the planet will be habitable for birds. The converse, presumably, is also true.

There follow profiles of sixty selected "songbirds" which are characteristic of the deciduous and mixed forests of the east, and of the open farmlands within it. It is hoped that the reader will now become more aware of some of the smaller and sometimes less conspicuous but usually quite common birds of our own man-made environment. Most of them have at least to some extent made their peace with human settlements and habitations, and almost all (at least in migration) can be seen within the limits of the typical eastern city. For a full description of the nature of the area under discussion, the reader is referred to the Introduction to Volume I.

A writer's life is fraught with complications. When there are deadlines to meet and potential conflicts to sort out, the survival of both project and author is to a great extent governed by the patience and ingenuity of publisher, agent, editors, and co-workers. My gratitude is warmly expressed to M. F. Feheley, J. G. McClelland, Peter Smith, Judith Symons, Anna Szigethy, and Michael Worek.

John A. Livingston

The work in this book owes much to the help of several people. The names of some of them have been mentioned in previous volumes, and if I do not repeat them now, my gratitude for their assistance has not diminished.

Most of the specimens used came from the Smithsonian Institution, through the kindness of Dr. S. Dillon Ripley who permitted me to keep more than a hundred skins for the two years it took me to do the paintings. As well, James L. Baillie, as he had done for years, chose and lent me fine skins from the Royal Ontario Museum whenever I needed them.

A difficulty ever-present in such works — that of finding the appropriate plants for the backgrounds — was greater in the case of this book. All the birds depicted on the following pages are small and spend their lives amid leaves and foliage not to be found on the West Coast where I work. Consequently, plants had to be shipped to me, and the office of picker and shipper of greens was filled by my friend Dudley Witney. Dudley showed incredible kindness, alacrity, and persistence in gathering the necessary things. Packages and boxes followed one another in a long procession to my door — each filled with carefully chosen, pressed, and labeled specimens, always quite fresh. I think Dudley must have spent months hunting, for many more plants came than I could possibly use.

The background of the Kentucky warblers was airmailed to me in an open carton, complete with insects and leaf-mould. Far from its Ontario woodlot home, this microcosmos went through its year of flowering and seeding. Now, still intact, it is sunk in the soil of my garden.

It may never notice the change.

J. Fenwick Lansdowne

plate 53—the sketch

BLUE JAY

Cyanocitta cristata

plate 53   BLUE JAY *Cyanocitta cristata*

IT is difficult to be indifferent to the crow family; all of them are noisy, conspicuous, aggressive, intelligent, and overflowing with personality. Audubon, never a man to let emotion go unexpressed, railed against the blue jay in particular, calling it a rogue, a thief, and a knave; he charged the bird with mischief, selfishness, duplicity, and even malice – words we usually reserve for creatures higher on the evolutionary scale. Audubon did concede, however, that the jay was a beautiful and cheerful bird and, by this qualification, joined the rest of us interested, delighted, and baffled by the cavalier behaviour of a bird which ranges from Alberta to Newfoundland, from Texas to Florida.

The facts, however, bear out very few of the many charges made against the blue jay. The blue jay will eat almost anything that is edible, but when, occasionally, it takes the eggs or chicks of another species, moralists should remember that the economy of nature stacks rather heavy odds against a young bird's survival. Ornithologists have estimated, furthermore, that a good three-quarters of a jay's food is vegetable, especially corn and cereal grains and acorns.

To deal with an acorn, a jay will hold the nut in its feet and crack it with its straight, strong bill. Jays are known frequently to bury acorns in the ground and, whether or not they ever find all of them, they thus help seed the oak forest.

In the early days, the blue jays were, no doubt, confined to the beech and oak woodlands which at that time provided most of their food. The birds have adjusted readily to the growth of cities and suburbs and are now common wherever there are suitable stands of trees. I, for example, have a boyhood memory of a jay's bulky, untidy nest in a slender ash just outside my bedroom window, in the heart of Toronto. I remember being surprised that the three-week-old fledglings, apart from the shortness of their still-growing tails, were almost indistinguishable from the adults.

Blue jays are uncharacteristically quiet during nesting time, but when the young are out and flying, families of them begin to make the racket we have learned to expect from this very garrulous tribe. The parties become larger as units of families drift together, and the din they make over a prowling house cat can be heard for blocks.

The jays' autumn flocking coincides with the appearance of the various nuts, berries, and fruits upon which the birds gorge as they gradually move southward.

There are few places better than Point Pelee National Park for watching a blue jay migration. The birds drift in a generally southwest direction in smallish, gradually merging groups; when they arrive at the southwest corner of Lake Erie, the individual flocks run into the hundreds. Taverner recalled a famous blue jay flight at Point Pelee on October 14, 1906. I have seen a good many, the greatest of which was on September 19, 1968, when at least three thousand jays passed overhead. James Baillie estimated at the time that they outnumbered the sharp-shinned hawks (always a feature at Pelee in the fall) by three to one.

Despite this massive migration, blue jays are with us all year. Local populations seem to shift southward during the winter, and, except in the South, the birds seen at that season are not usually the ones seen at breeding time. Their often tyrannical behaviour at feeding stations, to which they are easily attracted by peanuts and other seeds, probably helps to harm the jays' reputation. I have noticed that house sparrows and starlings almost invariably give way before the blue despot, but I have seen a jay and a male cardinal feeding (apparently amicably) side by side, with a few sturdy evening grosbeaks fluttering in from time to time without any undue disturbance.

Length 10 inches.   Female, Haliburton County, Ontario, September 3.

plate 54—the sketch

COMMON CROW
Corvus brachyrhynchos

plate 54   COMMON CROW *Corvus brachyrhynchos*

BLACK is an unfortunate colour for a large, omnivorous bird. Whatever redeeming traits the crow may have (and it has many), the bird's very blackness seems to condemn it. Few native animals have been persecuted with such savage persistence. In winter, crows often roost together in enormous flocks. These flocks may include tens or even scores of thousands of individuals who, one way and another, managed to elude the guns and poisoned baits set out earlier in the season. Then comes the most frightful onslaught of all: crow killers actually bomb the roosts with dynamite.

These witless, offensive measures against the crow are taken in the name of "control" – a widely used euphemism for wanton destruction of a species which does not happen to be protected by law. There is no blood-thirstiness like that of the self-righteous. Allegations against the crow have traditionally come from the duck hunters, who claim that the bird has a bad effect on the production of waterfowl they want to shoot; but these allegations have no basis in fact. Farmers also used to hate crows but, in latter years, they seem to be realizing that flocks of crows can be decidedly beneficial by devouring crop-destroying insects. Some "sportsmen," however, have achieved a certain notoriety by inventing sophisticated methods of luring crows to their guns, even resorting to tape-recorded assembly calls of the birds.

The standard "put-down" among birdwatchers is the question "Do you know the crow?" It is assumed that everyone knows the crow, and indeed almost everyone does, no matter where he lives. But the crow is a thoroughly uncommon animal. Large, strong, resourceful, and apparently cunning, it has withstood with notable success the best-organized and largest-scale onslaughts its persecutors have yet been able to devise. The crow continues to thrive.

In the latitude of the Great Lakes, the March migration of the crows is one of the most stirring events of the year. Long, loose skeins of birds in flight move along lakeshores and over empty, barren fields, fighting blustery winds all the way. From their occasional, raucous *caws* one might even believe that they were enjoying the whole thing to the fullest. When the flocks arrive on their breeding grounds, they stick together for a time, feeding sociably. Then the pairs gradually break off and become solitary quiet for the nesting period.

A crow's nest, usually well hidden in an evergreen, is large and somewhat awkward looking. It is well constructed, however, and withstands the effects of the elements so well that last year's crows' nests are frequently used by hawks and owls with a minimum of refurbishing. There are about five greenish eggs, usually spotted with browns or grays. The young birds eat exclusively animal matter (mostly insects and other invertebrates), but on a year-round basis, vegetable matter forms almost three-quarters of the birds' intake.

The crow's fondness for corn is well known. In winter, standing corn is its favourite place for gathering, feeding, and sheltering. The birds, it seems, are blessed with adaptability and a high degree of survival potential, and have benefited from wide stretches of agricultural land. They take not only the corn but also many of the small mammals which frequent such places – including mice, voles, and shrews.

Crows will also visit and even take up temporary residence around the breeding colonies of birds such as herons and gulls. If the nesting birds are not disturbed, the impact of the black hangers-on is minimal. The only significant predation by crows on colonial birds that I have witnessed takes place when curious people put the sitting birds off their nests. Then the crows move in swiftly, silently, and efficiently. In such cases, we would be wise to reserve judgement.

Length 18 inches.   Male, Wells Gray Park, British Columbia, May 14.

J.F. LANSDOWNE
· 1969 ·
Corvus brachyrhynchos ♂
Hemp Creek, Wells Gray Park, B.C.
May 14th, 1958   no. 10981
B.C. Prov. Mus.

plate 55—the sketch

BLACK-CAPPED CHICKADEE
Parus atricapillus

plate 55

BLACK-CAPPED CHICKADEE *Parus atricapillus*

CHICKADEES are year-round features of most of our range, tending to shift southward in winter. Some years their movements are more marked than usual. Very occasionally there is a chickadee flight large enough to constitute an "irruption," but irruptions are exceptional. In the non-breeding season we usually see parties of chickadees moving about in a somewhat aimless manner, often in company with other small birds such as kinglets and, in the migration period, warblers.

It is in the winter that we know the chickadee best. It appears to be the most fearless of our birds. Rare is the suet that does not attract a party of these hardy mites; with a little patience one can even encourage them to come to hand. There are few bird journals or family magazines which have not at one time or another shown photographs of children more or less festooned with these "cheerful" little birds.

The fiercest weather does not seem to bother them. This is a matter of physiology. Compared to a man, a bird is internally a raging inferno. The chickadee's heart, for example, beats five hundred times a minute when the bird is *asleep* and about twice that when it is exercising. This, compared to our sluggardly, near-reptilian seventy to eighty beats a minute, is a good indication why a small bird must eat almost constantly just to stay alive. Cold does not bother a winter bird; lack of food does. If the fires are kept supplied with fuel, the bird's high-powered metabolism – plus layers of loose, fluffy, insulating feathers – keep it going.

The chickadee is famous for its hyper-active way of feeding. In its search for the various invertebrates which make up its diet – insects and spiders, their egg masses and cocoons – it does all sorts of acrobatics. It hangs upside down, flutters and dances about, and adopts any number of strange and unlikely postures. Its sharp little bill can penetrate the most difficult and narrow cracks and crevices. Occasionally the bird will peck, almost like a woodpecker.

In the spring, breeding pairs of chickadees seem to be made up before the birds' final territories are declared. In the process, there is much chasing about, as the birds dart around the chosen area. Both sexes work at excavating the nesting hole (usually in an old and rotten stump, often that of a birch) jabbing vigorously at the pulpy, soft interior. They have little difficulty in digging and penetrate surprisingly sound wood.

The female may lay as many as ten eggs. (A small, vulnerable bird must have a high reproductive potential.) She does all the incubating, and, during those twelve days, the male brings food to her at the nest. Both share the duty of feeding the voracious young birds which will leave the nest after just a little over two weeks. The young, when they fly, are almost perfect replicas of the adults, except that they are somewhat scruffier.

Once they are out of the nest, young chickadees are quite competent to take care of themselves. This is where the chickadee's great agility comes into play. High-speed photographs have shown that when a flying chickadee is suddenly startled, it can react and begin to take evasive action within three one-hundredths of a second. You would expect this lightning response to be sufficient to protect it from most avian predators – which are so often notoriously inefficient – but I have seen a chickadee taken in mid-flight by a singularly nimble sparrow hawk.

The only species with which this bird can be confused is the very similar but more southern Carolina chickadee, which is somewhat smaller and grayer. The black-capped chickadee is thought to be the same species as the European willow tit; the phrase *tit-willow* is not included in the repertoire of either. The common call from which this bird gets its name is known to everyone. The so-called "spring" song, *phoebe*, can be heard at any season, and it is reported that "sixteen different vocalizations" have been listed.

244   *Length 4¹/₂ inches.*   *Male, Haliburton County, Ontario, September 4.*

plate 56—the sketch

TUFTED TITMOUSE

Parus bicolor

plate 56 # TUFTED TITMOUSE *Parus bicolor*

THE family of titmice is a large one; about sixty diminutive species are scattered over all the continents of the world, except South America and Antarctica. For such tiny creatures, their dispersal has been impressive; they are thought to have originated in Eurasia, upwards of forty million years ago. "Tit" is an old Anglo-Saxon word for something very small; in Britain they still use the word for the birds we know as chickadees.

In North America, we have fourteen representatives of this attractive family. Those species with crests, of which we have four (there is only one in Europe), we call titmice; those without, we call chickadees. Crested or uncrested, they all belong to the genus *Parus*. There are others – the bushtits (*Psaltriparus*) and the verdin (*Auriparus*) of the West – which have branched off somewhat from the ancestral family stem.

Although it is a common bird in the eastern United States, the tufted titmouse rarely manages to enter Canada, in extreme southern Ontario. It was first recorded in Canada in 1914, and although there have been occasional very local indications of some increase, its success has been tentative at best. The progress of the tufted titmouse stands in marked contrast to that of the cardinal, also originally a southerner, which has made such a spectacular northward advance in this century. Both birds are the same in one respect, however: both are non-migratory, and when they do establish themselves, they stay the year round, despite the climate.

The titmouse is a plain but subtly attractive little bird. Its generally gray colour, its crest, and its brown flanks are to be watched for. One of its best field marks is the surprisingly conspicuous black, beady eye, which contrasts brightly with the otherwise "mousy" plumage. The sexes look similar. Like any other chickadee, the titmouse is extremely active in its feeding, and does all the charming acrobatics characteristic of the family. Caterpillars are said to be regarded as a delicacy by titmice, and the birds depend all year chiefly on the eggs, larvae, and pupae of insects. In the appropriate season they are also known to eat beechnut mast and acorns.

Titmice seem to prefer dense hardwoods, with the forest floor dampish to downright wet. They will, however, come to residential areas if there is a sufficient number of large shade trees. They are not difficult to attract to bird feeders at any season; when we Canadians receive one of our rare glimpses of a titmouse, it is usually at a feeding station. (I have had my most intimate acquaintance with the bird at the attractive feeder maintained by the Roger Petersons in Connecticut.) In time, and with patience, the bird can be made to come to hand like a black-capped chickadee.

Titmice nest in cavities, natural and artificial. Often they are said to use old woodpecker holes. The one nest I have seen was in a bird box a little over eye level in a deep New Jersey woodland. (The box appeared to be crammed to overflowing with soft material.) There are usually about five or six eggs. In fall and winter the titmice associate in small flocks with other resident, non-migratory birds. During migration they frequently mingle with myrtle warblers.

Probably the most distinctive feature of the titmouse is its voice. It will call at any time of the year, and, at any distance, its loudly whistled three-note phrases will remind you of the Carolina wren or, possibly, of the cardinal. You can easily attract the bird to you by squeaking or by imitating its call – not a difficult one.

Length 5¹/₂ inches.   Female, Amelia Island, Florida, October 15.

plate 57—the sketch

WHITE-BREASTED NUTHATCH
Sitta carolinensis

plate 57 WHITE-BREASTED NUTHATCH *Sitta carolinensis*

Birds like crows and jays have made a great success of being "generalized." They can eat almost anything, and they obtain their food in almost as many ways as there are items in their diet. Under the right circumstances, however, it has paid some birds to be highly specialized. The world's fifteen species of nuthatches, of which we have four in North America, have managed to make the best of a style of survival which is uniquely their own.

When you see a bird which habitually clings upside-down to the bark of large trees, it is a nuthatch. There is one other species, the red-breasted, within the geographic scope of this book; it is slightly smaller, and has a black line through the eye. The more southern, white-breasted bird is identifiable by its size and its pure white cheek patch.

Nuthatches are characterized by their sturdy, "neckless" bodies and strong, tapered bills. The tail is short, the wings relatively long. The toes are quite long to assist in bark-clinging. One foot is usually braced at right angles to the body, the other pointed downward.

It has been suggested that nuthatches succeed in their upside-down approach to life because, in this way, they may spot food items that the more conventional, rightside-up creepers and woodpeckers might miss. It is true that forest insects in various stages of metamorphosis, and their eggs, are eaten by nuthatches, and this posture would be suitable for foraging, but a very high proportion of the birds' food is vegetable. (Anyone who operates a feeding station knows their fondness for sunflower seeds.) They will also take quantities of beechnuts and acorns, among a wide selection of berries and other fruits. To balance its winter diet, however, the nuthatch will vary its seed intake with quantities of suet. It has been known to come to salt.

A nuthatch opens nuts and hard seeds by breaking them open with the bill (hence the bird's name). It will attack a nut or seed on the ground or on your feeding tray; it will sometimes fly with it to a tree with good rough bark and lodge it there, and go about breaking it with hard strokes of its efficient beak. (Even if it is not hungry, it will continue to place nuts and seeds in the bark of trees; this "cache" may or may not be remembered later.) The bird has been known to forage on the ground.

Nuthatches are with us all year, but they are most conspicuous in winter, when they show little fear around our houses and their voices are among the very few bird sounds we hear. The familiar *yank, yank* is supplemented by various other calls we hear less often. The song is described by Godfrey as a hollow whistled *tew, tew, tew, tew.* In winter nuthatches are often accompanied by creepers, chickadees, and downy woodpeckers.

In spring courtship, the male pursues the female in mad, careening chases. The birds show great agility in the air, and good speed when they pass overhead, but they rarely fly far. They nest in a cavity in a tree – sometimes a natural rotten spot or knothole, sometimes a woodpecker hole. The birds will sometimes use a bird box, but they are perfectly capable of excavating their own premises, if need be. Look for them in oak and maple woods with plenty of decaying old trees (the kind of stands that economics-minded foresters delight in calling "over-mature"). The nest is softly lined with fine fibres, bits of wool or hair, and feathers. The male will feed the female as part of the courtship ritual, and will indulge in whatever strutting and posturing his upside-down position allows. The nuthatch is a fecund bird, producing ten or even more eggs, but the average is probably eight. Both sexes take care of the young, which look just like their parents when they emerge.

The white-breasted nuthatch is found over most of the United States and in Mexico, but is more scattered in Canada. It occurs in southern British Columbia, southeastern Manitoba, and the St. Lawrence Valley – rarely on the prairies.

Length 5 inches.   Male, Laurel, Maryland, October 8.

plate 58—the sketch

BROWN CREEPER
Certhia familiaris

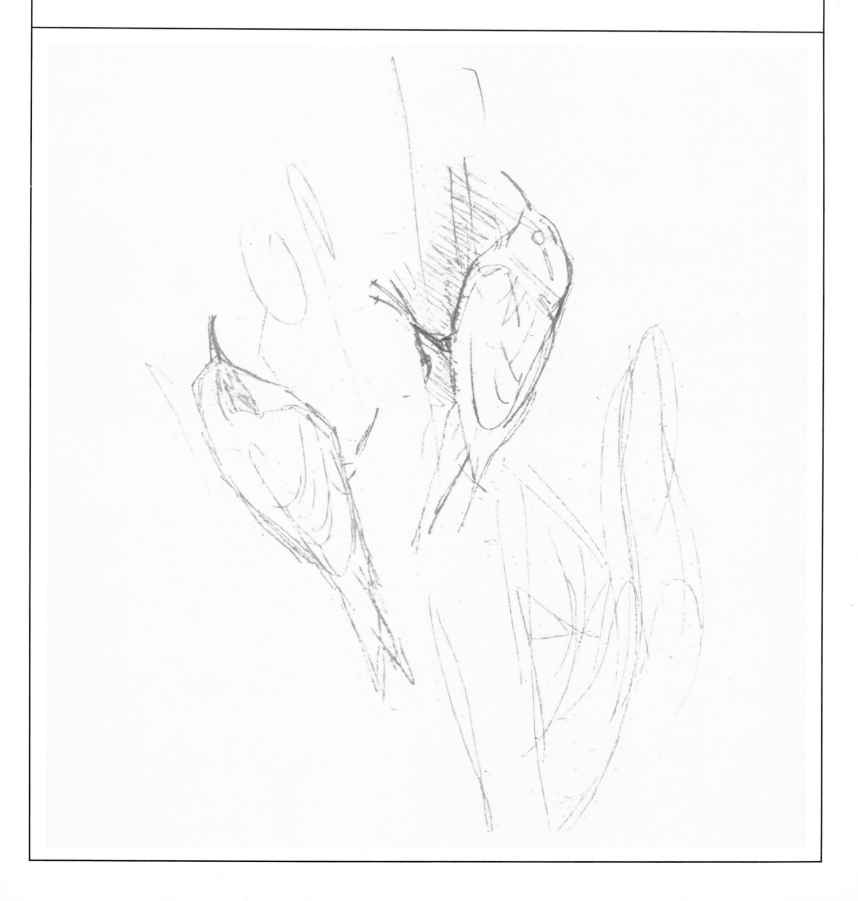

plate 58 BROWN CREEPER *Certhia familiaris*

Just because one is fascinated by birds in general, one does not have to like *all* birds. After saying that the brown creeper is the very model of dogged and patient industry, one finds it difficult to say anything else. A somewhat undistinguished bird, whose name describes it perfectly (it is brown and it creeps), it is one of five species of the northern hemisphere and the only one on our continent.

Our brown creeper is the same as the European tree creeper. All creepers are much alike in their adaptations to a special way of life, with slender body; long, curved, and delicate bill; long, stiff tail for propping against a tree trunk; and long-clawed toes for gripping. One does not need a close look to identify this bird; at almost any distance one will know a creeper by its behaviour. The nuthatch works head-downward. The creeper hitches its way upward, spiralling around the tree. When it reaches a certain height, the bird will fly down again (on somewhat longer wings than you might expect) to the base of an adjacent or nearby tree, there to begin circling upward again in its peculiar short hitches. Few birds are so predictable in their behaviour; perhaps none is so readily identified by its behaviour.

The creeper's probing, persistent pursuit of its insect prey is astonishingly thorough. This bird does not batter the tree as a woodpecker does, or pry at it the way a nuthatch does. In an utterly precise and painstaking way it delicately and methodically picks here and there, missing very little, so far as one can see. (Selous called its actions "dentistry," perhaps the most felicitous description ever). Of course it has all day to do it in, and very much gives that impression.

Usually creepers are solitary, although in winter you may run across small bands of them. These bands are usually transitory associations and not meaningful; the birds drift about with or without others of their kind, sometimes intermixed with golden-crowned kinglets and chickadees. Since the creeper has its own special niches to explore, it does not seem to come into competition with the other species.

Creepers are with us the year round in the eastern forest region, but many nest farther to the north, in the boreal forest. They move south from those latitudes, but apparently only as far as the prevailing weather dictates.

The nest of the brown creeper defied the most single-minded and determined searchers; it was not known for some time that the bird places its nest beneath a piece of projecting bark, superbly camouflaged and hidden, low down near the base of the trunk. When suitable trees are not available, the bird will resort to cavities, old woodpecker digs or knotholes, but these sites are exceptional. In the kind of forest it likes – deep woods with plenty of decaying timber – there is an abundance of nicely shredded tree trunks.

There are usually five or six white, brown-spotted eggs. The young – very like the adults except for their shorter tails – seem literally to disappear on the tree trunk as they clamber forth in their first exploratory venture. If they do not move, it is almost impossible to see them.

When I was young, I could discover few positive features about the brown creeper beyond its total devotion to duty. Then, one day, I heard a creeper singing in the nesting season. The song is quite remarkable in its strength; musical, and pleasant. It is high-pitched, however, and I suspect I shall not hear it much longer (as the years go by, one loses the top frequencies first). The quality of the call note is similar – excruciatingly weak and thin – a single *ss* rather like one-third of a golden-crowned kinglet's call.

Length 4³/₄ inches.   Male, Alexandria, Virginia, December 2.

plate 59—the sketch

HOUSE WREN

Troglodytes aedon

plate 59

HOUSE WREN *Troglodytes aedon*

THE wren family is of American origin. Of all the fifty-nine species of wrens in this hemisphere, only one has ventured to the Old World, where our winter wren has become "Jenny." Although the house wren has not followed its relative across the Bering Strait, it has spread (assuming its Central and South American counterpart to be the same species) from central Canada to Tierra del Fuego. A bewildering number of subspecific races have been recognized, but to all intents and purposes they are all house wrens.

Wrens are among the most volatile of birds, and the house wren is the most vigorous, aggressive, and mercurial of them all. Almost everyone knows a wren, and almost everyone knows this one, which has used man and his buildings to its fullest advantage. It readily accepts artificial nesting boxes, sometimes at the expense of other small birds, such as bluebirds, which we may want to attract.

The spring migration of house wrens goes almost unnoticed. One does not see flocks of them moving along, as in the case of so many other species. But on a bright spring morning, the bubbling, tempestuous song breaks out – and the tyrant of the backyard has arrived. As he sits on a fence, his throat and whole body quivering with the intensity of his song, the bird seems on the point of exploding with energy and emotion. Singing almost without pause, he forthwith begins to build a nest – or several of them – which may be in varying stages of completion when the females arrive.

During the nesting period, wrens are hard on other wrens, and even on birds of other species. They have been justly accused of scolding and chivvying larger birds, puncturing their eggs, killing their young and even the adults. (The house wren himself is known to have been evicted – by his cousin, the Carolina wren.) It almost seems that the wren's territorial urge is inversely proportioned to his size; he cannot tolerate anything with feathers near his nesting site.

Although we are most accustomed to thinking of wrens using bird houses, some bizarre sites have been recorded. Audubon placed his house wren family in an old felt hat, and said he had seen "many" in such quarters. Other unlikely nesting sites listed by Gross in Bent's *Life Histories* include a fish creel, watering pot, tin can, farm implements, teapots, a soap dish, boots and shoes, weathervanes, a coat pocket, and on the "rear axle of an automobile which was used daily." Gross says, "When the car was driven the wrens went along." They even hatched the eggs. No creature this adaptable could have failed to succeed.

A house wren's nest is typically a large, messy assortment of twigs and little sticks jammed into whatever space is available. As he may build several nests, he is kept frantically busy. Gross notes, "While so employed he often acquires a second mate while the first is still busy with household duties." Polygamy is fairly common with the house wren. In many cases, mates separate after the first brood. In fact, the female may already be looking for a second mate while her first brood is still in the nest, and the male is stuck with raising the fledglings.

There are a lot of house wrens; they nest twice, and the usual number of eggs is six or eight. It follows that there must be a very high mortality rate among the young, or we would have house wrens at pest proportions. Ninety percent or even more fail to reach breeding age. This is an excellent example of how nature ensures an inventory upon which to draw should there be a "crash" of adult house wrens. Otherwise, natural mortality keeps replacement at about par. A brutal method, perhaps, but utterly effective.

It is interesting that, as early as 1925, E. C. Hoffman noticed the adverse effects of pesticides on house wrens. He reported dead nestlings in abandoned nests in three successive years at a time when currant bushes were dusted with arsenate of lead. The adults disappeared shortly after they had carried arsenate-covered green currant worms to the nest. The pest control methods of forty-five years ago were primitive by comparison with the subtle synthetic compounds of today.

Length 4¹/₂ inches. Male, Washington, D.C., September 23.

plate 60—the sketch

CAROLINA WREN
Thryothorus ludovicianus

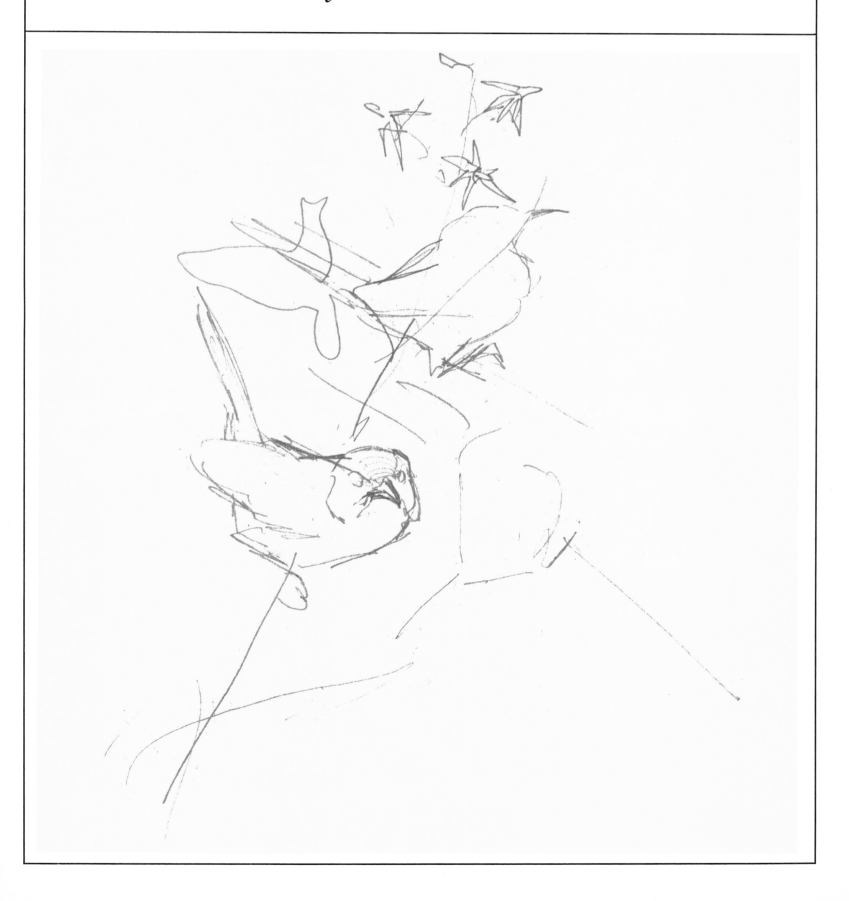

plate 60 # CAROLINA WREN *Thryothorus ludovicianus*

WRENS being the cautious, somewhat secretive creatures they are, chances are one will hear several Carolina wrens (and sometimes wonder whether they are titmice or cardinals) for every one seen. Its loud, rich carol has a rhythmic, rollicking nature which is characteristic: the song is usually a spirited three-part *tea-kettle, tea-kettle,* or a two-part *wheedle, wheedle* repeated half a dozen times. The song rings through the damp hardwood forests with authority and clarity at all seasons of the year. There are sundry variations, too, and a rich assortment of scolding, chattering notes.

The largest member of its family in the East is clearly identifiable as a wren by its shape and cocked-tail posture. The rich rufous upperparts and warm buffy underparts, together with a conspicuous eye-stripe, are unique. The Carolina wren is a sturdy-looking bird, perceptibly chunkier than its relatives. It is not common in Canada (where it is restricted to southern Ontario), but it occupies almost all of the eastern United States.

The bird is more aptly named than some, as it is unquestionably a southern animal, but in this century it has gradually pioneered its way northward, as have both the cardinal and, to a lesser extent, the tufted titmouse. It is sedentary and non-migratory, so wherever it happens to arrive in the north, there it will probably stay for the winter. The fact that it does not return to a more salubrious climate in the colder months has no doubt slowed its invasion of the North, but it now appears to have taken a reasonably firm hold along the north shores of Lakes Erie and Ontario.

Like all wrens, this bird is a confirmed "skulker"; it prefers dense, very brushy thickets. However, it will upon occasion become somewhat more confident and, especially in the South, it is often a familiar dooryard bird. It will even use buildings and other structures for nesting purposes; but it will do so only if there is good dense cover close by, into which it can retreat and angrily scold the passer-by. In a state of nature, the Carolina wren sticks to rich, wet woods, always with deep, tangled undergrowth.

The nest is rather large and looks somewhat informal from the outside, as so many wrens' nests do; the inner lining is composed of whatever soft materials are available. If it is forced to build in the open, the bird will often roof the nest over with a dome, with an opening in the side. As is the case with the house wren, the female is thought to incubate, but the final rearing of the young is often left to the male. Two or three broods are common in the south, each with from four to six young.

Birds as energetic, aggressive, and prolific as wrens commonly become involved in nuptial tangles. A. R. Laskey gave an interesting account in *Bird-Banding* of nest-building behaviour gone awry. A male Carolina wren became interested in a neighbourhood female and began to build a nest as part of his courtship ritual. Unfortunately he chose for its site the nest in which the female of his choice, and her mate, were already raising a brood of young. The parents kept on feeding the young birds despite the growing pile of twigs and other debris on top of them. The interloper was eventually removed a sufficient distance, and the brood was raised successfully.

Like most of our wrens, the Carolina is chiefly insectivorous, although in winter it will resort to a few seeds and berries. It will also come to your backyard feeding station. For those of us in the north to whom this is an uncommon species, feeders usually provide some of our best glimpses of the bird. It will not accept the offerings unless there is a deep tangled thicket somewhere close at hand, into which it may pop at an instant's notice. It is a curious bird and, even when it is in the depths of its retreat, it cannot restrain itself from coming forth to investigate the squeaking noises every birdwatcher learns to make. But it won't stay out long; its curiosity satisfied (or its attention span exhausted), it will again flit out of sight.

Length 4³/₄ inches.   Male, Statesville, North Carolina, October 6.

plate 61—the sketch

MOCKINGBIRD
Mimus polyglottos

plate 61

MOCKINGBIRD *Mimus polyglottos*

BIRDWATCHER learns to expect the unexpected, but the experience of Gerry Bennett at Petrolia, Ontario, near Windsor, richly deserves recording. It took place quite a number of years ago, at a time when Bennett had never seen a mockingbird. In the course of a morning's outing, he discovered a strange nest which was quite new to him. Baffled, he made a detailed description of nest and eggs, and on his next visit to the Royal Ontario Museum, he learned that he had found one of the then extremely rare Canadian nests of the mockingbird. A year or so later Bennett added the mockingbird to his personal list.

Mockingbirds are rarely seen in Canada. When one remembers that this elegant and personable species has been chosen the state bird of Arkansas, Florida, Mississippi, Tennessee, and Texas, one knows where to go to see it in its proper context. It was on my first visit to Texas, appropriately enough, that I first realized the mocker would sing all night long.

The song is the thing; the most eloquent and impassioned of American bird writers have striven to say the unspeakable. The mockingbird is, to be sure, an indefatigable singer, rather like the storied nightingale (which to my ear is more to be admired for the persistence of its rapid, disjointed, and extremely repetitive phrases than for euphony). As his name *Mimus polyglottos* (mimic of many tongues) implies, the mocker repeats the songs and calls of other birds. Many and remarkable have been the recorded feats of its mimicry. One or two examples will suffice. One "imitated thirty-two different kinds of birds in a space of ten minutes." Another is reported to have changed his tune eighty-seven times in seven minutes. Yet another changed one hundred and thirty-seven times in ten minutes. One of the most famous of all was said to imitate thirty-nine bird songs and fifty bird calls, plus the notes of a frog and a cricket. As Alexander Sprunt Jr. observes in Bent's *Life Histories* (source of the above records), the word for the mocker is "matchless."

The bird is, without question, matchless as a mimic. And it has delightful notes of its own. I think this is the most admirable bird we have – not only to listen to but also to watch. It sings from a very conpicuous perch, whether a telephone pole, a wire, or naked branch of a tree. But it soon stops singing when its year-round territorial prerogatives are threatened. No one transgresses the borders of a mocker's plot. He will fly fiercely at any other mockingbird and chase it away. He will chivvy cats and dogs – and people. He will "see off" birds of any species.

One winter evening, in a Florida garden, I saw the mockingbird's temper tested beyond reason. A very large flock of more than two hundred robins descended for food, drink, and bathing. The resident mockingbird was having fits as he attempted to drive them away. His rage and frustration mounted to terrible intensity; he flew repeatedly at the robins who came close to his favorite corner. He did manage to keep clear one small patch of lawn about thirty feet square, and within that area the robins appeared to defer to him. (I could not escape the anthropomorphic notion that the bigger birds were simply humouring him.) He was the picture of outraged fury, of course, and perhaps from a robin's eye view he may have appeared very fierce indeed.

The mockingbird is a slender, well-kept bird. It appears somewhat nondescript at rest – its most conspicuous feature being the long tail. Occasionally, a ruffle of feathers will reveal a pale highlight. In flight, however, the mocker becomes a different bird altogether, with flashing white patches in wings and tail.

The mocker does a good deal of foraging on the ground, poking for insects, picking up small fruits, and so on. It follows that a good number of the territorial incidents in the bird's life take place at ground level. Tails raised, heads tautly erect, the birds will face each other stiffly. They may hop about and then take to the air, one hotly pursuing the other. Or they may both go their own ways, their obligations satisfactorily concluded.

Length 9 inches. Male, Havana, Cuba, February 21.

plate 62—the sketch

CATBIRD

Dumetella carolinensis

plate 62

CATBIRD *Dumetella carolinensis*

I AM unmoveably persuaded that the catbird was placed upon this earth solely for the instruction and delight of small boys. It is common. Its voice is varied and attractive. It is secretive enough to provoke curiosity. Its nest is difficult to find (but not *too*). Its eggs are among the most handsome of any of the more common species. Sighting a catbird can recall almost-forgotten scents of spring lilacs, honeysuckles, and mock-oranges – the mysteries of dense Chinese elm hedges, hawthorn thickets, and hillside sumac groves.

This is the smallest of our eastern mimics (continentally, only the sage thrasher of the West is smaller), and the darkest. To all intents and purposes, it is a slate-gray bird with no remarkable features. Only on quite close inspection do you notice the black cap, and, on rather exceptional occasions, have a glimpse of the chestnut colouring under the tail. Usually the bird is in low silhouette against the sky or deep in the shadows of some thicket, even when it is singing at its best. Notice the slender shape and the long, flirting tail. It will occasionally emerge in response to your squeaks, but will quickly retire to its covert again.

The song of the catbird is not as varied as the mockingbird's, and it does not repeat its phrases. (Remember that the mockingbird makes many repetitions without pause, and that the brown thrasher speaks in couplets.) The catbird is every bit as musical as the mocker, however, and its own notes and phrases always take precedence over a rather minor degree of mimicry. The call note, the catlike *mew* which gives the bird its name, is often thrown into the pattern of the complete song. At the height of the season, this is one of the several species which will sing at night. A gentle, quiet "whisper song" has been noted in the autumn.

Under natural circumstances the catbird likes to nest in brushy, overgrown openings in the woods, shrubby meadows, and tangled ancient orchards. Run-down farmlands are ideal, in fact. Urban situations can be to its liking as long as there is plenty of dense shrubbery. There is every likelihood that an increase in this kind of habitat since settlement of the continent has been reflected in an increase in the catbird population. You will never find the bird in thick woods.

Although birds of this family have a tendency to stay close to their favourite singing perches, and not to move around much in the nesting season, when they do decide to move they are surprisingly swift and darting in their actions. This is particularly noticeable during courtship chases, when the male pursues the female across the lawn, in and out of the shrub borders, with a flickering speed that is quite unexpected.

The nest is large, and coarse-looking on the outside – a jumble of small sticks and twigs. But it is neatly lined within, with various soft materials. There is an average of four deep blue-green eggs, much darker than those of a robin, with an unusual glossy look to them – most beautiful. There are usually two broods, and the birds may or may not have the same mates the second time around. Catbirds' nests are occasionally parasitized by the cowbird, and sometimes the yellow-billed cuckoo has been known to contribute an egg to the catbird's clutch.

Catbird food is as varied as that of the other mimics; in season, various fruits and berries are important. In the south, there have been some allegations of serious catbird depredations on berry crops, but this seems to be of no significance in our area. In spring and summer, when young are being raised, the birds consume vast quantities of insects and other invertebrates, with emphasis on beetles and caterpillars of many kinds.

Most catbirds winter in the southern United States and Central America; the occasional individual roughs it out farther north.

Length 7³/₄ inches.   Male, Brandenburg, Kentucky, April 30.

plate 63—the sketch

BROWN THRASHER
Toxostoma rufum

plate 63 ## BROWN THRASHER *Toxostoma rufum*

Our largest eastern mimic is also the most colourful and the most elusive. While mockingbirds and (to a lesser extent) catbirds commonly frequent our gardens and door-yards, the thrasher keeps chiefly to itself. It is not as common as the other two, but is by no means scarce. It is trite to say a bird is more often heard than seen, but the saying is particularly true of the brown thrasher.

The bird's spring song is one of the more pronounced features of the season. Choosing a conspicuous, reasonably high station, the male sings strongly and vigorously; his loud notes carry for good distances. Although all rules have their exceptions, the thrasher *generally* sings in couplets, repeating each phrase only once before it moves on to another. It makes identification quite easy. The bird does not go in for mimicry nearly as much as the mockingbird does, or even the catbird. One may see the male while one is still a long way from him – his head will be raised, his long tail hanging below. But he will not allow a close approach; as you move toward him, he will hastily glide down to a suitably dense bit of shrubbery, there anxiously to await your passing. Photographs of singing thrashers are uncommon.

A brown thrasher can only be confused in the East with a large thrush, but it is much longer – by almost two inches – than any thrush. However, it does look superficially like one, and Audubon knew it as the "ferruginous thrush." His flamboyant plate illustrates three male thrashers, and a female, energetically defending a nest and four eggs against a black snake. In view of the strong territoriality of the thrasher, I have sometimes speculated about this plate, having in mind three adult males. But it is true that birds do tend to forget their internecine squabbles when there are dangerous predators around. And certainly the thrasher is dedicated in the defence of its plot. In any event, Audubon reported that the snake was finally done in, and that a "jubilee" was held over its carcass by a crowd of thrashers and other birds, "until the woods resounded with their notes of exultation"!

One's best look at a thrasher will probably come when it is foraging on the ground, as it commonly does. It is a long, tapered bird, bright cinnamon-rufous, with a graceful tail and a long, curved bill. At close quarters its gleaming yellow eye is surprisingly prominent. The bird will probe in your lawn for insects and their larvae, and will also "thrash" about noisily in the leaf litter at woodland edges. Its preferred food is insects – about two thirds of the total intake – but like its relatives it is also fond of wild fruit, including sumac, some cultivated berries, and acorn mast.

Nesting is always near the ground, or actually on it, invariably under good shelter such as thorn bushes, brush piles, tangled vines, and the like. I have found the nest remarkably difficult to find in view of the size and brilliant colour of the bird when it chooses to reveal itself. There are usually four eggs, not especially noteworthy for their beauty, being pale bluish with spotted brown. Like the other mimics, thrashers are impeccably clean about the nest, removing the fecal sacs of their offsprings religiously. They raise two broods, and may form new pairs for the second nesting. Thrashers have been known to lay eggs in the nests of other birds from time to time, including cardinals, robins, and wood thrushes.

This is the only thrasher in eastern North America; there are seven others in the West. Our bird will occasionally winter in the North, but generally it withdraws to the southern States.

276   *Length 10 inches.   Male, South Carolina, March 18.*

plate 64—the sketch

ROBIN

Turdus migratorius

plate 64 ROBIN *Turdus migratorius*

*I*F the first British colonists on the east coast of this continent had looked a little more closely at this hefty bird with the brick-red underparts, they might have realized it is much more closely related to the European blackbird than to the little robin redbreast of their homeland – although both are members of the thrush family. Many thrushes are spotted; our robins betray family characteristics in the plumage of the young birds and in their typically musical and varied songs.

There are sixty-odd members of the genus *Turdus*, most of them in the Old World. I have seen "robins" of one kind and another from Alaskan bogs to equatorial African jungles and forests of the Andes. They are all quite similar in build, posture, and behaviour – though not necessarily in colour. You can find our North American bird in deserts, woodlands, and cities – and from seashores to the high Rockies. It is one of our most widely distributed and successful birds.

Very few people do not know the robin. It seems to be one bird that has taken advantage of man and his works. All our settlements and other built-up areas are filled with robins. It is difficult to imagine a city park or a residential area without these birds; even industrial communities have robins. Frequently robins nest in unexpected locations – in parking lots, machine yards, and junkpiles, as well as on houses. But even though they have in a sense become human "satellites," robins are not as presumptuous as pigeons, house sparrows, and starlings. The robin remains very much a wild bird.

No robin in good health is self-effacing: it is a loud, strident, and vociferous bird. In spring and early summer, its clear carolling may begin well before dawn; for the birdwatcher arising while it is still dark, the robin is usually the first bird on the day's list. When it is not singing, the spring robin seems to be shrilling and screaming – wild courtship chases weave through our gardens and over our lawns always with piercing cries.

Birds of this genus build substantial nests, well-cemented with mud, easily recognizable. It is such a well-executed structure that you wonder why robins so frequently build a new nest in a new territory for their second brood. Usually there are four eggs. The robin has often been used as an example of population dynamics in nature. If both broods of four were successful, and all survived, we would have ten robins in the autumn for the two we had in the spring. It has been calculated that if this process were to go on uninterrupted, with adults and young continuing to survive for a period of ten years, there would be something of the order of nineteen *million* robins from that first pair. Of course this does not happen. Songbirds fall prey to predators, to diseases, to food shortages, and so on. Once out of the nest, the life expectancy of a young robin averages about a year and a half.

A sufficient number of robins do survive, however, to allow it to remain one of the most abundant birds on the continent. You need only see some of the spectacular flocks in Florida during the winter to realize what tremendous numbers of these birds there are. In the area just north of the entrance to Everglades National Park it is commonplace to see flocks of several hundred – often thousands. When they are on their way north, in the spring, they often roost en route in incredible numbers.

The robin's fondness for fruits, both wild and cultivated, is well-known. Large flocks can be a decided nuisance, sometimes, to cherry growers. But the bird's tastes are wide, and flocks seldom concentrate on any one item for very long. When young are in the nest they must have animal protein, and the birds' diligent search for earthworms is familiar to everyone. Unfortunately, earthworms containing DDT (often from elm leaves which they have eaten) can pass on lethal doses to the robins which prey on them.

*Length 8¹/₂ inches.   Male, Kershaw County, South Carolina, March 5.
Female, New Orleans, Louisiana, March 12.
Young, Victoria, British Columbia, May.*

plate 65—the sketch

WOOD THRUSH

Hylocichla mustelina

plate 65 # WOOD THRUSH *Hylocichla mustelina*

No sound in nature rivals the spring song of the wood thrush. When you first hear the strong, deliberately paced, incredibly musical phrases floating through the fresh green understorey of the hardwood forest, it is *the* high point of the year. No description of the song is adequate. For purity and richness, only the notes of the most sensitive woodwind seem comparable. The hermit thrush is the great singer of the boreal forest; but in the South, the wood thrush is in a category all its own.

Song is of course one of the chief characteristics of the great world family of thrushes. There are over three hundred species, including some of the most accomplished vocalists of all birds – nightingale, song thrush, and European blackbird among them. Thrushes are almost cosmopolitan as a family, but most of them are in the temperate zone and tropics of the Old World, where it is presumed they originated. On our continent, the thrushes are all strong migrants – most of them exceptionally hardy birds. This species winters in Central America, as far south as Panama.

In Canada, the wood thrush breeds only in southern Ontario and the extreme southernmost parts of Quebec, but its nesting range in the United States includes almost all of the eastern half of the country. This is the commonest thrush in the eastern hardwoods, with the exception of the robin. The latter has made itself much more at home in cities and otherwise built-up and populated areas; but in some places I suspect that wood thrushes are beginning to turn up more frequently in suburban gardens and well-wooded city ravines.

This bird is very much more like a robin than it is like the other brown *Hylocichla* thrushes – the veery, Swainson's, and gray-cheeked. Many authorities are now of the opinion that the wood thrush should join the robin in the genus *Turdus*, or rather that it should be restored to that genus. It used to be known (probably quite correctly) as *Turdus mustelinus*. In addition to more subtle pieces of evidence, the wood thrush is built rather differently from the others – heftier and chunkier – more like a robin. Had I not seen the owner of the first wood thrush nest I ever found, I would certainly have assumed it was that of a robin. Wood thrush spring courtship displays and chases are very robin-like. On the other hand, the occasional robin virtuoso can manage to sound something like a wood thrush.

We do not often see numbers of wood thrushes in migration. Usually the first evidence of the birds' presence is their song. The male is said to begin singing early in the season from high treetops, then, as the spring progresses, gradually to move to lower levels of vegetation. Certainly when the nesting period is well under way, the bird usually sounds as though it is singing from the ground, or very close to it. The flute-like phrases seem to echo and re-echo through the spring forest in delectable variety. But when you approach too closely, a sputtered, explosive alarm-note terminates the song. It is difficult actually to see a wood thrush singing; I still look forward to that pleasure.

In their study of the song of the wood thrush, Donald J. Borror and Carl R. Reese carefully checked the recorded songs of twenty-five different birds – no two of them sang identical songs. Their findings bore out a contention that had long been made by Aretas A. Saunders, one of the pioneers in this field, that one can recognize an individual wood thrush by his song. Borror and Reese discovered that beauty is only one of the features of this bird's voice. The song is, as well, incredibly complicated. Our ears miss most of its subtlety, but vibralyzer graphs illustrate the bird's "remarkable vocal gymnastics."

Length 7 inches. Male, Washington, D.C., May 3.

plate 66—the sketch

VEERY

Hylocichla fuscescens

plate 66

VEERY *Hylocichla fuscescens*

BIRDS do not usually come to birdwatchers; if an observer wants to see them, he must seek them out. Fortunately, there are occasional exceptions. As this book was being written, I was cooped up with my typewriter one May morning, too well aware that migration was at its peak. The birdwatcher's fidgety wanderlust was compensated for to some extent by a torrential rainstorm – the first big thundershower of the season. The rain pelted down harder and harder, with the noise level rising rapidly, when it was suddenly and cleanly interrupted by the glorious voice of a veery. The bird was singing in the height of the downpour, just a few feet from my studio window – but many miles from wherever it would nest. This is not an isolated phenomenon; I have several times heard veerys singing in the middle of the city; the rain seems to encourage them.

Usually one will hear the veery at its best at dawn and dusk, although the bird will sing throughout the day at the right season, and under cool, shady conditions. Associations play a large part in one's enjoyment of bird song; the veery's voice is always accompanied in my imagination by the clicks and peeps of frogs, the winnowing of snipe, the chirping of woodcock, the trills of amorous toads. One thinks of alder swales, willow thickets, and the depths of moist woodlands – and of uncountable mosquitoes.

The veery is rather easy to identify by its smooth warm colour over-all. The wood thrush has a reddish head; the hermit thrush has a reddish tail; gray-cheeked and Swainson's thrushes are more olive on the upperparts.

Winsor Marrett Tyler, in Bent's *Life Histories*, called the voice of the veery "one of the strangest sounds in nature." It has a quality which is strangely unbirdlike and almost impossible to describe. Each phrase is delivered at a lower pitch than the last, giving the full, rich song the effect of spiralling down the scale. One can often identify a bird by the quality of its voice with more assurance than by what it actually says. The veery's song has a husky nature which is quite characteristic. The notes are pure, but the voice has rich overtones – a "body" which makes it especially appealing. The call note is also distinctive – a whistled *wheeo*, with the emphasis dropping at the end.

The veery spends most of its time on or near the ground, searching the leaf litter for insects. Like all thrushes it eats fruits when they are available. The bird is often difficult to see in the forest. Walking along, one may glimpse a slender rufous-brown shape which darts from one hiding place to the next, and that will be all. Or, remaining perfectly still, one may see the bird perched, absolutely immobile, on a low twig. It is gone again in a wink, but the loud call-note will confirm the observation.

A veery's nest is built either on the ground or very close to it, deep in the ferns and low-growing shrubs of the forest carpet. The eggs are blue, rather like those of the wood thrush but smaller. Veerys nest almost right across the northern United States and southern Canada, but they do not quite reach the West Coast. They always adhere to hardwoods and mixed forests. They winter in northern and central South America.

Length 6 inches. Male, Cook County, Illinois, May 1.

plate 67 — the sketch

EASTERN BLUEBIRD

Sialia sialis

plate 67

EASTERN BLUEBIRD *Sialia sialis*

ROM the earliest days of settlement, few birds have prompted such exclamations of admiration as the gentle bluebird (although, as the tree swallow has learned, the bluebird is no gentler than any other under territorial conditions). It is unquestionably the most beautiful of our thrushes, with only its two western cousins, the mountain and western bluebirds, rivalling its pure, lovely colour.

Despite its rather ethereal appearance and its vulnerability to a number of natural and unnatural enemies, the bluebird is an extraordinarily hardy species. It goes no farther south in winter than it must; there are many records of birds wintering in Canada. In the East, most of them winter in the Carolinas, and often considerably farther north than that. In spring in our latitudes, the bluebird's throaty warble is one of the first signs of the new season; it drifts downward from fresh March winds as a promise of something better in store.

The ideal habitat for bluebirds is somewhat open country with scattered old trees; an abandoned farm or homestead is ideal, especially if there is a decrepit orchard to go with it. In colonial times and thereafter, bluebirds thrived; there was an abundance of nesting sites in rotten fruit trees and such places. Toward the end of the nineteenth century, however, stern competition arrived in the form of the tough, adaptable, and aggressive house sparrow, imported from Europe. The sparrows began forthwith to dispossess the bluebirds. No sooner had this happened than there was a second invasion – this time the even larger and more competitive European starling.

Worst of all, at about the same time as these invasions we began to go in for "clean farming" – the cutting down or pruning of old fruit trees, the removal of rotten fenceposts, and their replacement with metal posts. This had its effects almost overnight. The birds were driven from what remained of their habitat by the introduced exotics and had fewer and fewer places to which they could retreat.

Because bluebirds winter in large numbers in surprisingly high latitudes, they are vulnerable to sudden changes in the weather. A late February or early March freeze can catch them already on migration, and heavy losses have been suffered in late winter cold-snaps. Under normal conditions, no doubt, the birds' population dynamics had become adjusted to these occasional set-backs, but the additional pressures on their nesting grounds made it increasingly difficult for them to maintain their numbers. All these trials combined to bring the eastern bluebird population to a dangerously low level only a very few years ago.

Now, something positive may be happening. It is perhaps too early and over-optimistic to say so, but it *seems* that the imported Dutch elm disease may be giving the bluebird an unexpected "break." Many parts of its range are now filled with dead elm trees, which are attracting insects and, thus, woodpeckers. Many of the latter have provided new nesting sites for the bluebirds. Also, in the East there is evidence that the house sparrow populations have levelled off, and that starlings too may have become stabilized. If this is so, the dead elms may well contribute substantially to the beginning of a bluebird recovery.

Where nesting sites have been scarce, bluebirds have been assisted in many places by artificial nesting boxes. Many bird clubs and conservation societies have made projects of the building and setting up of bird houses designed especially for bluebirds. But even then, the bluebirds are not immune to the apparently "spiteful" attacks of house wrens. Also, tree swallows like to use bluebird boxes (although, as reported in Volume I, bluebirds have been known to dispossess the swallows).

*Length 5¹/₂ inches. Male, Mt. Vernon, Kentucky, October 3.
Female, Baton Rouge, Louisiana, January 3.*

plate 68—the sketch

BLUE-GRAY GNATCATCHER
Polioptila caerulea

plate 68 ## BLUE-GRAY GNATCATCHER *Polioptila caerulea*

GNATCATCHERS are treetop feeders so diminutive that one rarely has a good, clear look at them. When a gnatcatcher is seen for the first time, it is strĭkingly like a scaled-down mockingbird – gray coloration above, white below; long twitchy tail with white borders; slender bill. The two, of course, are not related, but the resemblance is strong. Unlike the mockingbird, however, the gnatcatcher is not zealous to advertise its presence. Were it not for the painfully thin, wheezy *twang* which is its call-note, uttered almost constantly as it feeds, one would rarely be aware of its presence.

There is some disagreement about the family relationships of gnatcatchers. They are among our smallest birds, but totally different from other small bird species. They have been considered members of the Old World warbler family (unrelated to our North American wood warblers), which also includes our kinglets. Some authorities, however, speculate that the gnatcatchers do not belong to this group, that they are actually of New World origin. Whatever their genealogy, they resemble no other birds in our area.

There are eight kinds of gnatcatchers (this is the only one in eastern North America) ranging from southern Canada to the southern parts of South America. This species is found from the most southern areas of Ontario, along lakes Erie and Ontario, across most of the eastern and southern United States. It winters from Florida and California south; I have seen it in winter in the Mexican provinces of Quintana Roo and Yucatan, and in Guatemala. But the birds breed in Mexico

as well, so one cannot be sure of the identity of Central American birds at that season.

It is said that the gnatcatcher has a soft, attractive, vireo-like song, but I have never heard it. The characteristic note is the call described above, which never seems to cease as the birds forage for food and work about their nest. In feeding, they are extremely active and fidgety – hovering like hummingbirds, darting out and back again in the manner of a flycatcher, restlessly working among the leaves of deciduous trees.

There is some evidence that insects may be the sole food of this species, barring a few items of vegetable matter under special circumstances, such as those offered at winter feeding trays in the south. But the long and tapered bill is not that of a confirmed fruit or seed eater. The bird's speciality is, as it were, as plain as the beak on its face.

The nest of the gnatcatcher is a delightful jewel, almost as delicate as a hummingbird's. A tiny cup is saddled across a horizontal branch, and the nest, as described by Francis Marion Weston in Bent's *Life Histories,* is "compactly built of plant down and similar materials bound together with insect silk and spider web and covered externally with bits of lichen."

There are four or five incredibly tiny eggs, pale blue-white, dotted brown. When the young emerge, the always frenetic activity of the birds builds to a new pitch of nervous excitement. Urgently flickering about in the leaves, tails flitting, the gnatcatchers resemble nothing so much as little mechanical birds wound tightly to an unbearable degree of explosive energy.

Length 4 inches.   Male, Baton Rouge, Louisiana, November 13.

plate 69—the sketch

CEDAR WAXWING
Bombycilla cedrorum

plate 69 CEDAR WAXWING *Bombycilla cedrorum*

However one chooses to look at them, waxwings are mysterious and unconventional birds. They are common enough, but their comings and goings, and even their familial ties, are for the most part poorly understood – if they are, in any sense, understood at all. They can be recognized by the uncommonly smooth and silky texture of the body feathering, by the crest and the brightly coloured wax-like droplets on the wing, the function of which is completely unknown. There are three kinds of waxwings in the world, but the cedar waxwing is restricted to North America. The larger and more colourful Bohemian waxwing lives in the northern forests of both America and Eurasia, and there is a third species in Japan.

For the sake of convenience, ornithologists have dumped the waxwings into what Austin calls a "trash-basket" family, along with the four silky flycatchers of Central America (one of which occurs in the United States), the strange palm chat of Hispaniola, and one waif in Asia Minor, the *Hypocolius*. All of these seem to be chiefly fruit-eaters; they live in trees, and they share the soft, attractive plumage. None is renowned for the quality of its voice. Beyond that, their relationship is obscure – if they are related at all.

Except in the breeding season, one is unlikely to see waxwings in the same place more than a day or two in a row. They are confirmed nomads, and seem to oscillate wildly in numbers from year to year. This is a common species, no question, but if one were in the position of having just a day in which to show one to a visiting European birdwatcher, it would be a challenge few of us could meet. These birds are utterly unpredictable, appearing one day to feed upon the fruit appropriate to the season, and disappearing the next.

Waxwings are strong fliers, and they are noticeably gregarious most of the year. They fly swiftly, looking something like starlings in their style, and as they move they give an almost continuous high-pitched, sibilant, lisping call note.

But when they alight, they often seem to disappear altogether. An entire flock may come to rest in the dead topmost spire of a tree, and then remain so perfectly still that if one hadn't seen them land, one could walk right by them.

Cedar waxwings nest unusually late in the season for birds in our latitudes – from midsummer and even later. Don't look for them in thick woods. They prefer partly open country, such as scattered cedar swamps among fields, loose orchards, and situations of that kind. The nest is big, and somewhat unkempt. Young birds are stuffed with insects and berries. Their appetites are enormous. Margaret Nice once reported that food fed to the young may pass through the digestive tract in as little as sixteen minutes. Adults, too, are gorgers. A good hatch of flying insects is snapped up in midair, and, when the mountain ash berries are orange and red, the waxwings never seem to know when they have had enough.

Unlike some birds, these do not seem to be closely tied to their nesting areas, or to the areas of their birth. In one experiment, of seventy-two banded adults only two came back to the same site next year. Of 174 banded young, not one turned up in the same area again. Cedar waxwings raise two broods, usually. They have been seen to begin courtship again, and even to copulate, while the first young are still in the nest. They have even been known to begin laying eggs before the first fledglings had left the nest.

Obviously waxwings are opportunists, nesting and wintering where food supplies are most propitious. Some years, when the pickings have been good for two or three breeding seasons in a row, the populations build up spectacularly. Then, there may be a "crash" in their favoured food, and we sometimes notice great irruptions of waxwings where they may not have been seen for quite some time. The populations have a way of levelling out again fairly soon, and things get back to normal. In winter, though, the birds are never predictable, and no one can anticipate where they will turn up next.

Length 5³/₄ inches.   Male, Kershaw County, South Carolina.

plate 70—the sketch

LOGGERHEAD SHRIKE
Lanius ludovicianus

plate 70

LOGGERHEAD SHRIKE *Lanius ludovicianus*

Most of us cherish certain immutable notions about birds (and about a long list of other things, for that matter). When something happens to challenge one of these hitherto unquestioned beliefs, it is worth remembering. Such was my experience with this species one winter day in North Carolina, where the loggerhead shrike is a very common bird.

The North American shrikes are not renowned for their voices, and most accounts of their songs and calls damn with faint praise. However, on the fine January day in question, I happened to be en route to Florida, with my wife and the Henry Barnetts. We stopped to look at some roadside birds, and were immediately struck by a sweet, almost bell-like and ringing note which none of us recognized. We spent some time searching for its source, which turned out to be a shrike; it called repeatedly for several minutes as we watched. It was a wholly unusual and lovely sound, in both quality and tone – sufficiently so to be distinctly remembered after many years. I have never heard it since.

The loggerhead is the only one of the world's seventy-odd shrikes restricted to North America. Its close and very similar relative, the northern shrike, lives in the boreal forests of both hemispheres. Most of the shrikes are in the Old World; there is none in South America. Some of the equatorial African species have extraordinarily beautiful and sometimes complex songs; the family potential is there, it would seem.

It could be said that the shrike is a songbird-turned-predator. The only physical evidence of its proclivity is the specialized beak – heavy, notched, and with a hooked tip – very effective for catching large insects, small birds, and other prey. The shrike does not use its feet for hunting; they are no different from those of any other songbird. When it must carry its prey, it usually does so in its bill. Incidentally, the shrikes have had plenty of time in which to undertake a new way of life and to develop their specialty; shrikes have been around for the better part of twenty-five million years.

A shrike often looks like a chunky, big-headed mockingbird as it sits immobile on some telephone wire, surveying its hunting domain. But when it flies, it zooms almost straight downward, scuds along close to ground level, then abruptly rises again to alight on the next wire, pole, or shrub. This flight pattern is absolutely characteristic. As the bird flies, one will notice white flashes in the tail and wings, but the latter are much smaller than those of the mockingbird.

This bird is not as large or aggressive as the northern shrike. It follows that birds and mammals play a lesser role in its food requirements. It spends most of its time working on large invertebrates and the occasional very tiny reptile and amphibian, though in winter and at other seasons it is not averse to the lesser birds, and some of the smallest mammals.

The old name for shrike was "butcher bird," not because it eats meat but because of its habit of impaling prey on a thorn or lodging it in the fork of a twig, the better to pull it to pieces. If you are equipped with the bill of a predator and the feet of a songbird, you need some additional purchase for cutting up your food. Sometimes the northern shrike returns to these "caches" in times of lean pickings; the loggerhead is rarely seen to do so. As Sprunt observes in Bent's *Life Histories*, "Food in the loggerhead's range is so abundant and constantly available that there is rarely an occasion when the bird has to resort to already secured prey. Conversely, there are doubtless times when the northern bird is hard put to it in winter and uses a larder far more frequently."

Loggerhead shrikes breed north to the southern limit of the coniferous forest. They are never ones to call undue attention to themselves, and while nesting they are especially self-effacing and inconspicuous. The bulky nest may be in a thick hawthorn or other impenetrable shrub, or in a dense tree. Look for shrikes in rural areas which provide plenty of open space for the bird to search from its lookout perch.

Length 7 inches.   Male, Fort Snelling, Minnesota, March 30.

plate 71—the sketch

WHITE-EYED VIREO

Vireo griseus

plate 71

WHITE-EYED VIREO *Vireo griseus*

ENEALOGIES of some birds are difficult to unravel, and that of the vireos is one of the more troublesome. Their ancestry is thought to lie somewhere between the shrikes and the warblers, but it is by no means certain. Some people believe that vireos are much closer to being shrikes; others even maintain they may have tanager affinities. The confusion probably arises from the fact that all these families of birds are relatively recently evolved, in terms of the geological time scale, and that clear-cut differences between them have not yet become manifest. Since vireos, warblers, blackbirds, and tanagers are all thought to have arisen in the American tropics, it is reasonable to think that at some distant stage they had a common ancestry. There are in the tropics today some birds which seem to overlap family boundaries, and which make the problem all the more vexatious – and fascinating.

There are about forty species of vireos, most of them in the tropics. In North America (north of Mexico) we have twelve; in Canada, eight, of which two are "fringe" species at best. The white-eyed is one of the latter.

No Canadian is going to learn much about the white-eyed vireo by staying at home. This is a bird of the south-eastern United States, which reaches its northern limit in New England and the southernmost parts of the Great Lakes area. It intrudes regularly but sparingly into Canada around Point Pelee, Ontario, but rarely elsewhere. The farther south one goes, the better one comes to know this attractive little bird, especially in the Gulf states, where it lives the year round. It winters as far south as Central America, and is common throughout the greater part of its range.

The smaller vireos – and the white-eyed vireo is one of them – are frequently mistaken for warblers. It will be noticed, however, that a vireo has a much more substantial bill than most warblers, and much less striking colour in its plumage. Vireos run to olive-greens and yellows; some have wing-bars, but they never show any streaks or spots of any kind. Also, vireos move in a much more sluggish fashion than warblers do. They will do some minor gymnastics, such as hanging upside-down occasionally, but even these tricks are done with a slow deliberation which is characteristic of the family. The white-eyed vireo is more active than most, and as the result it is more likely to be taken for a warbler than the others.

This species can instantly be recognized by its bright yellow sides, its wing bars, and the yellow "spectacles" around its white eye. The eye of the young bird is brown. Even more remarkable than its appearance, however, is its song; once it has been learned, it is rarely forgotten. There are always innumerable ways of attempting to express a bird song in an idiom understandable to people, but this one says something like *chick! widdo-weeo, chick!* with varying additional syllables. No matter what form the song may take, the *chick!* and the *weeo* are fairly standard. One will hear this song coming from virtually every thicket in Florida during the winter, where the white-eyed vireo sings all year.

This is fortunate, for this vireo inhabits the densest tangles, briars, thickets, and thorn bushes. It can be extremely hard to see, but when you hear one singing, have patience. Sooner or later it will come out to have a look at you, and if you do not startle it, it will inspect you at a surprisingly close range.

Like all our vireos, this species eats mostly insects, but in winter in the South it has been known to take food such as "sumac, grapes, and wax myrtle." As might be expected, it nests in the heaviest protective cover available. I have not seen the nest, which Pough describes as "fairly bulky for a vireo, and more cone- than cup-shaped ... often ragged-looking because of the leaves, moss, wasp paper, and sticks woven in with its soft woody fibres." The bird is a common victim of the cowbird, which shows an uncanny ability to find even the most deftly hidden nests.

Length 5 inches.   Male, Gulfport, Mississippi, March 23.

plate 72—the sketch

YELLOW-THROATED VIREO

Vireo flavifrons

plate 72 YELLOW-THROATED VIREO *Vireo flavifrons*

THOUGH vireos are not distinguished for their striking coloration, the yellow-throated vireo is without doubt handsomest in our area. It is also the easiest to identify, through the combination of white wing-bars and yellow spectacles, throat, and breast. But a glimpse that will afford you those several details simultaneously is rare; this is a bird that likes the high foliage of leafy hardwoods, and it is small and difficult to see. It pays to take your time, and to know its song.

This one sounds something like the red-eyed vireo (always the basic criterion for vireo songs and the one you must learn first), but it sings much more slowly, with longer pauses between phrases, more huskily, and at a lower pitch. To my ear, the quality of the sound is somewhat tanager-like. It drifts downward so slowly and lazily on a warm summer day that you would expect little difficulty in picking out the singer, but he manages to keep himself irritatingly well-hidden.

Yellow-throated vireos are not as common as the white-eyes, but they venture farther north in the Great Lakes region. They like gardens, parks, and farm woodlots where there are plenty of large shade trees, and generally avoid the depths of the forest.

I used to know a very dependable place for yellow-throated vireos just a few miles northwest of Toronto, but that place has been drastically changed, and I no longer have any choice spot at which to listen for these birds with any real expectation of success. They demand the biggest shade trees, and good stands of them, and apparently will not settle for anything less. In parts of its range where Dutch elm disease has had the greatest impact the effect has been clear.

Writing before 1950, Bent observed, "I have always suspected that its disappearance was largely due to the excessive spraying of our shade and orchard trees." Most of our certain knowledge of the effects of pesticides on birds is at the moment confined to some of the larger species such as the bald eagle and the peregrine falcon, each of which is at the apex of a long and often complex food chain. The situation with regard to smaller birds is much less clear, although there now is little doubt that chemical pesticides of many kinds influence every living thing in the environment. In any event, if pesticides have not been a factor in the changing fortunes of the yellow-throated vireo, other environmental changes certainly have. Mature deciduous woodland is its prime need, and there is not as much of that habitat as there once was.

Bent describes the nest as the handsomest of any of the vireos, "even prettier than the best examples of the nests of the blue-headed vireo, and fully as well decorated as the nests of the hummingbird, wood pewee, and blue-gray gnatcatcher, though differing from all these in shape and suspended from the prongs of a forked twig." Like the white-eyed and some other vireos, it is reluctant to leave its nest and is often remarkably tame when approached while sitting. Bent says "it cannot easily be driven from its nest and must often be removed forcibly, sometimes with difficulty," which calls forth in the imagination a picture which I am sure the author did not mean to convey!

For the winter, yellow-throated vireos **withdraw** to the tropics of their origin, spending the season in Central America, south to Panama.

Length 6 inches.   Male, Asheville, North Carolina, September 10.

plate 73—the sketch

RED-EYED VIREO
Vireo olivaceus

plate 73 # RED-EYED VIREO *Vireo olivaceus*

WITHOUT doubt, the most impressive way to introduce the red-eyed vireo is to report the famous contribution of Louise de Kiriline Lawrence, who counted 22,197 songs from one bird in the course of a single day! I have sometimes wondered whether that classic record was due more to Mrs. Lawrence's persistence or to the bird's. It is not only the best possible sidelight on the red-eyed vireo, but also a splendid example of ornithological dedication.

The song of the red-eyed vireo is heard in all its persistent continuity almost wherever there are shade trees. Robbins *et al.* call this "the most abundant bird of eastern deciduous forests." Peterson once calculated that it is probably more numerous than the robin. More people know the robin because robins are conspicuous in cities and suburbs, and they are big and to some extent flamboyant. However, it is difficult to picture any area of deciduous trees of any size whatever which does not support several pairs of red-eyed vireos. Listen on any sunny day in June, and be convinced.

The bird sounds rather like a robin, but the song is divided into deliberate phrases, with a pause between every phrase. It tends to go up the scale with one phrase, and to descend again with the next. The bird will sing for many minutes at a time without even appearing to stop for breath. For its indefatigability (or perhaps repetitiveness) it has been nicknamed "preacher" in parts of the South.

This is the largest vireo in our area and by far the most common, and should be your yardstick for identifying the others. The dull colours and sluggish, leisurely movements are characteristic. Notice the relatively heavy bill. You will know the bird not so much by its red eye (young have brown eyes) as by its general olive colour, the bold white stripe over the eye, and the grayish cap on the head. Once you know this vireo, and its song, the others will begin to fall into place.

Like any other vireo, this one is almost entirely insectivorous in spring and summer, methodically working its way along branches and small twigs, incessantly searching for insects, their eggs, larvae, and pupae. In the fall, Pough reports that the birds "relish blueberries, the berries of dogwood, spicebush, sassafras, and magnolia, as well as a great variety of small fruits." They need to stoke up well for their fall migration, which will carry them (flying at night) all the way to South America, from Brazil to Peru.

Although red-eyed vireos forage mostly in the widest canopy of leafy trees, they nest somewhat lower down. Vireos build attractive cup-like nests which are suspended from a suitable crotch or from a fork in a twig. This one is especially handsome, daintily decorated with lichens, bits of leaves, and mosses, and spider webs or similar material. There are three or four eggs. Both sexes are said to incubate, and both feed the young.

This is our most widely distributed vireo, from the Maritimes to the Mackenzie, south to the Gulf Coast.

Length 6¹/₂ inches.   Male, Roseboro, North Carolina, May 2.

plate 74—the sketch

WARBLING VIREO

Vireo gilvus

plate 74

WARBLING VIREO *Vireo gilvus*

Sometimes it would seem as though the vireos as a family had for some reason decided to make a policy of drab inconspicuousness and secretiveness. The most common species – and this is one of them – are surprisingly unfamiliar to most people. But you could never call it a conspiracy of silence. These are among the most vocal of our birds, and by their songs we know them.

Even the most highly coloured of the eastern vireos, the yellow-throated, is something less than brilliant. By comparison, the warbling vireo is very much a nonentity, a plain, gray little bird with a pale eye-stripe and a typical vireo bill.

There is nothing pedestrian about its voice, unique among our vireos. The song of no other species has its warbling quality, which sounds rather like a repetitive purple finch. The songs of most vireos are broken into discernible phrases, but this one is continuous: it spirals upward, ending on a higher pitch than it began. It is like most vireos, however, in its persistence; this species has been estimated to sing as many as four thousand times in a day, during the breeding season. The male is so intent on singing that he will even warble away quietly while he is doing his share of incubating the eggs. Hour after hour, the song continues, usually from a considerable height in the shade trees.

The nest is built in the usual vireo cup-shape, most often fairly high up in a big, leafy tree, frequently placed out near the swaying tip of a drooping branch. When he was living in New Jersey, Audubon watched the construction of a warbling vireo nest just outside his window, and he discovered that in this activity, as in their feeding, vireos can be exasperatingly slow and deliberate. He remarked that as the birds returned from material-gathering forays, "they moved so slowly from one tree to another, that my patience was severely tried." Things moved more quickly thereafter. Audubon reported that the eggs hatched in twelve days, and that the young were on the wing in sixteen days.

I think it is an experience common to most of us to think of a bird not necessarily in the surroundings where we see it most often, but in a special and individual context which for one reason or another made a lasting impression. There is in my memory an especially resolute singer in a small stand of willows on the bank of the St. Lawrence River near Montreal. Not having a vireo's staunch tenacity, I did not count his songs, but do recall that he sang all day long, without perceptible pause, as he made his quiet and leisurely way about, feeding all the while.

Winsor Marrett Tyler's contribution on the (eastern) warbling vireo in Bent's *Life Histories* was published in 1950, several years before the complicated links between synthetic chemical pesticides and birds had been worked out. He sensed, however, that something was wrong. "In recent years the warbling vireo has probably suffered more from the spraying of the shade trees with poison than from the natural enemies that commonly beset small arboreal birds. Their nests have been imperiled by the high-pressure spraying that rocks the elm branches at the vital points of the birds' summer distribution, the roadside trees of our country towns." This was a nice observation; all of us have seen the force generated by the large hoses of the sprayers. Little did we know, however, in 1950, of the insidious residual properties of DDT and its relatives. Perhaps one day we will recognize the total impact of pesticides on insectivorous birds.

Length 4³/₄ inches.   Male, Arnett, Oklahoma.

plate 75—the sketch

BLACK-AND-WHITE WARBLER

Mniotilta varia

plate 75 # BLACK-AND-WHITE WARBLER *Mniotilta varia*

ALTHOUGH this strangely-striped little bird is every bit the true warbler, with its slender bill, its size and shape, and its compulsive hyper-activity, it is marked like no other warbler and behaves like no other. When I was very young I knew it first as the black and white "creeper" (as did Wilson and some of the other early ornithologists, I discovered later). The bird in the hand is clearly recognizable as a warbler, but in the bush its actions are somewhat aberrant.

With the single exception of the similarly-inclined brown creeper, here is the very soul of assiduity and concentration. But where the creeper never varies from its feeding procedure, the warbler, like its kin, is given to improvisation. It works over the trunks and larger limbs of trees with delicacy and precision, flickering from place to place, probing and exploring for insects and other invertebrates. It commonly hangs upside-down, like a nuthatch, or works its way upward like a creeper. At other times it will catch insects in midair with the best of the flycatchers, or perform chickadee-like acrobatics. But generally it sticks to its job of bark-creeping, and it is impossible to confuse with any other warbler in our area.

The only other warbler which looks remotely like this one (and it takes a stretch of the imagination to create any real similarity) is the arrow-headed warbler *Dendroica pharetra* of Jamaica, a rather different, olive-coloured bird which does not creep. I once made an honest effort to turn a black-and-white warbler into the Jamaican species, without success. On June 13, 1968, on the island of Tobago, just a short distance from the Venezuelan mainland, my wife and I saw a warbler which was to all intents and purposes a black-and-white, but which simply could not be – on that date. Despite our efforts to consider the arrow-headed warbler, we had no success. It was clearly an erring black-and-white which had appeared after a heavy thundershower,

and was busily working in its specific fashion on a *Casuarina* – presumably the nearest thing to a northern tamarack it could find. The bird should by that time have been on its breeding territory in the northern United States or Canada, but there it was, a lonely waif undoubtedly lost to its species forever.

This sort of thing happens, of course, and the species is just as well-off without an individual who gets that far out of step. Black-and-white warblers have to know how to migrate and they have to get to the correct destinations. They are among the earliest warblers to arrive in our part of the world, often before the trees are in leaf. This could be a hindrance to those species which depend on insects in opening leaf-buds, but the black-and-white goes straight to work on the coarse bark of the larger trees.

As a rule warbler songs do not match the quality of the birds' plumage; at least they are not especially pleasant to human ears. The voice of this species is typically high-pitched, more remarkable for its upper frequencies than for structure or euphony. The song is wiry and agonizingly thin; it has been described as *wesee, wesee, wesee,* and so on. It is useful to think of the bird as rapidly inhaling and exhaling (which it is not) thus: *ss ss ss ss ss,* like the sound of an elfin saw in wood.

The nest is placed on the ground, and will hold four or five white, brown-spotted eggs. Bent includes a Michigan report from George W. Byers of a black-and-white warbler nest which contained two of the warbler's eggs and *eight* cowbirds' eggs. "His photograph of the eggs suggests that they were probably laid by four different cowbirds."

Black-and-white warblers are fairly common on Florida in winter, but most of them spend the winter in Central and South America as far south as Colombia. They appear to have no hesitation whatever about flying across the Gulf of Mexico, but Sprunt has seen them use the Dry Tortugas as stepping stones.

*Length 4³/₄ inches.   Male, Gainesville, Florida, May 10.
Female, Alexandria, Virginia, July 26.*

plate 76—the sketch

PROTHONOTARY WARBLER
Protonotaria citrea

plate 76 # PROTHONOTARY WARBLER *Protonotaria citrea*

MANY of the most evocative and historic North American place-names reflect the prevailing attitudes of colonial times so far as wild nature is concerned. There is none of these which I cherish more highly than the Great Dismal Swamp of Virginia and North Carolina. The male bird in the illustration came from there, and it may be difficult for some of us to reconcile the flaming splendour of the prothonotary warbler with all the overtones of dread and mystery which are implicit in the very name of the Great Dismal. As Joseph James Murray pointed out in *The Bird Watcher's America*, "At sun-up in the spring the Great Dismal is vibrant with sounds; at twilight it is truly dismal and any of its strange legends take on credence."

Too many of us think of a swamp as a smelly bog or an impenetrable marsh or some other tangled and muddy situation. A true swamp is a flooded forest with a dense canopy of tall trees (in the south, usually cypress) shading silent, open, fresh water. Too many of us also think only in terms of multitudes of biting insects, squadrons of deadly snakes, and a wide assortment of malevolent, otherworldly beings. Such a place is dark, to be sure, but it is the very gloom that provides the only possible setting for the *nonpareil* among warblers, the golden swamp bird.

"Prothonotary" is a ridiculous name, as all ornithologists have agreed. It means a chief papal notary, who wears a yellow hood. Unfortunately the pompous name was inflicted on the bird a long time ago, and the traditions of nomenclature are stubborn. For the present at least, we – and the undeserving bird – are stuck with it.

It is interesting to consider how many of the world's most brilliant birds live in the almost perpetual shadows of the deepest forests. One thinks of trogons, turacos, so many hummingbirds and cotingas, birds of paradise.

It is as though the intensity of their colouring were somehow too much to be revealed to open sunlight, and had been deliberately reserved for only the most fleeting disclosure. The prothonotary is one of these – an ephemeral flare which burns for an instant in the black mirror of a still pool, and is gone again.

This gorgeous warbler breeds over most of the eastern United States, wherever there are appropriate dark swamps with open water and plenty of drowned and otherwise dead trees for nesting sites. A favourite spot is the stump of a tree, standing in water, ideally containing the old excavation of a downy woodpecker.

This is the only eastern warbler which habitually nests in holes. In one study, Walkinshaw tried bird boxes on the prothonotaries with some success, but found that the birds had competition for tenancy with the much more aggressive house wrens. A small bird's life is difficult: one prothonotary nest in southern Ontario contained no eggs of the rightful owner, but seven of the cowbird.

As is often the case with birds of forests, where the understorey is in dense shadow, the voice of the golden swamp warbler is loud and ringing. It is as distinctive as its colouring – a clear and carrying *sweet, sweet, sweet*, which you will readily recall once you have heard it. The song is quite different from those of the two other warblers with which it might be confused. The blue-winged warbler, which it resembles superficially, lives in a different habitat, and has a black line through the eye together with wing bars. The yellow warbler has yellow wings, and at any distance appears all yellow.

This is a rare and very local bird in Canada. It occurs regularly only along the north shore of Lake Erie, especially at Rondeau Provincial Park, which is somewhat more dependable than Point Pelee. It winters in Central and South America.

*Length 4³/₄ inches.   Male, Great Dismal Swamp, Virginia, June 4.
Female, Mount Carmel, Illinois, May 8.*

plate 77 — the sketch

GOLDEN-WINGED WARBLER

Vermivora chrysoptera

plate 77 GOLDEN-WINGED WARBLER *Vermivora chrysoptera*

*A*T one time or another most of us have inflicted our special interests and enthusiasms on our children. It is possible, however, that we naturalists may be slightly more prone to the habit than some others. It seems that we do so at least until the children are of an age to make a choice, and we hope that we have done the right kind of "conditioning." When my daughter Sally was very small – at that truly magical age when everything is novel and ever so stimulating – I used to take her birdwatching from time to time.

One May morning we happened to find ourselves in the midst of an unusually large warbler "wave." Warblers were everywhere – redstart, magnolia, chestnut-sided, black-throated green, and all the rest. We enjoyed ourselves thoroughly for an hour or two (how pleasurable it is to see old treasures through new eyes), in the delightful process of giving names to new things. On our way home, the little girl stopped, pointed upward, and said, "There's one that's different. We haven't seen it before." I doubted that seriously – six-year-olds see any number of strange and unusual things – but, indulgently, I checked the bird. Of course, it was a fine male golden-wing, its occurrence infrequent enough in our area to be duly noted and filed.

It is always a joy to come across this splendid warbler. Even at the best of times the bird is elusive, and it does not seem to be really common anywhere. The odds against picking many up in spring migration are fairly long, and you need to find a nesting territory in order to be able to venture out with any real expectation of seeing one.

In my somewhat local experience with the golden-winged warbler, it has been a bird of rank, young deciduous growth. Except in migration, you will rarely see it in tall trees, but at that season it often seems to select the very tallest. It may turn up in somewhat dry situations, or in swamps and swales. For nesting, the common denominator appears to be the thickest and densest stands of alder, birch, poplar, and willow saplings. In so far as we have such habitat, it is a "jungle" bird.

When you have an opportunity to observe the golden-wing clearly and at length, you will unfailingly notice its acrobatic behaviour. Like a Nashville warbler, or any chickadee, it does much upside-down feeding. It moves, clings, and flutters from twig to twig with all the grace and dexterity of a kinglet, usually so swiftly that it is not always easy to distinguish its markings.

Essentially, this warbler is gray above, white below, with black face patch and throat. One may or may not see the yellow wing patch clearly. There is wide variation in the golden-wing's song, which is best described as buzzy. Usually the first buzz is followed by others on a lower pitch. The quality is rather different from that of any other warbler except for the blue-wing, and a visual check is always recommended.

Golden-winged warblers breed in the southern parts of the Great Lakes region and New England, and somewhat farther down in Appalachia. In Canada they barely extend through the southern parts of Ontario, but there are records elsewhere. The lower part of the golden-wing's range overlaps with that of the blue-winged warbler, which is so closely related that the two species frequently hybridize. Golden-wings winter in Central America and the northern parts of South America.

Length 4¼ inches.   Male, Gatlinburg, Tennessee, June 13.
Female, Bay St. Louis, Mississippi, September 20.

plate 78—the sketch

BLUE-WINGED WARBLER

Vermivora pinus

plate 78—the sketch

plate 78

BLUE-WINGED WARBLER *Vermivora pinus*

IN the experience of bird students in the North, this species is much less familiar than the golden-winged. One very occasionally sees a blue-winged warbler during migration. Farther south, in the east-central States, the bird nests over a reasonably large area, but it is nowhere common, and always difficult to find.

If the bird *is* in the neighbourhood, however, one's search is virtually ended, because it is a persistent singer with a distinctive voice. The first one-buzz note of its song sounds like a golden-winged warbler; this is followed by a peculiar and almost unbirdlike buzzy trill with a strange raspy quality which has always made me think of a miniature "Bronx cheer."

The blue-wing's preferred habitat is somewhat variable, and includes such places as dry, brushy gaps in stands of red cedar, moister edges of alder thickets, pastures grown up with large shrubs – always places with plenty of thick cover. The bird itself is readily identified: the black mark through the eye and the two white wing bars separate it immediately from any other largely yellow warbler.

In those places where the two species occur regularly, blue-wings regularly hybridize with golden-winged warblers. These crosses are fertile, but their appearance is not predictable. The most common form of hybrid, which is known as "Brewster's warbler," looks like a golden-wing with a white face and throat, and sometimes a dash of yellow on the breast. Much rarer is the cross called "Lawrence's warbler," which typically appears to be a blue-wing with a black face patch and throat. I have seen the "Brewster's" several times, "Lawrence's" but once.

Of course there are variants upon the variants, depending upon the (not always apparent) genealogy of the breeding pair. A very strange and mixed assortment of plumages is in the museum collections. The problem has been discussed in detail by Kenneth C. Parkes in the *Wilson Bulletin* (vol. 63, no. 1, March, 1951), and by Ludlow Griscom in *The Warblers of America*. The essence of the phenomenon would seem to be that blue-wing and golden-wing have so recently split away from a common antecedent that both are still having difficulties in establishing themselves as new and distinct species.

A rare event in Canada was the successful nesting at Milton, near Toronto, of a male blue-wing and a female golden-wing in 1956. They produced four hybrid young, and all six birds were taken for the collection of the Royal Ontario Museum. Those who occasionally express regret at the need to "sacrifice" a handful of birds in this way will understand that a clutch of hybrids means very little to the lifetime of the blue-winged and golden-winged warblers as species, but can mean a very great deal to the study of genetics. Such specimens are the raw material of science.

Unlike the active, even acrobatic golden-wing, the blue-winged warbler is somewhat deliberate and slow in its feeding. But it is a strong flier despite its size, spending the winter months in Central America.

Length 4¹/₄ inches. Male, Milledgeville, Georgia, August 29. Female, Atlanta, Georgia, September 1.

plate 79—the sketch

PARULA WARBLER
Parula americana

plate 79 PARULA WARBLER *Parula americana*

THE parula warbler is our smallest warbler and also one of the most rewarding: it is common, it is vocal, and it is pretty. Few warblers have such a characteristic song, which is an ascending very rapid trill with a buzzy quality, ending with an explosive *zip!* which is very distinctive. In the south, parula warblers are associated with Spanish "moss" (*Tillandsia*) groves, in the north, *Usnea* lichens.

The word "parula," from *Parus,* means "little chickadee." The bird is indeed very like a chickadee or a titmouse in the way it goes about its foraging. Rather than expending its energies in the constant, hither-and-yon, nervous movements of most warblers, it adheres to the work at hand, clinging, unhurriedly picking and poking. The name suits it, unless one prefers the elaborate and clinically descriptive "blue yellow-backed warbler" preferred by Bent and others. Names of this kind can be dangerous. If we were to adopt a literal approach, we would be forced to call the bird "Spanish moss warbler" in the South, "beard-moss warbler" in the North. It is rarely far away from either.

In the Brownsville area of south Texas, near the mouth of the Rio Grande, there is the Sennett's or olive-backed warbler, which is a tropical version of the parula minus the eye ring and breast band, plus a black mask in the male. This is also a bird of the *Tillandsia*. A third species, the Socorro parula, is confined to the island of that name in the Pacific off the tip of Baja California.

Parula warblers are so steadfastly addicted to their moss (or lichen) that they frequently incorporate the living material directly into the construction of their nest. A kind of cup is fashioned in the midst of the hanging vegetation, which admirably conceals it from all points of view. Often, most careful scrutiny will not reveal it.

Many remarkable observations have been made concerning the parula warbler's tameness in the vicinity of its nest. It will tolerate the closest approach – to the point that the young birds may sometimes be taken up in one's hand. There are even cases (a surprising number of them) where the adults have actually fed young birds which were being held. There are few birds so trusting.

In French Canada this bird is known as *la fauvette parula;* all warblers are *fauvette.* In France the word is reserved for members of the genus *Sylvia,* which includes the familiar European blackcap and the whitethroat. It may be that we have given English colonists an inordinate degree of blame for christening our robin and redstart as they did. The French settlers were homesick too.

In summer in our area, look for parula warblers in spruce woods, or cedar and hemlock groves. They winter in southern Florida, Central America, and the Caribbean.

Length 3³/₄ inches.   Male, Baton Rouge, Louisiana, April 11. Female, Georgia, April 20.

plate 80—the sketch

YELLOW WARBLER
Dendroica petechia

Yellow Warbler

plate 80

YELLOW WARBLER *Dendroica petechia*

THE fetching little yellow warbler is the most common of its family in our area, the most widespread geographically, and the easiest to recognize. Its vast breeding range extends from Alaska to Labrador and Newfoundland, south to Venezuela and Ecuador. This is our only bird which in the field appears to be all yellow, including the wings. Many rural people know it as "wild canary," or "yellowbird."

Except for the high Arctic, it is almost impossible to go anywhere in North America in summer without encountering a yellow warbler of one sort or another. Seven distinct subspecies, or races, are recognized on this continent, and there are others farther south. Since these races live in so many different kinds of country, it is difficult to generalize about the bird's habitat beyond saying that it seems to like rather small trees or largish shrubs, with plenty of space in between. It all depends where one comes from.

If one grew up in Ontario, and spent much time at Point Pelee, one would be convinced that the yellow warbler is the world's most abundant bird. There, it is most frequently seen in an old apple orchard now grown up with sundry dense vines and tangles and an assortment of young hardwoods, still relatively small. To me, the yellow warbler will always be associated with apple blossoms.

The bird's song is quite distinctive, and a good basis from which to compare and contrast the voices of less familiar species. It is a high-pitched and attractive series of musical notes, thus: *sweet, sweet, sweet, sweet, sweet,* with the last *sweet* higher than the rest. This is usefully differentiated from the louder, single-pitched notes of the prothonotary warbler, for example.

Yellow warblers have the misfortune to be well known for the frequency with which they are victimized by parasitic cowbirds in our part of the world. It should be pointed out, however, that despite the fact that it happens all the time, there does not seem to be any shortage of yellow warblers. These things have a way of working out. Many yellow warblers have actually taken steps to circumvent the cowbird by the admirably direct action of building a new nest on top of the old one, abandoning both cowbird and warbler eggs, and starting all over. As Snyder describes it, "the yellow warbler simply builds another bottom to its nest, literally putting a ceiling on cowbirds' eggs. It may repeat this procedure to the extent that a two or three storey nest results." Bent says the yellow warbler leaves "the alien egg to cool off in the cellar." Multiple nests of this kind with as many as five or even six storeys have been seen. Perhaps we can assume that eventually either warbler or cowbird will tire of the "escalation," and allow the season to proceed.

Any bird so widely distributed and of so many races is clearly a pioneer of sorts. It has even managed to invade such a distant and unlikely place as the equatorial Galapagos Islands. Indeed it may have hit upon the Galapagos more than once, or even several times. There would appear to be two different "kinds" of yellow warblers there now, co-existing at least for the present: one is a brightly-coloured form, the other much duller. Looking at these birds, one begins to wonder whether it might be possible that instead of two races living side by side (which seems rather unlikely), we are actually witnessing the emergence of a new yellow warbler species. The world of birds is really a long list of unanswered questions. It may well be that one day the yellow warblers of Galapagos will draw some of the scientific attention away from the famous finches of the islands.

Length 4 inches.   Male, Covington, Georgia, June 5.

plate 81—the sketch

CERULEAN WARBLER

Dendroica cerulea

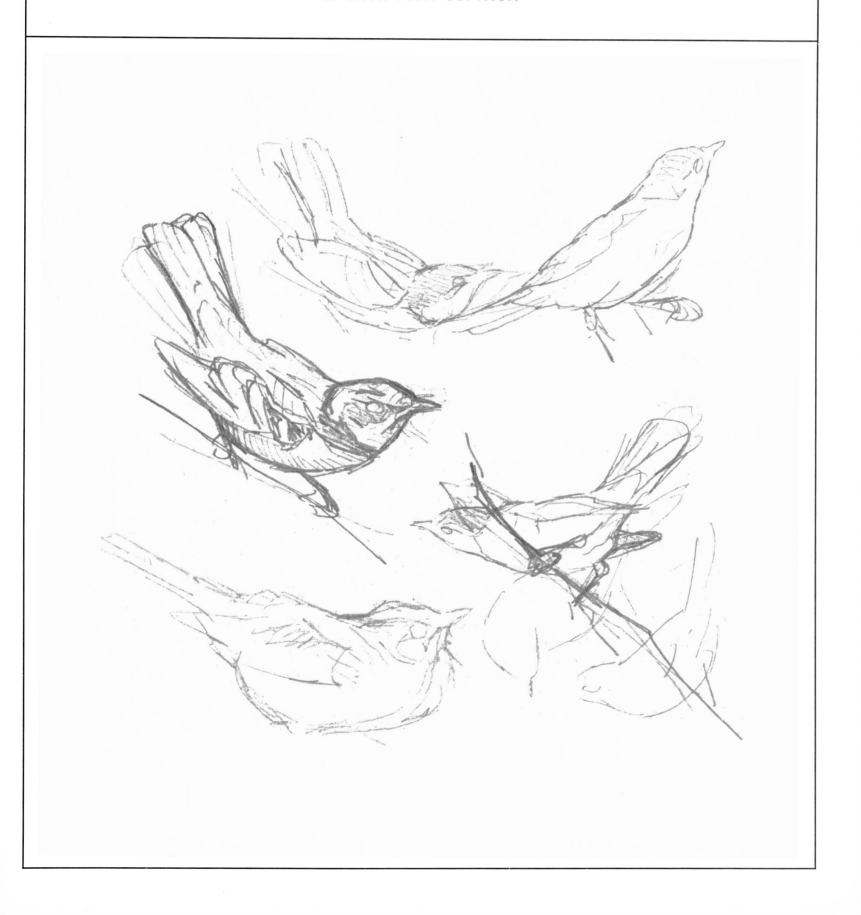

plate 81

CERULEAN WARBLER *Dendroica cerulea*

*A*VERY large part of the joy and excitement of birdwatching depends on where one does one's watching. This delicate species provides a case in point. If one lives, say, in central New York or Pennsylvania, in the heart of the big hardwood country, with scattered swamps, the cerulean warbler – delightful though it is – is no novelty. If one lives in Canada, a proper look at the cerulean warbler is rare and noteworthy.

The cerulean was one of the earliest "Carolinian" birds of my experience. I had been warned to expect it at Point Pelee, in southern Ontario. Before my first trip there in the late 1930s, James Baillie of the Royal Ontario Museum had schooled me to the form and quality of its dry, insectlike song – something like a parula, with buzzes on one pitch, the *zip!* at the end being replaced by a longer buzz. Even when so very young and so very much a beginner I had already learned to pay strict attention to anything Billie had to say about the songs of warblers – or any other birds, for that matter.

One unusually warm May morning I remember sitting propped against the base of a small red cedar near the tip of the Point, when the unmistakable series of buzzes I had been taught burst forth immediately over my head. It was unbelievable, but it *was* the cerulean warbler! There it sang, no more than eight or ten feet above me. In those days teen-agers had no access to binoculars, but there was no need for them. I shall never forget that moment, not only for the first sight of a beautiful new bird, but also for the realization that one *can* depend upon song – even for rarities.

My experience was an exception, so far as the cerulean warbler's normal behaviour is concerned. It usually prefers the highest of treetops and the heaviest foliage. The result is that one will not often manage to see its blue back, because the bird is nearly always directly overhead. All one will see in most cases are the white underparts and the black throat band which may or may not be fully developed. The individual illustrated has a solid bar, but this may very frequently be reduced to a series of spots, some of them joined together.

Since it favours substantial stands of the very largest hardwoods, preferably over swampland, the cerulean warbler is difficult to find in Canada. There is a handful of suitable places in southern Ontario, but they are becoming fewer every year. Virgin stands of Carolinian hardwood are almost extinct in Canada, and most of those that remain are being logged today. Point Pelee and Rondeau parks are the only places where one can reasonably depend on seeing the bird today. I suspect that sixty or seventy years ago the cerulean must have been much more widely distributed than it is now.

But the cerulean warbler is worth looking for. In the right kind of habitat one should listen for its highly individual song (luckily it sings continuously in season), and after much neck-stiffening searching of the tallest crowns of the trees, one may be rewarded. There are brighter, bluer, more readily observable warblers, but the cerulean warbler is special.

Length 4 inches.   Male, Deer Island, Mississippi, April 13.

plate 82—the sketch

CHESTNUT-SIDED WARBLER
Dendroica pensylvanica

plate 82

CHESTNUT-SIDED WARBLER *Dendroica pensylvanica*

It is fortunate that one of our best looking wood warblers is also one of the least skittish. The chestnut-sided warbler will allow exceptionally close observation, is fairly common in the right habitat, and advertises its presence with loud, emphatic, continuous song. One could not ask for very much more, and it is quite possible that this bird may be almost as well known to as many people in the east as the much more abundant yellow warbler.

It was not always this way. As it has been remarked time and time again by ornithologists, the chestnut-sided warbler was scarce during colonial times and for some time thereafter. It is difficult to believe this today, but the fact emphasizes that change is not inevitably for the worst. The chestnut-sided warbler, like the cardinal and the brown thrasher, is not a forest bird; it prefers areas which have been cut over or cleared in other ways, and then abandoned to deciduous second growth. It is easy to think of the chestnut-sided warbler as an avian counterpart of the white-tailed deer, in terms of its favoured habitat and the apparent advantage it gained from man-made changes in the original landscape.

Audubon and Wilson, both of whom travelled widely, scarcely knew this bird. It was extremely rare in their time – before widespread settlement, clearing, logging, and fire created such an abundance of choice chestnut-sided warbler country. Now, within its range, it is known to people with little more than a beginner's experience with birds. For an extremely interesting account of its gradual progress over the eastern part of the continent, one should read Bent's *Life Histories*.

Like the deer, the chestnut-sided warbler is now probably much more abundant than it was in pre-pioneer days.

In a natural state, no doubt the bird's fortunes as a species were closely linked to fire. The amount of clearing done by the Indians was probably negligible from the point of view of the species as a whole. Also, the unpredictability of lightning meant that burns were scattered at best. The warblers would possibly colonize a relatively small area for a few years after a local fire, then disappear as the forest succession proceeded beyond their requirements. There could never have been a great many of them until the white man arrived.

The chestnut-sided warbler's appearance is unmistakable; yellow crown, reddish-brown sides. It has two common songs, one of which is rather like that of the yellow warbler. The bird is immediately identifiable, however, by the ending of its song, which has a strong accent on the second-last syllable. It has often been paraphrased: *very, very, very pleased to meetcha!* The *meetcha* is the clincher. The song is powerful, sweet, and repetitive.

The nest is placed low, near the ground, in a well-concealing bush, small tree, or thicket. It usually contains four brown-spotted white eggs, and often cowbirds' eggs as well. Like the yellow warbler, this species will sometimes cover up the cowbird's egg with a new floor and start again.

Chestnut-sided warblers breed commonly from central Saskatchewan and Nova Scotia south to Ohio and New Jersey, and through the Appalachians south to Georgia. They winter in Central America.

*Length 4¹/₄ inches.   Male, Washington, D.C., May 5.
Female, Guayabo, Costa Rica, March 9.*

plate 83—the sketch

PRAIRIE WARBLER

Dendroica discolor

plate 83 ## PRAIRIE WARBLER *Dendroica discolor*

*A*LL of us know any number of singularly strange and inappropriate names for birds (Tennessee and Cape May warblers spring to mind, both of which are birds of the boreal forest), but there is none less well-advised than this one. The difficulty is that to change even the colloquial name of a bird requires something more, it seems, than a new decalogue from Sinai. Even then, of course, those of us who have spent a lifetime with one name for one species could never make the change successfully. But in this case an effort would seem worthwhile, if only for the benefit of succeeding generations of birdwatchers.

This is not a bird of the prairies. It is a small, attractive warbler of dry pine and oak scrub and similar brushy areas; in the far south it lives in mangroves. The name is justifiable only in Florida, where the birds are common during the winter, and where there is plenty of both coastal and inland prairie. No other vindication of the bird's name occurs to me, and even that one is tenuous.

But nomenclature is academic, and these things need not bother us so far as the living bird is concerned. This is one of our most interesting warblers because of its strangely rigid habitat requirements, and because its colonies have a way of moving around somewhat unexpectedly over a period of years. The birds may be common in one area for quite some time, then disappear altogether and turn up in a new environment to their taste, almost without warning. Pough, with his unerring ecological sensitivity, suggests that the prairie warbler's "spotty" distribution is because of the "unstable and temporary character of the plant communities it inhabits." It is rather like the rare Kirtland's warbler in its narrow and exceedingly demanding habitat requirements. It likes logged areas after a certain stage of recovery, and old farms which have relatively recently begun to return to a state of nature. Densely-standing tall trees are not its choice.

A bird this intolerant should not be expected to be common throughout its range. In our area the prairie warbler is numerous enough where the situation is exactly right, but it is scarce or completely absent where conditions have changed. It is abundant, however, in south Florida in winter. There is a resident subspecies in that state which lives on the coastal plains in and around the mangroves, and some of our northern birds winter there as well. Often the birds are surprisingly tame. They are also vocal; I have heard prairie warblers singing in south Florida in every month from December to March.

There is no difficulty in remembering the prairie warbler's voice. The song consists of a series of short buzzy trills, each higher in pitch than the last, which gradually ascend the scale. It is immediately recognizable. The bird is olive above, yellow below, with conspicuous black markings on the face and along the sides. You will notice too an obvious "nervous tic": it habitually flirts or tilts its tail – often a most valuable field mark.

Prairie warblers occur in Canada only in Ontario, especially along the piney shores of Georgian Bay. From there, the range extends to about the Mississippi, and south to Florida. Wintering birds reach the West Indies, the Mexican islands, and parts of adjacent Central America.

Length 4 inches.   Male, Greene, Rhode Island, May 15.

plate 84—the sketch

OVENBIRD

Seiurus aurocapillus

plate 84

OVENBIRD *Seiurus aurocapillus*

LMOST everyone who has walked in spring and summer woodlands has heard the voice of this bird, but relatively few know the source. Indeed when one does glimpse this strange but appealing little bird stepping about on the forest floor, the last thing that would conceivably occur to one is that it might be a warbler, and certainly not that it could be the author of a sound worthy of a creature twice its size.

The bird will be heard long before it is seen. Its strong and ringing call, *teacher, teacher, teacher, teacher, teacher (crescendo –* and then silence), is unmistakable. It is interesting to think how many birds of deep forests have lusty and penetrating voices. Presumably it is more necessary for them, because of the sound-absorbing properties of dense vegetation, than it is for prairie birds, so many of which have light and tinkling voices. This bird, and its relatives the waterthrushes, have the loudest voices of our warblers.

The ovenbird looks more like a thrush than anything else, as do the so-called waterthrushes, the other two *Seiurus* warblers. These three are terrestrial; the others are arboreal. They walk; most of the others hop. The name "ovenbird" derives not from any familial connection (the great South American family of ovenbirds is not represented north of Mexico), but from the odd shape of its nest. I have not seen an old-fashioned Dutch oven, but I know what an ovenbird's nest looks like, and the inference is easy. The nest is built on the ground; its base is not remarkable, but the top is arched or roofed over with materials from the forest floor – grasses, leaves, and bits of ferns; artfully camouflaged. There is a good-sized entrance (no mere tiny escape-hatch) to one side. The nest is astonishingly difficult to see, even when one knows where it is. I have watched a nest for a period of time, then looked away, only to find that it was impossible to pick it up again until the movements of the bird itself pointed it out once more.

Ovenbirds are frequent recipients of the graceless gift of cowbird eggs. Harry W. Hann, who over thirty years ago conducted a monumental study of the ovenbird *(Wilson Bulletin,* vol. 49 no. 3, 1937), reported that of nests studied by him in Michigan, no less than fifty-two percent contained cowbirds' eggs. It did not however appear to bother the ovenbirds unduly, and the cowbirds were remarkably unsuccessful. Of forty cowbirds' eggs, only ten young actually left the ovenbirds' nests.

Although its common *teacher* call is the best known vocal performance of the ovenbird, it also has a twilight song which is given on the wing. I have not heard this song (or, if I have, I did not attribute it to an ovenbird). It is described by Gross, in Bent's *Life Histories,* as "much more musical and beautiful" than the customary daytime call. Gunn remarks that it is sometimes given at night. "It is also given more frequently towards the end of the breeding season than during the early part of it." It is said that this melodic flight song is occasionally accompanied by a typical *teacher* call, which would leave identification beyond question.

Ovenbirds are common in broad-leaved woodlands east of the Rockies and south almost to the Gulf coast. They winter from south Florida to the northern parts of South America.

Length 5 inches.   Female, Baltimore, Maryland, May 17.

plate 85—the sketch

KENTUCKY WARBLER

Oporornis formosus

plate 85

KENTUCKY WARBLER *Oporornis formosus*

THIS handsome ground-dwelling warbler is not included because either artist or author has had any great personal experience of it – although both of us have watched the bird in the field many times – but rather because it is characteristic of the great hardwood areas of the eastern and central United States. In the moist woods of southern Illinois, for example, there is probably no more commonplace sound than the loud and emphatic songs of this well-favoured species.

Names of birds which carry geographic connotations may often be misleading, as we have commented elsewhere. The Connecticut warbler, for example, inhabits mid-Canada. In the present case, however, the geographical designation is a happy one. Wilson named the bird "for the state in which he found it most abundant," and, as Bent observes, "Kentucky is not far from the centre of its abundance in the breeding season." This was a far happier choice than Wilson's naming of the magnolia warbler, a bird of the northern spruce-fir-larch forest, which he shot out of a magnolia tree while the bird was on migration.

Warblers of the genus *Oporornis* are generally olive and yellow over-all; they generally live near the ground; and they are generally stockier in build and more deliberate in their movements than, say, the more arboreal *Dendroica* species. An adult male Kentucky warbler, with its black mask and yellow spectacles, cannot be mistaken for anything else. Females are duller, but recognizable. Young birds in the autumn are another story altogether however; all immature members of this genus are difficult to recognize at that time of year. Usually there is enough yellow and black around the eye to give you a clue.

The song of this bird is forceful and ringing; it carries a good distance through the forest understorey. Unlike some of its closest relatives, it often chooses a somewhat conspicuous place to perch for singing. I have seen one chanting away from a completely exposed site in a big cottonwood, thirty feet from the ground. Generally, however, the birds are more reclusive than that would indicate. The song is strongly reminiscent of that of the Carolina wren or tufted titmouse – a strongly enunciated *churdle, churdle, churdle* whistled endlessly.

I have never seen the nest of this bird. Sprunt says, "being on the ground, the nest is hard to find, both because it resembles nothing so much as a bunch of leaves, and for the reason that the bird is inclined to sneak away from it on the ground for some distance before flushing." There are said to be four or five brown-spotted white eggs.

Many observers have reported seeing the adult Kentucky warbler perform a "broken-wing act" when its nest was approached. The bird tumbles and flutters about on the ground, giving every appearance of being injured or otherwise in distress. This has the effect, often, of distracting the attention of an approaching predator away from the nest. There is no reason to think that the bird does this with forethought; its "tailspin" is the product of certain inherent impulses when its nest is threatened. (For a fuller discussion of this phenomenon, see the killdeer in Volume I.)

Peripheral in Canada, common in the eastern United States, Kentucky warblers winter from Central America to northern South America.

Length 4¹/₂ inches. Male, Alexandria, Virginia, April 30. Female, Baltimore County, Maryland, August 11.

plate 86—the sketch

MOURNING WARBLER

Oporornis philadelphia

plate 86 # MOURNING WARBLER *Oporornis philadelphia*

OURNING warblers are essentially Canadian birds in the breeding season; they range from north-central Alberta to the Gulf of St. Lawrence and Newfoundland, south only to the northernmost Great Lakes and New England states. Of course they are seen throughout the eastern United States in the migration seasons.

This is a bird of dense shrubbery and undergrowth, from which the male chooses to emerge to an exposed perch only to declare in song the limits of his territory. The thicker the understorey, the better the bird likes it – around the edges of swales and bogs, on steep ravine slopes, and in overgrown forest clearings.

It is a pity that this species is so elusive, for the male in breeding plumage is strikingly handsome. The adjective "mourning" comes from the black crape-like markings at the lower edge of his gray hood. But let it be known that there is nothing mournful about the bird's song or general behaviour. The only bird in the East with which it can be confused is the Connecticut warbler of north-central Canada, which lacks the crape and has a conspicuous white eye-ring. Where the mourning's range may to some extent overlap in western Alberta with that of its far western opposite number, MacGillivray's warbler, the latter has a broken white eye-ring. One cannot distinguish the young of these two closely-related species; there is no apparent difference between them.

The mourning warbler's staunch affinity for open, second-growth tangles on burned or logged forest country prompts Pough to remark that "it is another of the many birds that have benefited from the bad forestry practices of the past century." (The silver lining appears in the clouds when we least expect it.) There are many birds which have prospered since Europeans arrived: killdeer, mourning dove, and horned lark have all made increasing good use of the semi-deserts we have left in our wake; a host of warblers such as the chestnut-sided and the redstart have taken advantage of changes in forest conditions – most especially in the East.

If this bird is difficult to see most of the time, it is remarkably easy to hear. As with so many ground-favouring, thicket-dwelling birds, its voice is loud and clear. It is also emphatic and "swinging" – a series of notes that sound like *chory, chory, chory, chory.* The male is an absolutely indefatigable singer in spring, which makes the birds much easier to find than would otherwise be the case. Bent reports Wendell Taber's note of a male mourning warbler which sang forty-nine songs in twelve minutes, "the songs being regularly spaced."

Mourning warblers spend the winter in southern Central America and the northern parts of South America. Notice that the male bird figured here (above) was painted from a specimen taken in Colombia on February 15, but it is in good breeding plumage. It would not (had it lived) have arrived at the northern limits of its nesting range in our area until some time about the beginning of June. There is a partial pre-nuptial moult described in the literature as occurring in late February and early March, but this bird appears to have assumed high colour already.

Length 4¹/₂ inches.   Male, Rio Viejo, Colombia, February 15.
Female, Fortune Bay, Newfoundland, July 17.

plate 87 — the sketch

YELLOWTHROAT

Geothlypis trichas

plate 87

YELLOWTHROAT *Geothlypis trichas*

Wітн the exception of the ubiquitous yellow warbler, this personable little species, the yellowthroat, is the most widely distributed of its family in North America. There are about a dozen regional subspecies, or races, which are currently recognized. This is the only yellowthroat species north of Mexico, but there are perhaps ten more of various kinds in Central America, the West Indies, and South America.

This bird is quite unlike any other members of its family in our area. It is clearly a warbler, but in its general behaviour it is decidedly wren-like. It cocks its tail, scurries and jitters to and fro, scolds constantly and fiercely, and sings on buzzily fluttering wings. In its nervous excitement and hair-trigger irascibility, it acts much more like a typically volatile wren than one of the active but more generally peaceful and law-abiding warblers.

One will never find a yellowthroat nesting in dense woodland or in dry places. The bird invariably demands water of some kind. Its needs are modest though; sometimes the tiniest wet spot will suffice for a growth of rank vegetation of the size it needs. But the larger the piece of suitable habitat, the better; the edges of wide cattail marshes, the overgrown sides of weedy ponds and lagoons, and all such places teem with these vigourous little birds.

The most immediate evidence of the yellowthroat's presence is usually the male's continuous, rhythmic song. Many interpretations have been offered; the most popular is a repetitive *wichity, wichity, wichity, wichity,* although this is extremely variable from place to place – and even in one place. Gunn emphasizes this in *The Warblers of America:* "Yellowthroat songs in northern and central Ontario seldom adhere to the classic *witchity witchity*. There is much variation and some are scarcely recognizable as

Yellowthroat songs. Some are quite complex. Commonly, syllables are added to a phrase and notes in a phrase are repeated." It may be that regional song "dialects" will eventually be as good a clue as any to the race of the singing bird.

Song is constant and energetic through the spring and early summer. The male may sing from the cover of the reeds, or he may climb up a long stalk, hitching up in little jumps, singing as he goes. Sometimes he will fly up out of the marsh in much the style and manner of a long-billed marsh wren, chattering and chittering as he helicopters along like some vibrating insect, then he will drop back into the vegetation, still singing lustily.

The black mask of the male bird is unique; no other North American warbler resembles him. He retains the mask all year round. The female is more difficult to recognize, but notice her yellow throat and plain face, and her relatively large, bright eye. The characteristic movements, and the habitat, both help in identification.

In discussion of the yellow-shafted flicker (Volume I), the significance of sexual identification marks was raised. In the case of the flicker, the male is known by his black "moustache" marks. With the yellowthroat, it is the male's black mask. Peterson has reported on an experiment with yellowthroats conducted by the late great conservationist, William Vogt. He put out a stuffed female yellowthroat, which was duly courted, and copulated with two or three times by a wild male. Vogt then pasted a black mask on the dummy, and the male, in Peterson's words, "returned and was about to resume relations as before when he suddenly noticed the mask. He bounced a full two feet in the air and dashed away as if completely mortified."

Yellowthroats breed in suitable habitat over the entire continent south from the Alaska Panhandle, James Bay, and Newfoundland.

Length 4¹/₄ inches.   Male, Atlanta, Georgia, April 10.
Female, Whitewater Lake, Manitoba, June 6.

plate 88—the sketch

YELLOW-BREASTED CHAT

Icteria virens

plate 88 # YELLOW-BREASTED CHAT *Icteria virens*

On first acquaintance either with its voice or its appearance, one would never take this extraordinary bird for a warbler. No one readily forgets his first experience with it; I never shall. It was in my early teens, and it took at least two hours' determined work by five boys (mostly without field glasses) to glimpse and identify the author of an incredible medley of sounds emanating from a small, impenetrable bush.

A jumbled assortment of cackles, squeaks, and whistles was (only vaguely) reminiscent of one of the mimics, but this was clearly no thrasher or catbird. The bird "sang" without letup; chugging, tootling, and cawing, without any apparent pause for breath. Then it appeared, but only for a twinkling – a strange creature indeed, with a wild eye made even wilder by its weird spectacles, a bill which reminded us of no other bird, and brilliant yellow underparts.

The bird was at last identified, but not without difficulty. In the process of elimination, no one present thought of going through the list of warblers. In those days, Peterson had not yet published a field guide, nor had Pough – and Gunn and Borror's magnificent sound recordings were a long way in the future. Identifications took time, and they took perseverance. They also demanded expert help, but we had that in abundance through the long-suffering patience of the Royal Ontario Museum's James Baillie, who never failed to have time to answer just one more question, or to produce just one more specimen for confirmation. One way and another we learned our birds, and the ultimate reward came in Baillie's famous column in the Toronto *Telegram* (at the time of this writing, in its thirty-ninth year); the yellow-breasted chat, and its discoverers, appeared in print.

Everyone has difficulty with the chat. Despite its appearance, there are perfectly sound scientific reasons for including it in the warbler family. Superficially, however, it is a different story. Were it not for another strange little bird called *Chamaethlypis* or ground-chat, which appears to bridge the gap between the yellowthroat and the yellow-breasted chat, the experts would be less confident of the chat's relationships.

Its size, its curved bill, its long tail, and its short wings all add up to make this a highly unusual warbler. But of all its characteristics, the chat's voice is the most peculiar. Bent quotes Aretas A. Saunders: "The song of the yellow-breasted chat is not only entirely unlike that of any other warbler, but unlike that of any other bird with which I am acquainted. It is long-continued, and consists of a variety of notes and phrases delivered in an irregular, mixed order, with pauses between them. The phrases vary greatly in quality, consisting of whistles, harsh cackles, squawks, squeals, and various explosive noises, not always easy to describe. Some of these are single short notes, short series of notes, or long series, often retarded in time." A jumbled, disorganized, and utterly unforgettable performance.

As you would expect, chats nest quite close to the ground, always in the cover of thick shrubbery – the more tangle the better. Their breeding range extends over most of the United States, with only three slender "fingers" extending into Canada – in southern British Columbia, southern Saskatchewan and Alberta, and extreme southern Ontario. The birds are frequently victimized by cowbirds, and have been known to desert their nests on such occasions. Eric Nasmith has told me of a rare nest in the Toronto region in 1969. It contained two eggs of the yellow-breasted chat and two of the cowbird.

Chats are always difficult to see, because of their skulking habits. But if there is a chat in the neighbourhood, you will hear it.

Length 6¹/₄ inches.   Male, Washington, D.C., May 30.

plate 89—the sketch

HOODED WARBLER

Wilsonia citrina

plate 89

HOODED WARBLER *Wilsonia citrina*

ONE fine spring day shortly after the end of the Second World War, Donald Pace and I repaired to the grassy Toronto waterfront at the entrance to the Canadian National Exhibition grounds to eat our lunchtime sandwiches. It was a welcome relief from the stuffy confines of an industrial building in which we were working up the street. As we lounged on the grass – talking, no doubt, of birds, among other things – a tiny, brilliant yellow-and-black bird appeared on the lawn beside us. Neither of us had ever seen a hooded warbler before, but there was no mistaking it. The bird had absolutely no business being as far north as it was (hooded warblers are stragglers at best in the Toronto region), but it turned out later that a small aberrant "flight" of these elegant birds had appeared that week, soon to disappear again.

It was sufficient surprise to see a hooded warbler in our home region, but an even greater one to see it out in the open, in the middle of a close-cropped lawn the size of a football field. We knew it was a retiring, ground-loving bird of the deep southern woods; it must have been in a sorry predicament to allow itself to be so conspicuous.

In succeeding years, Pace and I became much more familiar with the bird in its proper haunts, which to a Canadian are those swiftly vanishing and infinitely precious stands of southern hardwoods – mostly poorly-drained maple and beech, with rank ground vegetation and plenty of young saplings, filled with the whine of mosquitoes and the flutes of wood thrushes. Hooded warbler country is deep green shade, dappled sunlight, and coolness. In Canada there are few such places – two or three along the north shore of Lake Erie, and a handful of ancient woodlots somewhat inland. For many years Fred Bodsworth, the noted naturalist-novelist who discovered the first Canadian hooded warbler nest, kept a close eye on the birds of the majestic Springwater Woods at Orwell, Ontario. The woods are diminished now; timber "management" is going ahead.

To see hooded warblers where they really belong, you must go to the great and extensive hardwood forests of the United States, east of the Mississippi. There, on lowlands covered by big trees, one can hear on every hand the characteristic ringing song of this lovely bird. The first time I heard it, I knew I had heard something like it before – the voice of the magnolia warbler of the northern forest is similar in form, but not so loud, or strong. There is another way of remembering it, if one does not know the magnolia. In rhythm, if not in pitch, the song repeats the opening notes of the *William Tell* overture, which people of a certain age recall as the theme-music of *The Lone Ranger*. Aretas A. Saunders' interpretation of the song, "*tawit tawit tawit tee too*," may thus be clarified.

The farther south you go, the more numerous the hooded warblers become. I know one spot in southern New Jersey where they are (to a Canadian) extraordinarily common. Bent quotes S. A. Grimes to the effect that in Florida, in the right swampy habitat, "it is usually the most abundant bird throughout the spring and summer. . . . In the swamps most favoured there is commonly a breeding pair every fifty to one hundred yards in any direction."

Like others of the genus *Wilsonia*, hooded warblers stick fairly close to the ground. They are active birds, constantly fanning the tail and revealing its white spots, often catching flying insects in midair. I have never seen the nest, which is described by Pough as "usually between two and three feet up in a fork in a shrub or small tree; made of dead leaves held together with plant fibers and spider webs; neatly lined with grass and fine bark shreds." The birds winter in Central America.

Length 4¹/₂ inches.   Male, Essex Co., Virginia, May 5.
Female, Christchurch Parish, South Carolina,
April 20.

plate 90—the sketch

CANADA WARBLER
Wilsonia canadensis

plate 90

CANADA WARBLER *Wilsonia canadensis*

THE breeding range of this pleasant little warbler extends from central Alberta to Nova Scotia, the northeastern states, and in the Appalachian mountains as far south as Georgia. From experience I tend to think of it chiefly in terms of the St. Lawrence Valley, most especially along the north shore of the river, east of Quebec City, where the dense, undergrown mixed forest is to its perfect satisfaction.

This species is remarkably free of shyness; on its nesting grounds and in migration one can often get surprisingly close to it. There is no mistaking the bird: plain gray upperparts uninterrupted by any white, yellow spectacles and underparts, and the characteristic black necklace. The female illustrated is an autumn bird; even at that season there is a suggestion of delicate dark markings on the breast. No other bird looks like it.

Some years the Canadian warbler is one of the most conspicuous birds in the cooler eastern forests. It likes mature areas, but ones which have a substantial understorey of second growth. Also, it shows a certain liking for water; sometimes it seems that the wetter and danker the surroundings the better the bird likes it. In *The Bird Watcher's America* Bodsworth has described typical nesting habitat in Ontario's Algonquin Park: "A widespread hardwood forest type in Algonquin today is aspen-white birch because these are the pioneering tree species that produced the first stage of new forest following the fires and lumbering of 50 to 100 years ago." He finds the Canada warblers less numerous in the other deciduous type, "typical of older forest stands that were not burned or leveled during the initial lumbering era . . . a hardwood association with sugar maple and yellow birch the dominant species."

The nest is described by Bent as "on or near the ground, often in a mossy hummock or moss-covered log or stump, or in a cavity in a bank or the upturned roots of a fallen tree." The nest is cruelly difficult to find, however; it always seems to be in the thickest tangles. But the breeding birds themselves are not difficult to discover. Where the area is to their taste they sing loudly and vigorously.

The song is not easily described, chiefly for the reason that it is so variable. It is fast and jumbled, with a mixture of loud *chips* and double *wichy* notes. It generally begins, however, with a loud and distinct *chip*, which is followed by a tumbled welter of notes which, taken together, achieve an attractive warbling effect. No North American wood warbler, however, actually warbles.

Like its closest *Wilsonia* relatives, the Canada warbler is an expert catcher of flying insects on the wing, and appears to take a substantial part of its food in this way. Audubon was so impressed by this that he first called the bird the "cypress swamp flycatcher." In a later plate he identified it as the "Canada flycatcher." When it is not doing aerial gymnastics, the bird actively forages like any other warbler, gleaning insects and their "grubs" from leaves, bark, and other small hiding places. It will not venture far from the ground even for food, and you will almost never see one any distance overhead. On migration stop-overs I have seen Canada warblers searching for insects directly on the ground.

Canada warblers winter a very long way from their breeding grounds – in Ecuador, and in Peru, as far south as Lima. It is said that in this season they move in flocks on both eastern and western sides of the Andes, at altitudes between four and five thousand feet.

*Length 4³/₄ inches. Male, Fort Lee, May 20.
Female, August 23.*

plate 91—the sketch

AMERICAN REDSTART
Setophaga ruticilla

plate 91

AMERICAN REDSTART *Setophaga ruticilla*

THE North American wood warblers have been called, over and over again, the "butterflies of the bird world." The description is most appropriate, and if any one species deserves it more than the others, it must be the charming *candelita*, as the Latin Americans call this scintillating and common bird.

From the Northwest Territories to Newfoundland, wherever there are suitable deciduous woods, and south through most of the United States except for arid regions and the far west, the active, flickering redstart displays its striking pattern and brilliant colour. It constantly fans its tail and wings, almost as though to demand attention. Since it is a bird of mixed second-growth, and since there is so much of that kind of habitat on the continent now, it is probable that redstarts are more common today than they used to be. In spring and early summer, their songs seem to be everywhere in wet woodlands and sapling groves.

Redstarts are unmistakable in any plumage, thanks to the bright patches in wings and tail. These may be flame-coloured, salmon pink, or yellow, depending upon the age and sex of the individual, but they are always present in some form, and the fluttering, butterfly-like motions leave no doubt. This is one species in which young males in their first year may sing, maintain and defend territories, and even breed before they have attained fully adult plumage. These birds look like females, but their flashes are more orange than yellow, and they show more or less sooty black around the face, throat, and wings. It allows one to speculate that (within certain limits) if the bird can deliver the right song for its species, he can attract a mate no matter what he looks like.

The nest is almost always in a young deciduous tree. I have had remarkably consistent luck by concentrating on (for example) birch saplings about two or three inches in diameter whose first crotch may be six or ten feet above the ground. There,

several times, I have found the sitting gray female redstart, as the male poured forth his high-pitched strangely sibilant song from the surrounding foliage.

Like all our warblers, redstarts are highly migratory, and there are so many of them that you sometimes see astonishing congregations when conditions are right (or, from the birds' point of view, wrong). One memorable morning at Point Pelee in May, a sudden cold snap had sharply reduced the supply of emergent insects. Large numbers of redstarts were moving about on the ground, in the grass, on the sandy beach, assiduously searching for those small invertebrates which might have been warmed up sufficiently to reveal themselves at ground level. They were so busy that you could walk right up to them.

Allan Cruickshank tells of an October migration when fifteen redstarts landed on his fishing boat in the Atlantic twenty miles east of Cocoa Beach, Florida. "They perched on railings, on fishing poles and even on the heads of the startled fishermen!" One should not, however, confuse this sort of thing with "tameness." The Pelee birds, and Cruickshank's, had no alternative, and when the pressure is on a bird, it may behave somewhat unusually. The "tameness" of migrating birds is almost always a sign of exhaustion or hunger.

It is noteworthy that this bird, a warbler, but one that does a lot of flycatching, has developed prominent bristles around the bill like those of the true flycatchers. This is an example of evolutionary convergence: totally unrelated birds who happen to be in the same "line of business" come to superficially resemble one another.

There is one other redstart in North America, the brilliant scarlet, black, and white painted redstart of the southwestern mountains. There are perhaps a dozen more in the American tropics. The true redstart is a small European thrush; this bird, like the robin and the others, got its name from homesick colonists.

Length 4¹/₂ inches.   Female, Gulfport, Mississippi, July 31.
Male, Alexandria County, Virginia, April 27.

plate 92—the sketch

BOBOLINK

Dolichonyx oryzivorus

plate 92

BOBOLINK *Dolichonyx oryzivorus*

As the horse gradually disappeared from the eastern part of the continent, the population of that imported European street urchin, the house sparrow, partially levelled out. As everyone knows, the birds depended for food to a great extent on undigested grain in the horses' droppings, and also on spilled grain around livery stables and such places. They now seem to have reached a relatively steady population level.

Not so, it seems, with the bobolink, which, if anything, appears to be steadily diminishing in the East. Bobolinks are not city birds, so they are in no way comparable to house sparrows – except that there would appear to be a common relationship to the horse. Bobolinks used to abound in the extensive hayfields which existed to support the horses. The horses are virtually gone; the hayfields are greatly diminished, and so are the bobolinks.

Although bobolinks, since my boyhood, are distinctly less numerous in the area covered by this book, they appear at the same time to have extended their range somewhat westward. They have now reached southern British Columbia, and in the United States they pretty well occupy the entire northern third of the country.

It is interesting that, despite its westward progress in relatively recent times, the bobolink still retains its ancestral migration route in the East. In the autumn, western birds appear to move east, then south, over the Caribbean to South America, where they winter. This would seem to be going out of their way somewhat; western birds should find it much more convenient to fly directly south overland via Central America. But they do not. Bobolink "tradition" is firmly ingrained.

There is a comparable situation with the wheatear, a thrush which has invaded both sides of the Canadian Arctic from Eurasia. Instead of migrating south in this hemisphere as do all the other birds with whom they nested during the summer, the wheatears go back to Europe, then south – all the way to Africa. Presumably they would not find this immense migration necessary if they "knew" that Florida and California were there. A few pioneers are beginning to turn up in the southern states in winter, however. Perhaps a few western bobolinks will begin to take the short cut one of these days. No doubt some already have.

It is the general rule among birds to be darker on the back and paler on the underparts. This arrangement has obvious survival value; the bird is less conspicuous when viewed from above, against the ground, and the same applies when it is seen from below, against the sky. The male bobolink outrageously defies this convention in the spring; he is jet black below and essentially white on the back. He appears to get away with it for the breeding season, but in the fall he reverts to a brown, sparrow-like plumage like that of the female.

All blackbirds are famous to at least some extent for their vigorous and often spectacular courtship displays. The spring flight-song of the bobolink is one of the most pleasing performances in North American nature. The song itself is a jumbled series of liquid notes something like the *plinks* of a small stringed instrument which bubble forth as though uncontrollable – copiously and loudly. As it sings, the bird may take to the air, fluttering on stiffly bowed wings over its field, fairly trembling with agitation and the force of its torrent of musical notes. Or it will sing from an exposed and prominent stalk of grass, raising its feathers to the fullest extent as its song cascades upon the ears of some impressionable female. It is said that even the redoubtable mockingbird cannot reproduce a bobolink's song.

In the South, bobolinks are sometimes known as "rice-birds." In migration they have always been strongly attracted to rice plantations; they like the sprouts in the springtime, and the ripening grain in the fall. At one point in history incredible numbers of birds were slaughtered in defence of the rice. Now, however, the birds are protected legally, and the rice-growing industry in the south has diminished in importance.

Length 6 inches.   Male, Laurel, Maryland, May 4.

plate 93—the sketch

EASTERN MEADOWLARK
Sturnella magna

plate 93

EASTERN MEADOWLARK *Sturnella magna*

ESPITE its name, this bird is not a lark. Like the bobolink – and admittedly neither looks the part – the eastern meadowlark is a member of the blackbird family. These are birds of American tropical origin; the large family includes some of our most widely ranging and abundant species, and also some of the most brilliant, including the resplendent orioles, troupials, and many more.

If the meadowlark is not a lark, and does not really look much like the blackbird it is, we can at least point to a strange and very strong resemblance to the European starling. On the ground, as it walks about with its long, pointed beak, short tail, and its waddling gait, it could be taken for a starling. The similarity continues in flight. With its arrow-shaped silhouette, and its habit of alternately flapping and sailing, the bird is remarkably starling-like. At close range, however, it is a different story. The meadowlark is exceptionally handsome and has a voice to match.

The song of the meadowlark is one of the earliest and most pleasant sounds of spring. It consists of a loud, very clear whistle, somewhat "slurred," with good carrying power. Its opposite number, the western meadowlark, is almost identical in appearance but its voice is totally different. The western's even more famous song is a rich, throaty, but musical "gurgle," in no way resembling that of our bird. As Godfrey remarks, "It amazes most people how two species can sound so different and yet look so much alike." Where the two species overlap, as in Wisconsin and Ontario, where you just might see them together, the western may appear to be slightly paler on the back. But do not count on it. You must hear the voice, and, to compound the problem, a bird that *sounds* like one or the other may well turn out to be a hybrid.

We hear the meadowlark's voice so early in the spring because it is a tough and redoubtable bird. It can endure a lot of cold, and goes no farther south in the winter than it absolutely must, and often lingers on windswept and thus relatively snow-free fields as far north as Ontario. But the farther south you go in winter the more meadowlarks one will see. Central Florida is full of them, on fields and roadsides, all winter long. If one looks out a car window, there will be, at almost any point, a brown bird with yellow underparts, a black V-neck, and white tail feathers which it flicks open as it jerkily moves along.

There is a fascinating phenomenon called "evolutionary convergence." This describes a situation in which two completely unrelated kinds of animals living in widely separated parts of the world come to resemble each other (at least superficially) and live in similar habitat. In Africa there is a group of birds called the longclaws, which are members of the family of wagtails and pipits. Some of these have come to bear an astonishing resemblance to our meadowlark; complete with V-neck, brown back, yellow underparts, and white, outer tail feathers. Even the voice is similar; perhaps clear whistled notes are the kind to have if one must compete with prairie breezes. No doubt white tail feathers are good specific recognition marks in the wide open spaces, and the brown and yellow coloration makes sense. But why the black breast mark?

The meadowlark builds a rather elaborate roofed-over nest on the ground. It is frustratingly well-hidden. Usually there are about five white, heavily-spotted eggs. In spring and summer the birds live chiefly on insects (their toll of grasshoppers must be immense), and in winter they concentrate on whatever seeds are left over when most of the other vegetarian birds have long since departed for more abundant pickings in the South.

Length 8¹/₂ inches.   Male, Fairfax County, Virginia, April 12.

plate 94—the sketch

REDWINGED BLACKBIRD

Agelaius phoeniceus

plate 94

REDWINGED BLACKBIRD *Agelaius phoeniceus*

WE have heard a great deal in recent years about the blackbird "problem." Several species of blackbirds, including this one, seem to have increased extraordinarily in the last few decades. In many areas, birds such as the redwing have been and are being denounced as "pests." When one thinks about it, of course, a pest is rather like a "weed," which is simply a flower that is not growing in the place one would like it to be growing in. A pest, a weed, a problem, or a nuisance, is a very subjective human declaration – the validity of which is frequently open to critical challenge.

In my childhood, the redwinged blackbird was strictly (or at least essentially) a bird of the marshes. There were plenty of redwings, and in some places their exuberant autumn gatherings represented a nuisance to some people, but not as a general rule. Since that time, however, they have proliferated explosively, to the point where one can find nesting redwings almost anywhere. The marshes no longer seem to be big enough to contain them all. They nest in fields now, and in drier areas, in brushy spots and the edges of woods – even in city parks and ravines.

Why this remarkable build-up? Why redwings? No one knows for certain, but it seems reasonable to think that it may well be related to a super-abundance of suitable (indeed ideal) habitat and food supply in both summer and winter. This is probably especially true of the winter, when wide stretches of standing crops in the South allow a much higher rate of redwing survival than used to be the case. The historic attrition of winter-kill may have been substantially reduced, allowing more birds to return to their nesting grounds and to breed successfully next spring. Here there may be a "pre-adaptation" involved. The redwing need not have originally evolved as a marsh bird at all – most of the blackbirds are arboreal – and so as their traditional nesting sites became over-crowded the adaptable birds simply moved into situations for which they had been perfectly well-suited all along.

A good example of the new-found blackbird bonanza is in southern Ontario, where mile after mile of uninterrupted cornfields offer an open invitation to immense flocks of blackbirds in the autumn. They stream out of the nearby marshes by the thousands and descend upon the corn like clouds of locusts. The corn growers react, and complain, and official steps are taken – sometimes drastic ones, sometimes humane ones, such as simple scaring devices.

The point of all this is that single-cropping is a grievous insult to nature. Nature responds accordingly. The only healthy ecological community is one that is sufficiently diversified to allow the operation of natural checks and balances to the end that no one species of plant or animal is permitted to reach "pest" proportions. Huge acreages of one crop – whether it be corn, rice, wheat, or whatever, encourage fast-breeding animals to increase beyond the ability of the natural community to sustain them. As a result, the animals resort to the unnatural food supply so bountifully provided for them.

There is no finer sight in our part of the world than the early spring flight of the redwings. A few aimlessly drifting birds seem to arrive first, and then there comes the huge flight of spring males. (The birds tend to segregate themselves by sex during the winter when you will see very large flocks mostly of one sex or the other.) Males set up their nesting territories upon arrival, announcing and identifying them with rollicking songs and vivid display. As the female flocks arrive, the males try to gather as many mates as possible into their territories; they are commonly polygamous.

The redwinged blackbird is colonial to the extent that the territories are quite small, and they adjoin each other closely. There may be several nests in one male's area. He will also build, after the fashion of some wrens, dummy nests which may be pressed into service as he attracts additional hens.

The prevalence of redwings, though a nuisance to some agricultural people, does not seem to have had any deleterious effect on other native birdlife with the possible exception of the bobolink. The verdict on that is still "not proven."

Length 7¼ inches.   Male, Cranberry Glades, West Virginia, June 16. Female, Slovac, Arkansas, April 2.

plate 95—the sketch

ORCHARD ORIOLE

Icterus spurius

plate 95

ORCHARD ORIOLE *Icterus spurius*

THE common name of this bird is more apt than many; it is indeed to be associated with orchards. The scientific name, on the other hand, has an interesting background. At one time there was some confusion between this species and the Baltimore oriole, the female of which was confused with the male orchard oriole – hence, a "spurious" Baltimore. However, that is all straightened out now, although female and sub-adult male plumages of both species sometimes cause confusion for the inexperienced bird watcher.

Most of the eastern United States is home for this uncommonly attractive bird, but it is very local in Canada, occurring only in a slim ribbon of extreme southern Ontario, with a solitary outpost in Manitoba. It is not really common anywhere, however, and if one wants to see it in any numbers, one should go to Point Pelee in the spring. That is the only place I know where one can depend on seeing plenty of these immaculate blackbirds, and hear their pleasant songs in profusion. To my ear, the orchard oriole is somewhat reminiscent of the fox sparrow; for some, the robin is brought to mind. There are references to the bird's singing in flight, which I have not observed.

Like the much more common Baltimore oriole, this species has no hesitation about taking up residence around human habitations. Orchards are their special delight, as are quiet rural areas with plenty of shade trees. They appear to especially like trees which overhang roadways. Where the birds occur in numbers, they are willing to nest at much closer quarters with each other than any Baltimore oriole would tolerate.

The adult male in spring is unmistakable in his impeccable black and seal-brown plumage. First year males are more difficult; they are chiefly olive-green but they have a black throat. They will sing, and breed, in this plumage. Females are greenish-drab; unlike the hen Baltimores they show no hint of orange. Autumn comes early for these tropic-oriented birds; they leave us by midsummer,

at which time the young birds look very like the females. During the winter the adult male's colours are still recognizable, though much muted. At that season I have seen orchard orioles in southern Mexico and Guatemala, although they retreat as far south as Colombia.

Bird study is full of imponderables and inexplicables but there are few ornithological phenomena so tantalizing as the strange activity indulged in by many birds, known as "anting." For reasons which are still far from being clear, a bird will upon occasion crouch down on an ant hill, pick up ants in its bill, and busily rub them through all parts of its plumage, almost as though it were dressing its feathers. L. M. Whitaker reported in *The Wilson Bulletin* (Vol. 69, no. 3, 1957) on a captive orchard oriole which would go through this puzzling performance for as much as three-quarters of an hour at a time. A total of 148 species of birds have been known to "ant."

In the absence of a better explanation, some of the earlier observers concluded that the bird so engaged was storing ants away in its plumage for convenient transport to some other place where they could be eaten at leisure, or for delivery to its young. This is not as fantastic as it sounds; certain parakeets are known to carry nesting material by lodging it in their feathers. But it does not seem to be the answer to "anting."

It is known that worker ants contain formic acid, and it may be that formic acid is useful or desirable for the maintenance of a bird's feathers. It is known that formic acid has some properties as an insecticide, so perhaps it discourages parasites. I think it not completely beyond possibility that the bird may also enjoy the tickling sensations so produced; all mammals like to be scratched – so why not birds? When ants are not available, however, birds have been known to use some bizarre substitutes. Welty lists "beetles, bugs, wasps, orange peel, raw onion, hot chocolate, vinegar, hair tonic, cigarette butts, burning matches, and smoke."

*Length 6 inches.   Female, Canal Zone, Panama, February 28.
Male, Whitmore, South Carolina, June 4.
Sub-adult male, Fort Snelling, Minnesota, June 3.*

plate 96—the sketch

BALTIMORE ORIOLE

Icterus galbula

plate 96

BALTIMORE ORIOLE *Icterus galbula*

THE word "oriole" is the result of another one of those historic misunderstandings which have confused and bedevilled bird watchers for many years. The true orioles are Old World birds, none of which is represented in this hemisphere. Our orioles are members of the American blackbird family; they are more properly called troupials. Many of these birds are brilliantly coloured; the American tropics abound with them. We have in our area, however, only two that we call "oriole" – the natty black-and-brown orchard oriole, and this one, which wears the orange and black colours of the colonizing Calvert family, the Barons Baltimore, whose territorial grant north of the Potomac eventually became Maryland.

We are singularly fortunate that so many of our most ornamental birds are so common in cities, gardens, and parks. On a sunny spring day, if one were actually to count the individual sources of the whistled notes of orioles from city elms, one might be surprised at how many there are. During the height of the nesting season, city streets and town squares, country lanes, and open woodlands are filled with the rich songs of these blazingly colourful tropic invaders. Elm trees are always especially favoured, but in their absence almost any broad-spreading shade tree may be used.

For all their dedication to song, the birds are singularly difficult to see, as they forage somewhat sluggishly and inconspicuously in the heart of the green canopy. At the height of courtship proceedings, one may glimpse a fiery dart streaking from tree to tree, or perhaps two of them as the males chase each other from breeding territories or pursue the somewhat duller-coloured females of their choice.

Many of our American blackbirds are distinguished for their artistry in nest-building – among them the troupials, caciques, oropendolas, and the orioles. Some of the swinging, pendant nests of the colonial oropendolas may dangle for as much as six feet. The nest of the Baltimore oriole is more modest in size, but it is a masterpiece of delicate weaving. In Bent's *Life Histories*, Winsor Marrett Tyler described this species as "perhaps the most skilful artisan of any North American bird."

The hanging nest, which is ingeniously fastened to a twig crotch toward the tip of a drooping elm branch perhaps thirty feet or more from the ground, is a delicately-woven, purselike structure. It hangs six inches or more from its branch and has an opening at the top. These nests are strong; they are whipped about cruelly in some summer storms. They are not easy to see; in the midst of dense summer foliage they are very inconspicuous. When the leaves fall in autumn, however, they are so very apparent that you wonder how you could have possibly missed them during the season.

For their weaving, the orioles use any suitably long, slender and pliable plant material or other string-like substance. Usually it consists of delicate fibres, but twine is often used, and in the horse-and-buggy days horsehair was common. The cavity is lined with finer material. Despite their strength and durability, the nests are rarely used in another breeding season. The number of blackened old nests you will see along a street or country lane does not in fact reflect the abundance of the Baltimore orioles in any given year.

Pendant nests are common in all the tropics of the world. No doubt they evolved as a means of foiling arboreal predators of various kinds. But predators evolve, too, and in equatorial regions there are many sorts of slender and agile tree snakes quite capable of entering a hangnest no matter how skilfully it is constructed.

The Baltimore oriole summers over the greater part of eastern North America east of the Rockies, north to the limit of broad-leaved trees. It winters in Central and South America. Bullock's oriole, its counterpart in the West, has an orange face and much more white in the wing.

Length 6¹/₂ inches.   *Male, Panama, February 26.*
Female, Costa Rica, April 8.

plate 97 — the sketch

COMMON GRACKLE

Quiscalus quiscula

plate 97 # COMMON GRACKLE *Quiscalus quiscula*

IN the latitude where I live, the third week of March is often blustery, cold, and unpleasant. It does have its very occasional springlike days, but not many of them. Year in year out, however, the period between the middle and the end of March is enlivened by the arrival of the first male grackles – rude, noisy, arrogant, and utterly captivating in their roguishness. Big, sturdy fowl (they use to call them crow blackbirds), the grackles announce their presence loudly and obstreperously. There is no missing them. They make their occupation of a garden evident immediately, with strident, creaking voices; they march stolidly across lawns that may or may not be free of snow. They will roost for a while in sheltering evergreens, then move steadily northward again through the gales. Flocks of females will follow somewhat later.

Grackles are extremely abundant birds in North America, especially in farming areas, where they like to nest in loose colonies in the rows of Norway spruces that were so widely planted in earlier days. At non-breeding times they gather in incredible numbers. One count at a favourite wintering site in Georgia revealed over two million birds. It is anyone's guess how many grackles there are on this continent, but there is scarcely a farmyard or city park east of the Rockies and south of the boreal forest that does not have a high density of these uproarious rowdies.

The authorities used to recognize two distinct species of common grackles – the "purple" grackle of the Southeast and the "bronzed" of inland areas and the North. The two have now been joined under the collective name; they remain only as subspecies. There is no disputing the difference in their colour; these are races that *are* identifiable in the field by the average bird watcher. Both are illustrated here. The top one is a southern individual from Georgia, a typically purple bird.

These usually have bars of iridescence on the back. The lower one, the only form which occurs in Canada, is clearly bronzy, with no bars on its back. Both are males. Head colour is extremely variable, and is not a good subspecific mark. Females are smaller and not so brilliantly coloured, although the intensity of colouring varies with the individual. In the deep South, including Florida, there is a smaller purple form.

Apart from its size (the grackle is much larger than any other blackbird in our area), this bird is recognizable by its especially long tail which, in the male, is folded in a way that makes it resemble the keel of a boat. This is particularly noticeable when the bird is in flight.

Grackles will discover and eat almost anything, and their feeding habits are as diverse as their food items. They will poke their long bills into a lawn in search of "white grubs;" they will carefully explore hedges and shrubs for the nests (and eggs and young) of smaller birds; they will linger around garbage cans and dumps for whatever tidbits may come along; they will follow plows in order to pick up worms, beetles, and other invertebrates; they will patrol beaches for flotsam; they will even eat acorns.

Their manner of dealing with acorns is interesting. Where a jay will hold an acorn in its feet and break it with blows of its beak, a grackle will take an acorn in its bill and simply crack it, with great pressure. This feat is apparently accomplished by means of a "palatal keel" in the roof of the mouth, which holds the acorn steady. The grackle has a lot of accomplishment going for it. In its general food habits it is rather more like a crow than the other blackbirds, and all share a deep fondness of grain in season. The bird's resourcefulness and high adaptability have resulted in the species' spectacular success in the face of human settlement.

Length 12 inches.   Male, Georgia, March 4.
Male, Tompkins, Newfoundland, May 6.

plate 98—the sketch

BROWN-HEADED COWBIRD
Molothrus ater

plate 98

BROWN-HEADED COWBIRD *Molothrus ater*

THE North American blackbirds are a varied and diverse lot, but none is stranger than the cowbird. Its name derives from the fact that small flocks habitually associate with domestic cattle in fields (in the old days they called it "buffalo bird"). I have seen one perched on the back of a moose. It would seem that the birds avail themselves of small insects stirred up out of the grass by their larger companions, in much the same way that African cattle egrets benefit by walking about between the legs of elephants and buffalo.

Its partiality for the company of larger creatures is by no means the most remarkable thing about the cowbird. Like the well-known European cuckoo, it customarily lays its eggs in the nests of other birds, leaving the foster parents to raise the young cowbirds. Nest parasitism in a family of birds which includes such renowned weavers as oropendolas and orioles seems a strange anomaly. But there is nothing ordinary about any blackbird.

Cowbirds appear to be of South American origin. There are eight species all told, four of which are known to be parasitic. But the habit is not restricted to those birds and the European cuckoo. Ducks of several species are known to lay at least occasionally in the nests of other ducks, and so are some rails. There are records of American cuckoos doing the same. The honey-guides of the Old World tropics have developed an especially heinous technique: the young honey-guide hatches out of its egg equipped with a fearsome hook on its bill, with which it forthwith does in the rightful nestlings, thus taking over sole occupancy so there is no competition for food brought by the foster parents. Its infamous deed accomplished, the young honey-guide then loses the hook on its bill and becomes a perfectly ordinary and innocent-looking baby bird.

The young cowbird does not kill or evict its nest mates in anything resembling the style of a honey-guide (although a female cowbird will on occasion remove the owner's egg before depositing her own). In general, the cowbird nestling is much larger and stronger than its nest mates, which are usually birds the size of warblers or sparrows, and in the ten days or so of its nest life it undoubtedly has some effect on the other birds through crowding. Cowbirds are known to have parasitized some two hundred and fifty different species of birds.

Scientists have wracked their imaginations in attempts to understand how the parasitic habit evolved in the first place. It has been suggested that the birds had to do it in order to keep up with the nomadic bison. This hardly seems likely; certainly there is no evidence upon which to base it. Another thought has been that a female bird "caught short" and unable to retain her egg simply dropped it in the first available nest, and the habit became part of the normal cycle of the species. This seems unlikely also, in view of the fact that many birds at least occasionally drop eggs away from the nest, and they have not developed the parasitic habit.

Better explanations have been put forward by Francis Herrick, the famous authority on the bald eagle, and Herbert Friedman, who has studied the cowbird exhaustively. It is suggested that the habit originated not on the Great Plains but in the tropics, where the birds evolved. In some way the birds may have lost the delicate synchronization between inherited urges to build nests and to lay. If these got turned around somehow, so that courtship, mating, and laying preceded the nest-building drive, then parasitism could result.

When I was a boy I was always at pains to remove a cowbird's egg (white, speckled with brown, usually larger than the host's) if I came across one in the nest of a little chipping sparrow, yellow warbler, or some other. But later reflection has indicated that there is a healthy balance here; there would seem to be many more host birds than there are cowbirds, and absolutely no sign whatever of undesirable effects on the species victimized.

Next spring, watch cowbirds more closely. Notice especially their mating displays. There are few birds in our area which are so rewarding.

Length 6¹/₂ inches.   Male, Virginia, March 4.
Female, Baton Rouge, Louisiana, January 20.

plate 99—the sketch

SCARLET TANAGER

Piranga olivacea

plate 99

SCARLET TANAGER *Piranga olivacea*

*I*LIKE to recall Lansdowne's remark on seeing his first male scarlet tanager on a spring trip to the East many years ago. His face lighted, not so much with sheer aesthetic delight as with dawning comprehension. *"Now* I understand," he said. "It's impossible to paint that bird – there aren't the pigments to match it." Perhaps not, and of course the difficulties of mechanical reproduction stand in the way of duplicating such super-saturated colours, but I feel that his painting belies Lansdowne's first impression. There is a definitely unreal quality about the colour of the male bird, which seems fairly to glow and shimmer with some internal energy against the cool green background of spring leaves. There is no North American species the equal of this one.

Tanagers are birds of the tropical Americas, where there are over two hundred different species. Only two manage to make their way as far north as Canada for breeding – this one, and the red, yellow, and black western tanager. A third, the all-pinkish summer tanager, visits the southernmost parts of Ontario occasionally, but it is not known to have nested there.

As a family, tanagers are not really much different from finches. In general they live on softer food – much fruit, and insect "grubs" – and the bill is thus less stout and conical than that of a grosbeak or a sparrow. It is perfectly substantial, however, and its structure is characteristic – curved downward somewhat, with a slightly hooked tip.

Despite their colouring, these are strangely inconspicuous birds. One could never call them furtive, but they are perceptibly sluggish and phlegmatic in their movements and deportment, and they live in the dense canopy of the highest shade trees. Except during migration one will almost never find a tanager by seeing it first. If one knows the song, however, one may be surprised at how many of the birds there actually are, even within cities. The song is quite like that of a robin in style, but somewhat slower and huskier,

with a characteristic raspy, coarse "burr." The male clearly enjoys his singing, and the sound will eventually lead one to him – his unbelievable brilliance well-hidden in the thickest foliage around the nesting site.

In the tropics, most of the tanagers do not change their colour from season to season; in this species, the change is dramatic. The male turns green in winter, but he keeps the black wings and tail. The centre bird illustrated is an autumn adult male in the midst of his post-breeding moult at the end of August. The lower bird, a female, retains that colour all year round (female tanagers of the tropics are usually more highly coloured than this species). Occasionally one will see a spring male tanager that is orange or orange-yellow instead of scarlet, though he will have the black wings and tail. These birds are usually young males in their first adult plumage, the strange hue perhaps a manifestation of some kind of food deficiency or metabolic imbalance. They are said to assume the proper shade of scarlet in subsequent years.

The four species of tanagers in North America are all very migratory. As is natural for birds which originated in the tropics, the tanagers move out of our area quite early in the fall and do not return until spring is nicely advanced. Scarlet tanagers follow a very interesting migration route, outlined by Lincoln. They breed from southeastern Manitoba and southern New Brunswick to Oklahoma and Georgia. When they begin to move south in the autumn, they do so in a band which is as wide as their nesting range. Then the migratory band begins to narrow more and more rapidly, until when they arrive at the Gulf Coast they are moving only between Texas and Florida. The funnel then narrows even more swiftly, as the tanagers fly over the slim land mass of Costa Rica and Panama. Once in northwestern South America, however, the birds fan out again to cover an area nearly as large as their breeding range.

Length 6¹/₄ inches.   Male, Washington, D.C., May 15.
Male, Maryland, August 31.
Female, Highland Falls, New York, May 24.

plate 100—the sketch

CARDINAL

Richmondena cardinalis

plate 100—the sketch

plate 100   # CARDINAL *Richmondena ʼardinalis*

BIRD zealots become all too accustomed to a full measure of grief – the decimation of seabird populations by oil pollution of the sea, for example, or pesticidal obliteration of birds of prey, loss of habitat for the ivory-billed woodpecker, over-shooting of game fowl, and so on. So when a genuine success story comes along – especially one involving a bird so striking as the cardinal – it is eminently noteworthy.

Prior to this century the cardinal was unknown as a breeding bird in Canada, and in the United States it was regarded as strictly a "Carolinian" species. In the intervening years it has expanded its range remarkably: Snyder calculated at least 250 miles northward in one thirty-year period. The cardinal first nested in Toronto the year before I was born; in less than fifty years it has become one of our more familiar garden birds, and now has moved as far north as the edge of the Laurentian Shield. Cardinals now turn up at least occasionally around Montreal and as far north as southern Saskatchewan.

There are those who have said that this reflects a warming trend in our climate. Climatic change is a very slow process, and it is difficult to relate the rapidity of the cardinal's range expansion to that. In Toronto, for example, where records have been kept since 1840, it has been calculated that the historic increase in temperature has been about 3°F. a century, not marked enough to account for the bird's having taken advantage of it to the extent that it has.

The reason for the cardinal's advance would appear to be the widespread availability of optimum habitat. This is not a bird of the deep forest. In earlier times no doubt the extensive stands of original woodlands kept it hemmed in to the south. Then, as clearing took place on such a vast scale, as farmlands became overgrown with tangled shrubbery, and as city parks and ravines became available, the cardinals took advantage of this situation. It seems to have taken the birds longer to make the jump in the East because of the wooded nature of so much of New England. The northward movement probably took place by way of Ohio,

where conditions were more suitable, then over into southwestern Ontario (the first Canadian nest was at Point Pelee in 1901), thence eastward and northward. It may well be that in due course those areas of New England not yet occupied by cardinals will receive their first birds from the eastward-moving Canadian population rather than from the south.

Cardinals are sedentary: they do not migrate. Their northward pioneering is all the more noteworthy for this. We can picture birds taking their chances during the nesting season, then withdrawing quickly at the onset of a northern winter, but where the cardinal breeds, there it stays the year round.

A cardinal was involved in one of the most curious observations of bird behaviour ever recorded. We all know that birds obey certain innate impulses or drives at various times of the year. The drive to migrate, the drive to indulge in territoriality and courtship, the drive to nest, to feed young, and so on. The last impulse led one female far beyond the limits of biological need. For several days, this bird fed worms to *goldfish* in a small ornamental pond! The fish would come to the edge of the pool, open their mouths, and the bird would pop in the worms. Welty suggests that "it seems likely that the cardinal, bereft of its young, approached the pool to drink, and was met by gaping goldfish accustomed to being fed by humans. The two instinctive appetites, one to feed, the other to be fed, magnetically attracted each other, and a temporary, satisfying bond was set up." A photograph of this otherwise incredible event, by Paul Lemmons of Shelby, North Carolina, appears in Welty's *The Life of Birds*.

One of the earliest cardinal nests in my recollection was also the strangest. It was in the very middle of the city, where a florist's shop maintained a large greenhouse. A broken pane of glass allowed the birds access to the warm and green interior, where they built a nest and raised a brood of young. The secret of the cardinal's success is adaptability.

Length 7³/₄ inches.   Female, Athens, Georgia, February 14. Male, Houma, Louisiana, May 10.

plate 101—the sketch

ROSE-BREASTED GROSBEAK

Pheucticus ludovicianus

plate 101 ## ROSE-BREASTED GROSBEAK *Pheucticus ludovicianus*

THERE are certain birds which have an indefinable quality about them. No matter how familiar one may have become with them, they never fail to evoke special enthusiasm and delight. The splendid rose-breast is one of them. It is by no means an uncommon bird – there are plenty of them in our hardwood forests – but they have a kind of magic about them that many of their closest relatives and other even more beautiful species for some reason lack.

This robust finch is an aggregation of contrasts – the male is so resplendent, the female so prosaic. At times the grosbeak is frustratingly difficult to see; at others, especially in migration, it is almost ludicrously approachable. The voice of the bird in full song is so gracious, lilting, and melodious, but its wretched little call note would scarcely do credit to a hummingbird.

Birds are supposed to be well-camouflaged, for perfectly practical reasons of survival. Yet in this species the conspicuous male does his share of incubating and brooding, and even dares to sing while he is at it. This is an arboreal bird, nesting in shade trees, yet at times it will feed on the ground. It is a finch, yet in some of its attitudes and movements it acts like some sort of small parrot. It is extremely migratory, successfully making a voyage which at its greatest extent is between points as distant as northwestern Canada and Ecuador, yet it often seems strangely awkward and inept in flight when one comes upon it in the woods. The sum of its parts is much more than just one more finch.

I have a childhood memory of an ancient and faded rose-breasted grosbeak mounted and gathering dust in an old glass case at school. One day a teacher showed this bird to the class and announced to my utter astonishment that this was a relatively common nesting species right there in our city. I simply could not believe it; although the specimen was by no means bright, all the potential was there. When spring came around, it was time to try to find one. It developed that the search did not take long at all. The grosbeaks, travelling in their somewhat languid bands, often in company with scarlet tanagers, were surprisingly evident. Once one had been taught the thin *pink!* which is the call note, the rest was relatively easy. In life, of course, the male turned out to be infinitely more sensational than any specimen or portrait. As he moves, the bird seems to become more striking every instant, with his rosy wing linings (obscured at rest), and the eye-catching black and white pattern of wings, back, and tail as he flutters away from you.

Rose-breasts will sit tightly, and it is remarkable how easily one can miss a male bird or even a small group of them; they sit stolidly and unmoving as one passes. Obviously the hens are even more difficult; they look like overgrown stalwart house sparrows, but on closer inspection they have a subtle, gentle beauty of their own. The female of the black-headed grosbeak, this bird's opposite number in the West, is very similar but more orange. The males are completely different, but due to the similarity of the females, it is no surprise that the birds occasionally hybridize where their ranges overlap. To me, their voices are indistinguishable.

We are fortunate in our grosbeaks. In the winter we have occasional and unheralded visits from the attractive but unassuming pine grosbeaks, and more regular invasions by the aggressive and obstreperous flocks of evening grosbeaks. The gorgeous cardinal sings all year round. But for a few brief weeks in summer we enjoy the loveliest of them all. The apt but unappealing popular name of the rose-breast, "potato bug bird," sheds more light on its food habits than on its form and nature.

Length 7¼ inches.   Male, Cook County, Illinois, May 9. Female, North Carolina, June 22.

plate 102—the sketch

INDIGO BUNTING

Passerina cyanea

plate 102   # INDIGO BUNTING *Passerina cyanea*

UNFORTUNATELY some of our most intensely blue birds are a great deal less colourful in actuality than they appear to be in illustrations and museums. It is a question of light. One must have perfect light conditions for the appearance of the blue, a mechanical effect of light refraction.

The indigo bunting is a small bird, and it likes to sing from a high perch. The most one usually sees of it (despite its great numbers) is a little black silhouette against the sky. On those uncommon occasions when one can contrive to manoeuvre the bird into full sunlight, below eye level, the brilliance thus revealed is almost unbelievable.

A fully adult male indigo bunting is our only all-blue bird. First-year males are usually not all blue, however, and this frequently leads to reports of blue grosbeaks in areas where blue grosbeaks have no business being observed. It is a southern bird, rarely venturing as far north as our area. It is much larger than a bunting, and the blue male shows two conspicuous brown wing bars. The difficulty is that so many young male indigo buntings also show more or less brown in their wings.

Indigo buntings have several distinct plumages, but since most of the illustrations in the guide books were painted from immaculate adults, we are not always completely aware of them all. In spring migration a fully blue male bunting is the exception rather than the rule. Indeed, some of the birds may well still be in the process of completing their prenuptial molt while they are moving northward. (The males turn brown in winter, with bits of blue in the wings and tail.) There are sundry dappled, in-between plumages.

There are a lot of indigo buntings. Our city parks, ravines, and tree'd suburbs are filled with them – wherever there are good-sized trees with plenty of ground cover and thickets for nesting. A rather drastic but very illuminating experiment by Griscom points out how many birds there are – including surplus individuals ready to move into someone else's vacated territory. Griscom removed the male of one pair; the female had found a new mate by the next day. He removed that male also, and continued to similarly treat each successive male until he had taken nine. The tenth he left to "help raise the family." This is an excellent example of the way nature provides for and anticipates population disasters; there is always an inventory of "unemployed" birds ready to take over.

The indigo bunting is an indefatigable singer, and the song has volume and character. It consists of a rapid succession of notes, in which strongly accented phrases are often repeated, but so swiftly that a jumbled effect is the result. The opening phrases are the loudest, and the song tends to trail off at the end. But no matter. In a few seconds the bird will sing again, often from the dead tip of a shade tree, or from a telephone wire. Borror states that he has no record of any two birds singing exactly the same pattern. This variability is part of the song's charm. The characteristic style of phrasing and a somewhat "brassy" quality make the song quite distinctive from that of the somewhat similar goldfinch. As Tyler says, the bird "throws the notes out for all he is worth."

These charming little birds breed over almost the entire eastern half of the United States, coming into Canada only in southern Manitoba and the Great Lakes region and southern Quebec. They winter in the West Indies and Central America. At least one individual bird migrated so successfully and accurately that two years running it was found in the "same jungle clearing" in Guatemala.

Length 4¹/₂ inches.   Male, Sugar Creek Prairie, Richland County, Illinois, June 2.
Female, Arnoldsburg, West Virginia, May 23.

plate 103—the sketch

AMERICAN GOLDFINCH

Spinus tristis

plate 103

AMERICAN GOLDFINCH *Spinus tristis*

Though very few of our songbirds are gregarious at all times of the year, the little goldfinch is the acme of amiable sociability. You will scarcely ever see a solitary individual. Even in the nesting season goldfinches are remarkably easy about territorial prerogatives, although males will pursue males, and females will chase females. The accessibility of food and the company of their kind seem to outweigh other considerations. In the non-breeding season, flocks often number hundreds of birds.

This is the familiar "wild canary" (not to be confused with the yellow warbler) of open farmlands. Small flocks of steeply undulating, softly twittering yellow birds are characteristic over open country with scattered trees and brush. The true canary is an Old World serin of the Canary Islands, but this is the nearest thing we have to it on this continent.

Goldfinches are notoriously late nesters. It seems that they must await not only the ripening of the seeds they require for their young but also of some of the plant materials they use for nest-building. Always sociable, the birds pair before they begin to build the nest, and good-sized flocks are well known even in midsummer, long after most other birds have gotten their broods well-advanced, or even on the wing.

Shaped like a cup, the nest is an attractive and delicate structure made of mosses and bits of grass, with the inner portion exquisitely lined with thistledown. It is reported that the nest is so well woven together that it will actually hold water, and that in times of severe rain, young birds have even been drowned. The fact that the birds must wait until the season is sufficiently advanced that suitable plant materials are available is illustrated by the fact that it takes them about twice as long to build a nest in July as it does in August, when the thistles, milkweed, dandelions and others are at their best. The nest height is variable, but it is generally within a few feet of the ground. The birds have been known to dismantle the old nests of yellow warblers, Baltimore orioles, and others, and to use the materials for their own nests.

The female appears to do all the nest building and incubation. She sits remarkably closely, rarely leaving the nest, and perforce she must be fed. The male comes to the nest with his throat or crop distended with tiny weed seeds, which he feeds to his mate by regurgitation. Skutch described the food as a "white, viscid mass," which suggests that something may have been added to the seeds, over and above partial digestion. One wonders whether there may be some fatty additive here along the lines of pigeon "milk." Similar masses of seeds are fed to the young, also by regurgitation.

The song of the goldfinch is as lilting, light, and bouncy as the bird's flight. It is especially sweet and high pitched. At any season of the year you may hear a gentle twittering while the birds are in flight. During the winter, when a few weed stalks remain above the frozen surface of the snow, the cheerful and vivacious companies of goldfinches are joined by relatives from farther north, such as pine siskins and common redpolls. In times of stress, the goldfinches will desert the open fields for birch and alder groves, and occasionally you will even find them in the heart of the forest. This is a matter of the availability of food, not of the temperature.

Length 4¹/₄ inches.   Male, Asheville, North Carolina, July 29.
Female, Athens, Georgia, May 26.

plate 104—the sketch

RUFOUS-SIDED TOWHEE
Pipilo erythrophthalmus

plate 104 # RUFOUS-SIDED TOWHEE *Pipilo erythrophthalmus*

It would be difficult to mistake the towhee for any other bird; no species resembles it to any extent. This unusually good-looking finch customarily dwells on the ground, where it is often more difficult to see than its "splashy" pattern would indicate. Ornithologists regard the bird as a sort of "super-species" which occurs over almost all of the United States and in a strip across most of southern Canada, with the exception of western Ontario, Quebec, and the Maritimes.

Some fifteen different races, or subspecies, are recognized, and they reduce to essentially three major forms: the one illustrated, which has a black back and a red eye (the species used to be known as the red-eyed towhee); a southern form in which the iris of the eye is white; and the western bird, which is more or less heavily spotted with white on the back and wings. It has been decided, however, that these are all one species, and the rufous sides are common to all of them.

The female towhee is one of those females very handsome in their own right. In the spotted form, the head and back of the female are much darker than in the race illustrated; in fact, they are almost black.

The name of the bird is a valiant attempt to express its call, *to-whee*. Another common interpretation is *chewink*, which has also been used as a nick-name for the bird. The song is most frequently interpreted as *drink-your-teeeea*, consisting of two notes followed by a quavering trill. As Peterson so rightly observes, a verbalized description "conveys but a wretched idea of the voice of a bird." It does help, however, to give us some kind of reference for the next time we hear a particular sound. It is a kind of mental short-hand, really, and one which is very personal, because in every one of us hearing is just as individual as eyesight. Some basis for comparison usually helps, no matter how flimsy.

The towhee is a bird of dense brush, tangles, and thickets. One will rarely see one in a tree, except on those occasions when the male ascends to his singing perch. Even then, he makes frequent returns to ground level and the cover he requires. As they feed on the ground, the birds behave very like brown thrashers or fox sparrows. They work among the dead leaves with purpose and great vigour, often making a perceptible disturbance. A towhee will scratch with both feet at once, leaping into the air in order to do so, and the resulting turmoil on the forest floor sounds like the product of the efforts of a much larger animal. The purpose of the exercise is to get at insects in the humus during spring and summer, but when autumn comes the birds also eat a good deal of vegetable matter, including seeds and wild fruits of various kinds – as a proper sparrow's diet should be.

This is a tough species. It often winters a long distance north, even in southern Canada. Most of the population, however, appears to drift somewhat south for the coldest months, and they are absent then from the northernmost parts of their range. This is frequently a familiar bird at winter feeding stations, but only in those cases where there is sufficient adjacent cover to satisfy it. It is always careful to keep its distance.

*Length 7¹/₄ inches.   Male, Atlanta, Georgia, March 30.
Female, Athens, Georgia, March 8.*

plate 105—the sketch

SAVANNAH SPARROW

Passerculus sandwichensis

plate 105

SAVANNAH SPARROW *Passerculus sandwichensis*

NY small bird that lives, is fruitful, and multiplies from Alaska to Mexico and from Labrador to the West Indies, is hardy, adaptable, and (at least to some extent) opportunistic. All habitats seem apt for this abundant and attractive little sparrow. It survives in some of the most extreme conditions imaginable – barren seacoasts, arid deserts, chilly boglands, windswept sand dunes, as well as more congenial pastures and meadowlands. Its flexibility as a species in accommodating itself to this welter of varied environments is reflected in the fact that the American Ornithologists' Union recognized sixteen distinct subspecies in its most recent (1957) *Check-List*.

From the general, day-to-day point of view, subspecies are strictly for professional taxonomists working with museum specimens; they are of limited interest or value to field observers, simply because so many of them are not safely distinguishable in the field. But in this species the *extremes* are obvious, both in size and in colour. Usually the birds in the coldest parts of the range are the largest. Coloration can vary with habitat: paler birds on dunes and in deserts, darker birds in the forested regions. But these generalizations are elastic, and it takes a bird in the hand and an expert eye to distinguish the sundry forms. The bird illustrated is the typical nesting Savannah sparrow of the Canadian Maritime provinces.

Small sparrows are frustrating, to put it mildly, for the inexperienced bird watcher. Once one becomes familiar with some of the "basic" ones, however, one can gradually fill in the rest by the process of elimination. This species is exceptionally common in the right short-grass habitat. It is superficially like a song sparrow, in the sense that it is heavily streaked, and the streaks on the breast may converge to form a central spot in much the way they do on the song sparrow. However, the Savannah's crown has a pale central line, its tail is much shorter and has a notch at the end, and its legs are pink or flesh-coloured. It is perceptibly smaller than a song sparrow. Notice a yellowish line over the eye; in the spring a more pronounced yellow mark will develop *in front* of the eye.

A Savannah sparrow is extremely active on the ground. Usually it will hop about, but if one frightens it, it will take off mouselike through the grass at a dead run. The male commonly climbs up a grass stalk to sing. The song is thin, and buzzy, though soft. (Other "buzzing" sparrows are harsher, and sound more like insects.) Of the many and varied published descriptions of the song, I like Godfrey's – "A lisping *tsip, tsip, tsip, tsip, tse-wheeeeeeeeee-you* (the *wheeeeee* is trilled, the final *you* abrupt and much lower)." The Savannah's call note is an almost inaudible, sibilant *tseep*.

The name "Savannah" would seem to be extremely appropriate for this bird – wherever it may be in a geographic sense, it always seems to gravitate toward flat, open, grassy places. But in fact that is not the reason for the bird's name. It was named for Savannah, Georgia, by Wilson. The irony is that the bird does not in fact nest much south of New England, although it winters in considerable numbers right down the coast to Florida and beyond.

The migratory movements of the birds are exact. In South Carolina there has been a number of cases of banded birds returning to precisely the same place in successive winters. During that season, the many races are freely intermingled, but they seem to sort themselves out again for the spring journey northward.

Length 4³/₄ inches.   Female, Alligator Point, Florida.

plate 106—the sketch

VESPER SPARROW

Pooecetes gramineus

plate 106 VESPER SPARROW *Pooecetes gramineus*

THE beginner will soon come to realize that sparrows are by no means as dull as he might have expected. None is more attractive than the vesper sparrow. It is immediately identifiable by the white outer feathers of its notched tail which are especially conspicuous when the bird flies. At closer range one will be able to see a slight eye-ring, a cheek patch, and a reddish "shoulder" patch, but the combination of typically sparrow-streaked upperparts and white tail flashes will confirm the identification.

The bird is a good singer. It does not limit itself to vespers, but is in fine voice all day long. Since it is willing to sing late in the day, sometimes after dark, we may perhaps hear it more clearly in the evening, after the competing and more abundant blackbirds, meadowlarks, and others have fallen silent. The song is pretty and characteristic; it "begins with two similar clear unhurried whistles, followed by higher ones and then by a descending jumble of twitters and trills" (Godfrey). The latter part of the song can be confused with that of the song sparrow, but the opening whistled notes are characteristic, and the combination of the two is diagnostic.

Although it frequents low places, the vesper sparrow likes them dry. Well-drained pastures are to its liking – places with short grass for cover, such as roadsides and burnt-over forest clearings. Unlike many songbirds, it may actually scratch a shallow depression in the ground before constructing its cup-shaped nest. As late spring and early summer grasses sprout and grow, a nest which may have been precariously visible a few weeks before can be completely obscured. Although its nest is at ground level, and the birds customarily forage there, the male chooses whatever eminence may be available from which to sing – a weed stalk, small bush, apple tree, fencepost, or telephone line.

Since vesper sparrows prefer the ground to be dry – even arid – it follows that, like so many other birds of such places, they often enjoy "dust-bathing." Obviously this dusting is not a matter of true bathing; it cannot accomplish the same result. Possibly it helps to get rid of small body parasites in some way analogous to the presumed purpose of "anting" (see orchard oriole, *plate 95*), but neither of these activities is properly understood. It is interesting, however, that there seem to be no reports of bird species which both dust *and* ant their feathers, so it may be reasonably safe to assume that the two activities have parallel functions in personal maintenance.

Sutton reported in Bent's *Life Histories* that the vesper sparrow does not seem to require a reliable water supply either for bathing or drinking. Many arid-country creatures are able to obtain sufficient moisture from dew and from the food they eat. As one might expect for such a sparrow, the vesper's diet consists largely of weed seeds, although it does also take a substantial number of insects. A certain amount of moisture is, of course, available in both.

The vesper sparrow breeds over most of the southern half of Canada (except western British Columbia) and the northern half of the United States. It winters in the southern states and Mexico. Although it is rarely out of earshot in the summer, the bird is by no means as common as, say, the song sparrow.

It seems to be comparatively quite demanding in terms of breeding territory. Berger has made this very interesting remark: "It seems likely that the number of pairs inhabiting extensive cultivated tracts planted to hay, wheat, or corn is limited by the number of available song perches rather than by actual territorial conflict." A provocative thought; territory involves much more than sheer acreage.

Length 5¹/₂ inches. Female, May 18.

plate 107—the sketch

SLATE-COLORED JUNCO
Junco hyemalis

plate 107

SLATE-COLORED JUNCO *Junco hyemalis*

Juncos are small sparrows, immediately recognizable by their even-coloured, unstreaked bodies and their conspicuous white outer tail feathers. There is at least one kind of junco in almost every place in North America south of the tundra. This species is by far the most numerous and widespread; it breeds south of the treeline in every Canadian province, and in those parts of the northeastern United States where there is a typically northern evergreen forest. Slate-colored juncos winter almost everywhere except southern Florida and the most arid parts of the southwest.

In the winter months most people are familiar with the juncos. Juncos roam snowy fields, hedgerows, backyards, and vacant lots in their search for weed seeds and the other simple fare of the season in small parties of a dozen or two. In their wanderings they mingle frequently with little bands of tree sparrows.

No matter what the season, juncos keep up an almost constant "talking" as they move about – a series of short, sharp *chip* notes as though to keep the individual members of a group in touch with each other at all times. This may also be a role of the white tail flashes, which very probably (as species identification markers) help birds of a feather to flock together. When one sees a small winter party of juncos, one may notice that they seem to move more purposefully and swiftly than most other birds, almost as though they had a definite goal in mind, as opposed to sheer nomadism.

The song of the slate-colored junco is a simple pleasing trill on one pitch, more musical than the drier trill of the chipping sparrow. Once I had the delightful experience of hearing a junco singing its "whisper song," a beautiful and lengthy *sotto voce* warble which was almost inaudible – completely unlike its regular song. I cannot help feeling that since the bird was a migrant and since the song under the circumstances could meet no mating or territorial need, that individual may simply have been enjoying the sound of his own voice. But that would be most difficult to prove.

We have five juncos in North America, and in areas where species overlap, several of them hybridize. In the East we have only the one breeding species, the slate-colored, but in winter we very occasionally have western visitors in the form of Oregon juncos. These birds are quite readily identified; they have a black head and hood in sharp contrast with a brown back and sides. However, intermediate birds do occasionally occur and it is safest not to call them Oregon juncos. The two interbreed in the Canadian Rockies.

The slate-colored junco was the subject of some pioneer studies by William Rowan of Edmonton, Alberta, who was interested in photo-periodicity and the way in which bird physiology and behaviour may be governed by seasonal changes in the length of day. Rowan exposed captive juncos to artificially lengthened days over a period of time, adjusting the electric lights in their cages so that the birds "thought" spring must be coming. When they were examined in midwinter, it was discovered that the sexual organs of birds so treated had become enlarged to spring breeding condition – in some of them, even to a greater size than "normal" birds were known to achieve in spring.

Length 5¹/₄ inches.   Male, Asheville, North Carolina, March 28.

plate 108—the sketch

CHIPPING SPARROW
Spizella passerina

plate 108

CHIPPING SPARROW *Spizella passerina*

WITH the Savannah sparrow the chipping sparrow shares the distinction of being the smallest common sparrow in our area. In farmyards, village squares, and gardens any very tiny sparrow is almost certainly a chipping sparrow, with its (summer) red cap, white eye-line, and plain gray breast. Audubon claimed 130 years ago that it was one of the most common birds in the United States, and, keeping in mind the degree of agricultural development at that time, we have little reason to doubt his statement.

This sparrow shows a special liking for country plots, gardens, orchards, and even residential areas. It is particularly happy with open lawns sheltered by large shade trees. One could speculate that the relatively quiet towns and villages of Audubon's period, and the general pastoral nature of the land then settled, must have been ideal for this bird. Modern cities are not so attractive. Judging by the bird's willingness to live in proximity with man, one might guess that it may not have been so common a hundred years *before* Audubon, when so much of the land was still uncleared.

Of course, in the good old days, there were the horses. All the old bird books, without exception, emphasize the chipping sparrow's almost invariable use of horsehair with which to line its nest. In my boyhood that was one way of being sure of the identity of the nest without even seeing the bird or its eggs. With the decline of the horse population, however, things have changed, and the birds have to use substitutes. They will use any kind of animal hair when they can get it. In a remote part of Minnesota, where there were no horses, William DeMott Stull took with him some horsehair with which to bait chipping sparrows into his banding traps. He reports, in Bent's *Life Histories*, "It worked very well. At nest lining time the females readily entered traps containing a few strands of horse hair."

One wonders why this attraction to hair arose in these sparrows, birds which were unfamiliar with horses. Why has it persisted? Small songbirds are not long-lived creatures, and from his description of the area it is reasonable to assume that Stull's birds had had little if any previous experience with horse hair. The birds may well have had no more than one (if that) breeding season in their lives, yet they quickly used the ancestrally-favoured material when it became available.

Birds have some fascinating built-in predilections. I remember one of the Darwin's finches in the Galapagos, a *Geospiza scandens* (they have no English names) which availed itself of a beakful of Roger Tory Peterson's silver locks as he was being barbered by the Royal Ontario Museum's T. M. Shortt. Showing no fear, the bird hopped over and upon our feet to gather nesting material with which we were certain it had had no prior experience!

In early summer, one of the finer sounds is the loud trill of the chipping sparrow, uttered from some high vantage point. It consists of a series of dry *chips* uttered in such rapid succession that the individual notes melt together and form a continuous buzz. The voice of the pine warbler, which is sometimes confused with that of this bird, is very similar but slightly more musical. It is also ever so slightly slower, so that (to my ear) the individual notes are still distinguishable, albeit barely.

When feeding their young, chipping sparrows concentrate on insect food, but for the balance of the year their diet consists almost entirely of seeds, chiefly those of weeds of no economic significance. They winter in the southern states and beyond.

Length 4³/₄ inches.   Male, Clear Lake, Michigan, June 12.

plate 109—the sketch

FIELD SPARROW

Spizella pusilla

plate 109   # FIELD SPARROW *Spizella pusilla*

Tʜe only sparrow with which this one can be confused in summertime is the chipping sparrow, which has a conspicuous black and white eye line and a dark bill. In winter, when our area entertains great flocks of tree sparrows from the subarctic, field sparrows are largely gone. The tree sparrow is bigger, brighter, and has a large black spot in the middle of its breast. The best clues to the field sparrow are its pinkish bill and legs, and its pale eye ring. Peterson, always uncannily apt (but, in this instance, somewhat ungracious) says of the field sparrow that it has a "blank" expression.

While it is not noted for its appearance, the field sparrow richly merits praise as a singer. Its distinctive song consists of a series of plaintive and high-pitched sweet whistles which begin slowly, then gradually accelerate into a trill, which at its conclusion may ascend or descend the scale, or remain steady. It is not a strong or powerful song, and one has to listen for it, but it is one of the more pleasant and appealing sounds of spring.

Males sing almost constantly while they are establishing territories and awaiting the arrival of the females, but then the song tapers off quite dramatically, and you will hear little further from them until the young are fledged and the birds are getting ready for a second (and perhaps third) brood.

Field sparrows are somewhat more stand-offish than some of their close relatives. They do not usually make use of human settlements and buildings; for the most part they eschew our company. But they are quite common, for all of that, and in suitably brushy fields and over-grown pastures they are often present in surprising numbers. The nest is usually on the ground, although small shrubs may be used later in the year. The most common enemy of field sparrows seems to be the ever-present cowbird, but there seems to be no lessening of field sparrows on the cowbird's account. All ground nesters are of course subject to attack by the usual number of small predators – dogs, cats, squirrels, snakes, and all the rest.

Lawrence Walkinshaw, who has studied field sparrows in great depth, and who contributed the chapter on this species to Bent's *Life Histories*, has noted that not even the vigorous territorial singing of the males prevents occasional border incidents. One of the functions of song, of course, is to help define territorial boundaries. Field sparrows are also said to have a "specially patterned flight to intimidate territorial competitors." Walkinshaw noticed that the males "each came back to the identical spot he had defended the previous year." Now, the life of a small songbird is usually short, but Walkinshaw did have one male over six seasons. This individual had a different mate each of those years, but he remained constant to the mate of the year for two or three broods each summer. There are records of some female promiscuity: Walkinshaw observed one female which copulated with her mate and with two neighbouring males in swift succession.

Field sparrows nest over the greater part of the eastern United States, except the extreme south, and their normal range in Canada extends only into the southernmost parts of Ontario and Quebec. In winter they withdraw to the southern states, but one will see occasional individuals in the North at that season, usually mingling with tree sparrows. In the non-breeding season the birds are somewhat warmer in colour than they are at nesting time. The individual opposite, a late November bird ir his wintering quarters in Florida, would have been slightly grayer in colour come spring.

460   *Length 5 inches.   Male, Pensacola, Florida, November 24.*

plate 110—the sketch

WHITE-THROATED SPARROW

Zonotrichia albicollis

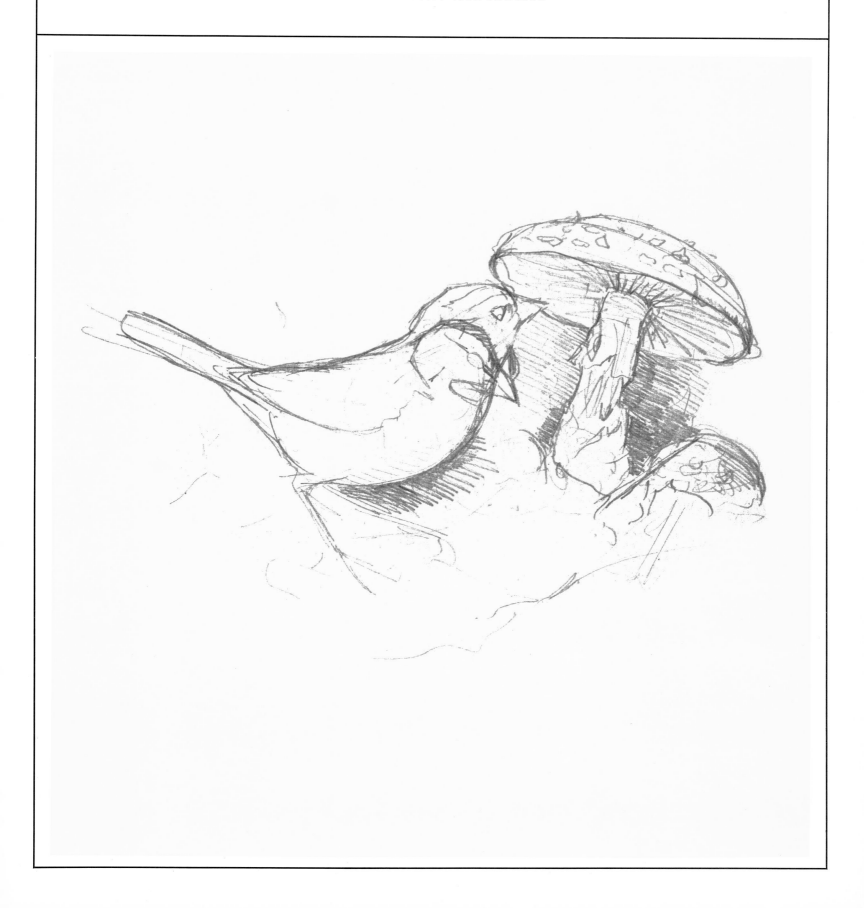

plate 110 WHITE-THROATED SPARROW *Zonotrichia albicollis*

FTER an apparently endless winter, the white-throat's song is an unfailing boost to morale. I feel certain that many more people are familiar with its song than know the bird's appearance. The clear, sweet but quavering notes are heard everywhere during spring migration – in the country, in city parks and gardens, and of course on the bird's nesting grounds in wooded areas mostly east of the mountains, from the Yukon to Newfoundland and Labrador, south to the Great Lakes and New England.

Surely I cannot be the only watcher of birds who spent almost an entire lifetime wondering, from time to time, why one sees brown-headed, apparently young white-throats in spring migration. They were not females, because the sexes are similar. But very few small songbirds come north to their breeding grounds in immature dress, and it was assumed until quite recently that fully adult garb was the one pictured here, complete with black and white stripes on the bird's crown.

Now, this question is resolved. Since 1958, James K. Lowther and J. Bruce Falls have been studying the white-throat on its breeding grounds, and in 1961 Lowther dropped the bombshell that the spring birds with brown-and-tan-striped heads were in fact adults, just as those with black-and-white heads are. The white-throat comes in two colour types, and the two interbreed. This was a new and fascinating development in our understanding of a bird which is so common that most of us simply took it for granted.

According to Lowther and Falls, who worked with white-throats for several years in Ontario's Algonquin Provincial Park, four-fifths of the nests they examined had incorporated some kind of "structural canopy" such as that afforded by clumps of dead ferns and grasses. They report, in Bent's *Life Histories*, that only the female builds the nest, which is usually "on the ground at the edge of a clearing." There are occasional records of white-throats nesting above ground level.

An interesting observation sheds light on the way in which somewhat similar birds "share" the available landscape in their choices of nesting sites. The authors report that the white-throats choose conditions "intermediate between the open areas in which song sparrows nest and the dense woodland in which juncos nest." Thus, three very closely related species can live at very close quarters, and without competition can make the optimum use of the opportunities offered by their environment.

No characteristic of the white-throat is so memorable as its song. A series of whistled notes, which usually change in pitch in the course of the song, it takes a characteristic pattern, of which the best known is the tendency to be grouped in "triplets" interspersed with steady notes. The traditional interpretation of the song has been *Poor Sam Peabody, Peabody, Peabody*, or, depending upon where you may be listening to it, *Oh sweet Canada, Canada, Canada*. At one period, the word *Kennedy* was elicited at the expense of *Canada*. Falls remarks that the more usual form, as described by Borror and Gunn, comes out thus: *Poor Peabody, Sam, Peabody, Peabody, Peabody*. Whatever the form, however, the plaintive quality of the white-throat's whistle is almost instantly recognizable most of the time, and the typical three-syllable *Peabody* is unmistakable.

As this is being written (mid-October) a white-throat is bathing with spirit and vigour in a small puddle formed in a depression in some fallen leaves, within two feet of my window. It has a head with brown and tan stripes. Before 1961 I would not have given it a second look. Now, however, I shall never know whether it is in fact an adult of the brown-and-tan form or a young bird...

Length 5³/₄ inches.   Male, Herndon, Virginia, April 24.

plate 111—the sketch

SWAMP SPARROW

Melospiza georgiana

plate 111 SWAMP SPARROW *Melospiza georgiana*

THE large and world-wide family of seed-eating finches is represented on all continents except Antarctica where, at the moment, there are no seeds to eat. There are nearly seven hundred species of these birds, and almost half of them are thought to have originated in the New World. Our birds vary tremendously in appearance, from the showy, brilliant cardinal and indigo bunting to the unobtrusive brown and streaked sparrows.

What seed-eating finches have in common, among other things, is the stout, conical bill and heavy jaw muscles with which they crack the hard shells of the seeds they live on for the greater part of the year. The size of the bill can range from the massive and heavy equipment of the evening grosbeak to the slender, almost delicate beak of the swamp sparrow and some of its relatives. The swamp sparrow happens to be more committed to a diet of insects than some of the other *Melospiza* sparrows, and this is evidenced in its lighter bill and, anatomists tell us, its smaller skull.

Of course, any species is simply a convenient and arbitrary expression of a moment in time: tomorrow's swamp sparrow may not look like today's – or yesterday's. In the tropics, where one sees a wider variety of small birds of this kind, it is often difficult to decide whether the bird one is looking at is finch, tanager, or blackbird. Intermediate forms abound, and perhaps the swamp sparrow is on its way to becoming a new kind of little marsh "blackbird," and not a finch at all.

This is a shy, furtive, and (except when it is singing) unobtrusive bird of marshes, swamps, and wherever there is grassy vegetation and shallow water. It likes large cat-tail marshes, but nests also in rank growth at the edges of streams, ponds, and bays. It has often been observed to feed by actually wading in the water. Such places abound with insects in season, and, like its neighbours the yellowthroats and the long-billed marsh wrens, the swamp sparrow makes a relatively easy living.

The bird is not much to look at – rather a dark sparrow, with reddish crown and wings. At closer range one will notice the pale throat and gray breast. The swamp sparrow is most readily identified by its voice, and in the breeding season it is notably vociferous. The song is a series of *chips* strung together so quickly as to become a trill. It is much louder than that of the chipping sparrow, noticeably slower, and somewhat more musical. The call note is an emphatic metallic *chink*. Like the marsh wren, the swamp sparrow will readily sing at night.

A swamp sparrow's nest may be on the ground, in grass tussocks, or in the tangled lower stalks of cat-tails, or in low bushes. Wherever they are placed, the nests are critically vulnerable to rapidly changing water levels, and many a brood has been wiped out by sudden flooding. As Wetherbee puts it, in Bent's *Life Histories*, "Each year the birds take two or three of these 20-day gambles, that the water will not rise until their young are fledged." The period referred to is about twelve days for the incubation of the eggs, and another nine or so for the young to leave the nest. It all happens in quite a hurry. But then small birds do not have much time – their lives are short.

468   *Length 5 inches.   New Jersey, April 23.*

plate 112–the sketch

SONG SPARROW
Melospiza melodia

plate 112

SONG SPARROW *Melospiza melodia*

*A*NYONE attempting to learn the sparrows should begin by acquainting himself thoroughly with the song sparrow, so abundant almost everywhere as to be *the* yardstick for the identification of some of the less common species. The song sparrow is brown, and it is streaked, as are so many sparrows. It has especially heavy markings on the back and sides, and the streaks on the breast converge to a central spot. The tail is rather long (several somewhat similar species have much shorter tails). The bird has a habit of working it up and down as it flies. This habit is especially noticeable when the song sparrow drops down into a shrub or other cover – the tail gives a final derisive flick as the bird disappears. Notice the head and face markings. Once one has learned this sparrow thoroughly, one will have much less difficulty with the others.

Song sparrows are found in summer over a vast portion of the continent – from Alaska and Newfoundland to Mexico and the Carolinas. But they are not all the same song sparrows. To make the best possible use of the varying kinds of habitat in that enormous area, the song sparrow has demonstrated the height of adaptability as a species. Thirty-one separate subspecies were recognized in the most recent A.O.U. *Check-List*, which makes the song sparrow the most variable bird we have.

This wide splitting-up of a species is evolution in action. Every race, should it become sufficiently isolated from the others, is potentially a new species. Looking at a random collection of the many races on a museum table – some large, some small, some dusky, some pale – one will wonder immediately how long it will take until there are more than one song sparrow species. It is rather like looking at the wide assortment of Galapagos finches today. Birds descended from a common ancestor begin to look and act different from each other as they invade different kinds of habitat and take up different styles of living.

Except for the swamp sparrow, we have few finches – or any other songbirds, for that matter – which show such an affinity for water. Song sparrows are found almost wherever there is fresh water, from open ponds to soggy ground, with enough brush and dense cover to suit their foraging and nesting purposes.

Nests are placed either right at the level of the ground or at a modest height above it. Depending upon the length of summer (and thus the latitude), the weather, and other circumstances, song sparrows may raise two, three, or even four broods of young in the course of a season. When conditions are good, breeding territories are quite small, and song sparrows will nest at unusually close quarters with their own species. Their nests are heavily parasitized by cowbirds and, like others at such low levels, the nests are vulnerable to predators. But the clutches run from three to six eggs, and as in most small birds there is a mortality of about eighty per cent.

The song sparrow sings throughout spring and summer, and is even heard sometimes in the dead of winter. It is difficult to generalize about the song. Typically, in our region, it "begins with two or three loud notes which sound like *sweet, sweet, sweet*, followed by a trill, then several short notes that run down to the end of the song" (Godfrey). I was brought up on the dreadful verbalization *"Hip, hip, hurray, boys, spring is here!"* The call note is almost impossible to describe; it is a distinctive, short metallic chirp. The best thing to do is to isolate a song sparrow, memorize its call note, and proceed from there.

Length 5¹/₂ inches.   Male, Stafford, Virginia, December 6.

Bibliography and Index

Birds of the Eastern Forest

Bibliography

*The birdwatcher is blessed with an extremely wide range of reading —
from books especially for the beginner to the vast advanced literature
of ornithology. The selection of titles presented here does not pretend
to be more than a sample of the sources available; it is offered merely as
an introduction to the subject, and includes both elementary and more
advanced references.*

Identification

PETERSON, ROGER TORY, *A Field Guide to the Birds*. Boston: Houghton
Mifflin, 1947.

POUGH, RICHARD H., *Audubon Land Bird Guide*. Garden City: Doubleday, 1946. *Audubon Water Bird Guide*. Garden City: Doubleday, 1951.

ROBBINS, CHANDLER S., BRUNN, BERTEL, *and* ZIM, HERBERT S., *illustrated by*
ARTHUR SINGER, *Birds of North America*. New York: Golden Press, 1966.

*These books are visual aids to bird identification. In many cases, how-
ever, the song or call note of a bird may serve as corroboration of a
sighting, and occasionally may be even more important than the appearance of a bird. A number of long-play bird recordings of excellent
quality has appeared in recent years, and the number is growing. Some
are collections of birds of geographic regions; others contain families of
birds. For details, the reader is referred to the Federation of Ontario
Naturalists, Don Mills, Ontario, Canada.*

General and Reference

AMERICAN ORNITHOLOGISTS' UNION, *Check-list of North American Birds*
(5th edition). Baltimore: A.O.U., 1957.

AUSTIN, OLIVER L. JR., *and* SINGER, ARTHUR, *Birds of the World*. New York:
Golden Press, 1961.

BENT, ARTHUR C., *Life Histories of North American Birds* (21 vols.).
Washington: United States National Museum, 1919-1968.

BERGER, ANDREW J., *Bird Study*. New York: J. Wiley and Sons, 1961.

CRUICKSHANK, ALLAN *and* HELEN, *1001 Questions Answered About Birds*.
New York: Dodd, Mead, 1958.

DARLING, LOIS *and* LOUIS, *Bird*. Boston: Houghton Mifflin, 1962.

DORST, JEAN, *The Migrations of Birds*. Boston: Houghton Mifflin, 1963.

FISHER, JAMES, *and* PETERSON, ROGER TORY, *The World of Birds*. Garden
City: Doubleday, 1963.

FORBUSH, E. H., *and* MAY, JOHN B., *A Natural History of the Birds of
Eastern and Central North America*. Boston: Houghton Mifflin, 1939.

HALL, HENRY MARION, *edited by* ROLAND C. CLEMENT, *A Gathering of Shore
Birds*. New York: Devin Adair, 1960.

HICKEY, J. J., *A Guide to Bird Watching*. New York: Oxford University
Press, 1943.

KORTRIGHT, F. H., *Ducks, Geese and Swans of North America*. Washington: American Wildlife Institute, 1942.

LINCOLN, FREDERICK C., *Migration of Birds*. Washington: United States
Department of the Interior, Fish and Wildlife Service Circular 16, 1950.

PALMER, RALPH S. (ed.), *Handbook of North American Birds* (Vol. 1). New Haven: Yale University Press, 1962.

PETERSON, ROGER TORY (ed.), *The Bird Watcher's Anthology*. New York: Harcourt, Brace, 1957. *Birds Over America*. New York: Dodd, Mead, 1964.

PETERSON, ROGER TORY, *The Bird Watcher's Anthology* (ed.), New York: Time Inc., 1963.

PETTINGILL, OLIN SEWALL JR., *A Guide to Bird Finding (East)*. New York: Oxford University Press, 1951. (ed.), *The Bird Watcher's America*. New York: McGraw-Hill, 1965.

THOMSON, A. LANDSBOROUGH (ed.), *A New Dictionary of Birds*. London: Nelson, 1964.

VAN TYNE, JOSSELYN, *and* BERGER, ANDREW J., *Fundamentals of Ornithology*. New York: J. Wiley and Sons, 1959.

WELTY, JOEL CARL, *The Life of Birds*. New York: Alfred A. Knopf, 1963.

Canadian

GODFREY, W. EARL, *The Birds of Canada*. Ottawa: National Museum of Canada Bulletin No. 203, 1966.

LIVINGSTON, JOHN A., *illustrated by* J. FENWICK LANSDOWNE, *Birds of the Northern Forest*. Toronto: McClelland and Stewart; Boston: Houghton Mifflin, 1966.

MUNRO, J. A., *and* COWAN, IAN MCTAGGART, *A Review of the Bird Fauna of British Columbia*. Victoria: B.C. Provincial Museum, Special Publication No. 2, 1947.

PETERS, H. S. *and* BURLEIGH, T. D., *The Birds of Newfoundland*. St. John's: Newfoundland Department of Natural Resources, 1951.

SALT, W. RAY, *and* WILK, A. L., *The Birds of Alberta*. Edmonton: Alberta Department of Economic Affairs, 1958.

SNYDER, L. L., *Ontario Birds*. Toronto: Clarke, Irwin, 1950.

SQUIRES, W. AUSTIN, *The Birds of New Brunswick*. Saint John: The New Brunswick Museum (Monographic Series No. 4), 1952.

TAVERNER, P. A., *Birds of Canada*. Ottawa: Canadian Department of Mines Bulletin No. 72, 1934.

TUFTS, ROBIE W., *The Birds of Nova Scotia*. Halifax: Nova Scotia Museum, 1961.

Periodicals

There are many publications produced regularly by local, provincial and other bird clubs and organizations. The following brief selection is considered fundamental for the birdwatcher in this region:

AMERICAN ORNITHOLOGISTS' UNION, *The Auk*.

CANADIAN AUDUBON SOCIETY, *Canadian Audubon*.

FEDERATION OF ONTARIO NATURALISTS, *The Ontario Naturalist*.

NATIONAL AUDUBON SOCIETY, *Audubon*.

SASKATCHEWAN NATURAL HISTORY SOCIETY, *The Blue Jay*.

WILSON ORNITHOLOGICAL SOCIETY, *The Wilson Bulletin*.

Index

Birds of the Northern Forest

Contents

Introduction

A SUBSTANTIAL part of Canada is forested, and the greater part of that forest consists of cone-bearing evergreens. When most of us speak of "the North" we do not usually mean the arctic – that remote fastness scarcely occurs to any of us – but we do mean the vast expanse of spruce, fir, and larch that lies between us and the truly northern regions. The northern forest we think of is the harsh and exacting land of moose, otter, and red squirrel, of lynx and snowshoe hare. It is a land of insects. It is also the land of the fifty-six species of birds presented in this volume. If Canada can be said to have characteristic birds, they are these.

But the northern forest is not uniquely Canadian, or even North American. If you were to look down on the globe, viewing it from above the north pole, you would see (ignoring water masses) a series of concentric circles. The bull's eye in the middle is the polar ice cap. It is ringed by the wide and treeless tundra. Immediately to the south of the barren grounds is suspended the great mantle of evergreen woods, the northern forest of this book.

Since the huge coniferous blanket is essentially the same in both Eurasia and America, it is not surprising that the two land masses have many of the same forms of wildlife. Bears, wolves, moose, and weasels are common to both. Siberia and Scandinavia are not too radically different from Canada; twenty-one of the birds appearing in this book occur in the Old World (one of them, the Canada goose, was introduced). Some, like the winter wren and the gray-cheeked thrush, made their way into Asia from North America. Others, shrike and kinglets among them, reversed the process, and were immigrants. For an animal with wings, the Bering Strait is no great challenge. In addition to the twenty-one circumpolar species, several more in this book have very closely related "opposite numbers" living in the Old World in much the same way.

In Canada, the northern forest extends from the edge of the barrens south to central Alberta and Saskatchewan, the north shore of Lake Superior, the Gaspé peninsula, and the northern tip of Newfoundland. At its southern fringe in the Great Lakes region and the Maritimes, there is a mixed forest of evergreens and broad-leafed trees which blends the coniferous belt with the hardwood zone of the south. Still farther south, in areas such as Appalachia, elevation has much the same effect as latitude, and stands of evergreens extend the "northern" forest deep into the eastern United States. In the west, the high mountains carry a similar and related cover of cone-bearing trees, and support many of the same birds.

The coniferous woodland roughly parallels the southern limits of Ice Age glaciation. It is the most recent area to have become treed following the retreat of the Pleistocene ice sheet. The north woods support the fewest species of plants and wildlife of any Canadian region with the exception of the arctic, which is still in the process of escaping the glaciers. In comparison with the south, relatively few animals have yet invaded the northern forest. There is a general uniformity in terms of habitat; if an animal likes a handful of evergreen species, that is one thing; if it must have a broad and rich selection of leafy hardwoods then it cannot live in the north.

But even here, in a land that seems nothing but one great stand of conifers, there are different environmental opportunities within the more general habitat, and different kinds of birds have taken advantage of them. The northernmost tree-line with its impoverished vegetation has its special nesting birds, such as the gray-cheeked thrush and the blackpoll warbler. The denser forest is the haunt of owls and spruce grouse. In cool bogs you find the solitary sandpiper, rusty blackbird, and palm warbler. Where fire or flood have opened the forest and begun to promote the growth of aspen, birch, and other deciduous trees, birds such as the lesser yellowlegs and purple finch move in. The lake country is the home of loons, mergansers, and ospreys. The forest is extensive, but it is varied; its birds reflect that variety in the ways in which they have become adapted for existence there.

Not all of the following fifty-six birds are restricted to the northern forest to the exclusion of other habitats. Birds such as the peregrine falcon, the osprey, and the raven are almost cosmopolitan; in Canada, they are found chiefly in the evergreen forest. This is extreme and demanding country, and the summers are short. Many birds of the area are forced to migrate – flycatchers, thrushes, vireos, and warblers among them. They nest in the north, but winter in tropic America. Others stay in the higher latitudes much of the time, but occasionally move south in great numbers according to fluctuations in their food supply. If their populations build up to a point where the local environment can no longer support them, chickadees, several finches, and others will leave the northern forest in some winters for the better possibilities offered by more southern regions. A few species, for example the gray jay, desert the evergreen forest only on very rare occasions.

As a result, many of the birds in this volume are familiar to most Canadians only as spring and fall migrants or occasional winter visitors. Others are best known to wilderness campers, canoe-trippers, and those who have summer cottages in the spruce country. Most are quite widely distributed in Canada, and can be seen fairly predictably at the appropriate seasons. Only one or two, such as the great gray and boreal owls, are "rare," and even they can be encountered from time to time. Their "rarity" is probably a matter of their being thinly distributed over an enormous wilderness area, and of their normally sedentary nature.

Though none of the birds included here is rare in the strict sense, some have endured lamentable population losses in recent times. Since it is impossible, we believe, to be even casually interested in birds without a concomitant interest in their welfare, it is also impossible to prepare a book about birds without reference to their conservation.

The word "conservation" means many things to many people. It is used frequently as a synonym for "wise use" – though we are not altogether sure what *that* means, either. The word seems to convey whatever the user wants it to. "Conservation" is commonly used by the forest industry, for example, to describe its minimal gestures toward the restoration of the resource it has so sadly mutilated – especially on the Pacific coast. It is almost as commonly used by organized fishing and shooting groups to justify such activities as the poisoning of water systems so that a pure culture of some exotic game fish may replace the diverse and wonderful natural community of fishes that developed there. The name of conservation is invoked in connection with the fervently righteous slaughter of crows and magpies. Self-perpetuating government "predator control" agencies poison wolves and coyotes and destroy bears and cougars in the name of "conservation." The word has lost its meaning.

But conservation the ethic – the state of mind – is very much alive. Some people have it; some haven't. Happily, more have it today than did a generation ago. This is due in major degree to the work of such national organizations as the Canadian Audubon Society and other private groups and government agencies at national, provincial, and local levels.

If we are not precisely sure what "conservation" means any more, we do know, however, what "preservation" means, and we do not blush to say that we are preservationists. We believe that the preservation of birds – *all* birds – is a legitimate aim that does not need justification on economic or any other grounds. Birds should be preserved because they are there – because they happened. That, to us, is reason enough.

How the peregrine falcon and the osprey are to be preserved from the insidious chronic effects of chemical pesticides, we do not pretend to know.

Probably it will involve legislative bans on the most lethal compounds and insistence upon the use of non-residual materials. Neither do we really know how to preserve the loon from the deafening, stinking invasion of its forest lakes by the outboard motorboat. You cannot legislate engines out of existence; perhaps we will have sufficient foresight and wisdom to legislate sufficient nature preserves *into* existence.

But we do think we know how to preserve the great gray owl and the hooded merganser from the farm boy with the .22 rifle. That is why we do not hesitate to add one more volume to the already great store of books about our native birds. The greater the number and variety and form and availability of books on birds, the greater the chances of at least some information – and hopefully some inspiration – reaching the right destination. That is sufficient motive in itself for doing another book on birds.

In the three thousand million (or so) years of life on this earth, an awe-inspiring multitude of complex organisms has arisen in response to the opportunities offered by an infinite number of changing environmental conditions. These organisms are specialists. Some convert radiant energy into plant material. Some convert plant material into animal protein. Others convert animal protein into yet another animal protein. They do it in as many different ways as there are different kinds of organisms. In the bird world, there are between eight and nine thousand distinct species, each one unique, each exploiting its environment in a separate, individual way. Even the least of these, in its uniqueness, is irreplaceable both in terms of science and in terms of the maturing conscience of man. Our current sovereignty over much of the living world carries with it a profound responsibility.

Most birds and other wildlife suffer most severely not from overt aggression against them, but from rapid alteration or disruption of their natural environments. Animals are inextricably adjusted to the particular kinds of places they live in; most of them can live nowhere else. Polluted water, levelled woodlots, burned grasslands, and drained marshes all eliminate the special wildlife of each type of area as surely as any conscious campaign of liquidation. But habitat change, though it does occur locally, has not yet affected the bulk of the northern forest. No doubt it will in due course, but at the moment most of the birds in this book (with critical exceptions) are among those least affected by man's gradual scouring of the face of North America.

There are many more than fifty-six species of birds in the northern forest, and thus any selection must be arbitrary. We have tried to include a representative collection of the *kinds* of birds to be found there, and to spread our selection as evenly as possible across the spectrum of the families of northern birds and the varieties of habitat to be found within the region as a whole.

The result of our selection is eleven water birds, nine hawks and owls, thirty-one songbirds, and five miscellaneous species not allied to the others. We consider it a reasonable sample, but only a sample, of the birdlife of the northern forest. If the reader regrets the absence of a favourite species, chances are that it will appear in a future volume of this series of books. Our plan is to deal similarly with other major Canadian environments, such as the eastern hardwood forests, the prairies, the sea coasts, the mountains, the arctic, etc.

The birds are presented in systematic order – loons to sparrows – according to what is generally agreed to be their evolutionary sequence. Finches are thought to have evolved more recently than loons and grebes. (Birds are such perishable, soft-boned creatures, however, that the fossil record of ornithology is regrettably slim.) The order and the nomenclature are those of the 1957 *Check-list of North American Birds* published by the American Ornithologists' Union.

In dealing with a collection of birds ranging in bulk from geese to kinglets, it is clearly impossible to illustrate them in relative size. A book that could accomodate a life-size warbler would run into difficulty with a loon. Accordingly, as a guide, the length in *inches* of each species is provided in a footnote. In the case of hawks, where wingspread is important to identification, that is indicated in *feet*.

The birds were painted from skins loaned to the artist from the large and representative collections of the Royal Ontario Museum in Toronto. James L. Baillie of the ROM's Department of Birds, to whom the author has a life-long indebtedness for inspiration, guidance, and instruction, has devoted countless hours and days to the selection of bird skins for the artist's reference over many years. Since these are portraits of actual birds that once were living, accompanying each plate for which the data are available there is a note of the place and month of capture. Both are significant to the bird student, and we feel that this additional information will be interesting also to both residents and visitors in the regions concerned.

In many species of birds, the sexes are distinctly different in pattern and coloration. In others, they are to all intents and purposes identical. In still others, the sexes are distinguishable in the field, but there is sufficient similarity between the two that identification of the species is not in doubt. This has guided the artist throughout. The Tennessee warbler is a good example; it was not considered necessary to illustrate the female, even though she is not precisely like the male. The "family" resemblance is sufficient.

The text is not formalized under standard sub-headings for each species (description, field marks, distribution, habits, nest, eggs, etc.). This information is available from a long list of sources in the rich and exhaustive bird literature, a small selection from which is presented in a brief bibliography. Of course it is the fact of this literature, the product of countless field observers and laboratory workers, writers, and artists, to which this book owes its existence. The interdependence of bird students and naturalists generally is just as vital as the interdependence of the wildlife community itself.

The aim of the text has been to point out merely a few interesting or noteworthy points about each bird or group of birds, in the hope that the result will be not only a somewhat closer acquaintance with the species selected and their forest home, but also some appreciation of the nature of birds in general, and the pleasure and wonder that artist and author have derived from them since boyhood.

We love birds. We love painting them, writing and talking about them, watching them and listening to them, and attempting to learn something about them. That is really what this book is all about.

It is dedicated to Budd.

JOHN A. LIVINGSTON

J. F. LANSDOWNE

1

Common Loon

GAVIA IMMER

plate 1

Common Loon - GAVIA IMMER

T HERE have been loons of one kind or another in the world for at least sixty million years. They are thought to be the most ancient of Canadian birds; this seniority places them first on our list. For convenience, students arrange birds in sequence from the most "primitive" (those with the oldest fossil record) to those thought to be the most recently evolved – in Canada's case the finches, ending with the longspurs and the snow bunting. This in no sense means that the loon is a simple organism. It is one of the world's more sophisticated animals, superbly adapted to getting a living in the water.

You could imagine that the loon was deliberately designed as a fish-catching machine. It has a projectile-shaped body, strong propulsive feet mounted well to the rear, remarkable vision, and a javelin-like bill, all of which add up to awesome efficiency. It can stay submerged for three minutes or more, and can dive to depths of two hundred feet. Elaborate physiological processes conserve oxygen. Also, it can alter its specific gravity at will, sinking into the water like a submarine until only its head is showing. This is possible because it has relatively solid bones for a bird, and it is able to press air from its lungs, plumage, and elsewhere to give it the desired level of buoyancy.

But if an animal wants to specialize, it cannot have everything, and to achieve such fine adjustments to the water, the loon had to sacrifice some things. One of these was mobility on land. Its legs are set so far back on its body that the bird can scarcely move, and is forced to hump itself along, seal-like, on its breast and belly, or to use its wings as props.

The process of adaptation is mostly a matter of give and take. Large appendages would only get in the way under water, so evolution has drastically cut down on the loon's wing. The result is evident when the heavy, goose-sized bird takes off; it has to taxi quite a distance to become airborne, and once aloft must beat its wings very rapidly to maintain altitude. Like a stubby-winged aircraft, it substitutes power for "lift" area. It cannot take off at all from land. Descent has similar problems; there is no grace in the loon's return to the water. Its small wings allow no hovering and little braking, and the bird sets down in a shallow, inelegant crash-glide with water flying wildly in all directions.

The voice of the common loon, like "woman wailing for her demon lover," is an unforgettable, spine-tingling feature of the northern forest. Its weird yodels and *tremulo* cries are especially stirring after nightfall, when the air is still.

Where they can find seclusion from the increasingly ubiquitous outboard motorboat (bane of the lake country and its wildlife), loons breed throughout the northern part of the northern hemisphere. There are four species, all of which occur in Canada.

Length 28-36 inches. Female, Kamloops, British Columbia, April.

2
Horned Grebe
PODICEPS AURITUS

plate 2

Horned Grebe - PODICEPS AURITUS

*A*LTHOUGH grebes look and behave superficially like loons, the two are not related. This pint-sized species is known in Britain as the Slavonian grebe; its "horns" are erectile golden feathers which both sexes display in their mutual courtship ceremonies.

Like those of loons, grebes' legs are set very far back on the body for maximum driving power under water, but the feet are totally different. A loon's feet are webbed; a grebe has separate, extraordinarily lobate toes, which give plenty of area for thrust when pushing backward. On the return stroke, the foot folds to ruler-edge thinness to avoid water resistance as much as possible. Grebes are expert divers and underwater hunters, and have all the appropriate physiological as well as anatomical specializations. When they are swimming on the surface, they can regulate the amount of body area that shows above the water. Because of their relatively small wings, grebes are not graceful fliers, but by means of rapid strokes and sheer power manage a reasonable turn of speed.

The nest of a grebe is noteworthy. It consists of a floating, tangled heap of marsh vegetation artlessly thrown together, often anchored to standing water plants. Sometimes it becomes sheltered in the course of incubation by the rapid early-summer growth of adjacent green shoots. Often the whole soggy mass is quite wet, including the eggs, which are covered by a few strands of vegetable matter when the bird leaves the nest.

Young grebes are vividly striped and fuzzy, and look quite unlike their elders. They can swim at birth, but when they are very small they commonly ride about on one of their parents. They mount the adult bird from the rear, make their way along its back and pop into a soft "pocket" under the old bird's wing.

Canada has five grebes, the world, twenty. This species is to be found almost countrywide.

Length 12-15 inches. Male, Lake St. Martin, Manitoba, June.

3

Canada Goose

BRANTA CANADENSIS

plate 3   *Canada Goose* - BRANTA CANADENSIS

THE big gray "honker" is unquestionably the most storied and honoured of Canadian waterfowl. In fact it has a world reputation for sagacity, fidelity, altruism, and related manners and motives bordering on the incredible. It is a splendid bird regardless; the anthropomorphic and uncritical legends were spawned by men, not geese.

The Canada goose has been "broken down" by students into nine or ten different races, or subspecies. These range from the small, duck-sized, three-pound version in Alaska to a huge prairie form which may weigh eighteen pounds or more. It is interesting that these several varieties maintain their identities; no doubt they resulted from and are perpetuated by the bird's seemingly unalterable traditional behaviour. Its habit of returning as a family unit to the same nesting grounds year after year apparently promotes enough in-breeding to keep the various populations undiluted genetically.

In spring migration, the northward advance of the geese is exquisitely tied to the thermometer. The birds may be expected to follow immediately in the wake of the 35° isotherm as it moves up the continent in March and April, bringing them to the nesting grounds at virtually the moment after ice break-up.

Canada geese breed when they are two years old and appear to mate for life. If one partner is lost, the survivor remates. Although they are very sociable and gregarious in the off-season, they do not like too much crowding at nesting time, and they demand a certain degree of "elbow-room" from others of their kind.

In common with loons, ducks, and others, geese in the summer moult lose all their flight feathers simultaneously (most birds do not), and are grounded for about three weeks when the young are still half-grown. The very nicely timed result is that both young and adults take to the wing at about the same date.

Numbers of Canada geese appear to remain fairly stable. Despite their popularity with gunners, the geese have been fortunate in the remoteness of their breeding grounds and the usual freedom of these areas from drought. Losses in the shooting season are normally replaced next summer with gratifying regularity – or they have been so far.

Length 22-42 inches. Male.

Lesser Scaup

AYTHYA AFFINIS

Lesser Scaup ♀

plate 4

Lesser Scaup - AYTHYA AFFINIS

*T*HE vernacular name of this duck is a bastardization of the word "scalp." This in turn is related to "scallop" and the shellfish and other invertebrates upon which flocks of scaups feed at low tide, when many of them move to the sea coasts for the winter.

Lesser scaups are known to the duck shooters as "bluebills." They are among the most abundant species of the western continental flyways. Their breeding success is partly due to the fact that they are northern nesters, and thus they are not affected to too great an extent by seasonal droughts and the gradual but inexorable dropping of the prairie water table. They nest late in the season and begin their autumn migration only just ahead of the changing weather.

Their preferred nesting sites are the borders of ponds and freshwater marshes. The nest is a depression in the grass, lined with down which the hen plucks from her breast. Like most ducks, the male deserts the female when the full clutch of nine to twelve buffy-olive eggs has been laid and incubation begins. He moves to a larger body of water, there to flock with other males and wait for the flightless moult period in safety from land predators. Back at the nest, the female has to depend on her camouflaging plumage.

The peculiar laterally-compressed shape of a duck's head, and the unusually high placement of its eyes, are for a very good purpose. Ducks have a range of binocular vision, not only to the front, but also to the rear. Everyone knows how difficult it is to surprise a duck, though lesser scaups can become among the more confiding of their family when encouraged by artificial feeding.

This species is distinguished from the closely related and very similar greater scaup (an Old World as well as North American bird) by the purplish head of the male, its slight crest, and, when in flight, by a relatively short white wing stripe. The greater scaup has a round, green-glossed head and a longer white stripe in the wing.

Length 15-18¹/₂ inches. Male, Niagara Falls, Ontario, April.
Female, Niagara Falls, Ontario, April.

5

Common Goldeneye

BUCEPHALA CLANGULA

plate 5

Common Goldeneye - BUCEPHALA CLANGULA

THE goldeneye is known as a "sea duck," although it breeds on freshwater lakes in the forested area of Canada and Alaska. Gunners have nicknamed it "whistler" for the distinctive sound delivered by its stiffly vibrating wing feathers.

This is a particularly hardy bird; it is no stranger to cold. In spring, migrating flocks of goldeneyes follow close upon the break-up of ice, and move into lakes and rivers the very moment they are even partially open.

Unlike a great many ducks, the goldeneye does not breed until it is more than one year old. Nesting is in a cavity in a tree, as much as fifty feet from the ground, often some distance from water. The hole is lined with down. After the clutch of eight to twelve greenish-white eggs has been laid, the male departs. The brood hatches in about twenty days, whereupon the downy youngsters are faced with their first major decision in life: how to get to the ground.

They seem to manage this successfully, judging by the numbers of goldeneyes, but just how they do it has long been debated. It has been said that the hen bird may transport the chicks by means of her bill, her back, or her feet. It seems more likely that they simply tumble out and take their chances. Since a little blob of duckling does not weigh much more than the equivalent volume of thistle down, it seems doubtful that many are seriously injured.

With the approach of winter, goldeneyes move only as far south as they absolutely have to. Great rafts concentrate at the southern edges of the ice. If water is open inland, the birds will remain there, but in most winters they are gradually forced toward the coast as the fresh waters close up.

The goldeneye eats a wide variety of food, including mussels, aquatic insects, and the shoots and roots of water plants.

Length 17-23 inches. Female, Niagara Falls, Ontario, May.

6

White-winged Scoter

MELANITTA DEGLANDI

plate 6

White-winged Scoter - MELANITTA DEGLANDI

*I*N swimming and diving, different water birds use different techniques. Penguins, for example, literally fly under water, propelling themselves with their wings, using the feet to assist in steering. Scoters do it the other way round. Propulsion is with the feet, and the wings seem to serve as rudders.

Notice in the plate the way in which the bird's wings are raised away from the body somewhat, with their tips crossed over the tail. At the wrist, a thumb-like "bastard wing" called the *alula* is extended away at an angle from the rest of the wing. This may be a particularly specialized underwater propulsive device, or it may act as a stabilizer. The alula is present in all birds, but its use in this way is especially noticeable in the scoters.

The bird pictured is a female. The male white-winged scoter is velvety-black with the same white patch at the rear edge of the wing, and a brilliant orange bill. Like the goldeneye, this species emits a peculiar whistling note which is thought to be produced by the wings.

White-winged scoters nest in a wide variety of locations, including forested lakes, prairie potholes, and the arctic tundra. In winter they concentrate in saltwater bays. At that season, their food consists mostly of mussels and other shellfish; they seem to feed most commonly at depths of fifteen to twenty feet.

Nesting birds of this species have the curious habit of covering their eggs with loose soil as the clutch accumulates. Once all the eggs are laid, down is used instead, as with other ducks. In the meantime, looking for scoter eggs has been described (by Herbert K. Job) as "like digging potatoes."

Length 19-23¹/₂ inches. Female, Swan Lake, British Columbia, November.

Hooded Merganser

LOPHODYTES CUCULLATUS

plate 7

Hooded Merganser - LOPHODYTES CUCULLATUS

THE merganser or "fish duck" tribe has come up with the most extreme specialization in the duck family. In the small hooded merganser it has produced what some consider one of the world's loveliest waterfowl. The little drake is able to fan his black-tipped white crest forward to a fully erect position and habitually does so. This flashing white "heliograph" is one way to recognize him at a distance.

The peculiar bill of a merganser is unique among waterfowl. Instead of the broad, spatulate bill of other ducks, evolution has provided just the instrument for catching and hanging onto slippery fish. Long, narrow, and with backward-directed "teeth" in both mandibles, the merganser's bill is a classic example of extreme adaptation to a very specialized line of work. Of course no bird has true teeth. The sharp points are fine but sturdy serrations in the bill itself.

The hooded merganser is another of the tree-nesting ducks. It looks for streams and ponds that are well wooded right to the edge. Occasionally it will use a stump standing in the water, and, rarely, it may come to a bird box.

Look for this bird in flooded forests with open patches of water. But you may look in vain; the beautiful hooded merganser is no longer common. North America underwent and is still enduring the last paroxysms of a widespread trophy-shooting dementia, manifest still in uncountable hooded mergansers picking up dust on mantelpieces and gathering cobwebs on boathouse ledges throughout the vacation country. This is a most unwary species – too tame for its own good. Any dolt can kill one.

As you would expect, the hooded merganser is an expert swimmer and diver. It can make its living in rather fast water, unlike most other diving ducks. Small pond fish are its normal fare – rarely or never those of any commercial value.

Length 16-19 inches. Male, Seven Oaks, Florida, December.
Female, Lake Scugog, Ontario, October.

8

Red-breasted Merganser

MERGUS SERRATOR

plate 8

Red-breasted Merganser - MERGUS SERRATOR

*A*NY bird that eats fish is faced, sooner or later, with the problem that is common to all animals that eat anything that man also eats. Mergansers eat fish; *ergo* mergansers are bad. If, like so many other ducks, they ate pondweed (man cannot digest pondweed), mergansers would be good. They would also be good to eat. But they are not at all good to eat, and this, plus their diet, weights the balance against them. Mergansers are often described by some gunners and fishermen as "worthless" or "undesirable."

It is true that these birds occasionally eat fish when and where they should not; usually this is a very local event. A merganser in a fish hatchery must be discouraged immediately. So must an intruding mink, but a mink is anything but worthless. The isolated malfeasance of one individual should never be allowed to develop into a blanket indictment of a species as a whole. In fact, most mergansers (like all other predators) take the line of least resistance; they use the prey species most readily available and most easily caught. Slow-moving coarse fish are much easier to catch than fast and agile game fish, and they are much more abundant in the waters occupied by this species. The odds favour the taking of coarse fish, which, not surprisingly, is exactly what happens.

The red-breasted merganser is somewhat more gregarious than other species and even acts co-operatively upon occasion. A string of birds will take position in line abreast and drive a school of fish into shallow water where it is easier to catch them. Whether this is an abstract relating of cause and effect or only an "instinctive" pattern of behaviour is open to question.

This species always nests on the ground, usually on the shore of a spruce-rimmed lake. Eight to ten buffy-olive eggs are laid in a downy depression, usually beneath a sheltering bush or small tree. In the late autumn, after the breeding season, enormous flocks of these birds may be seen in migration on the southern Great Lakes, streaming toward the coast and their winter fishing grounds on salt water in the southern states.

Length 19¹/₂-26 inches. Female, Departure Bay, British Columbia, March.
Male, Long Point, Ontario, November.

9

Goshawk

ACCIPITER GENTILIS

plate 9   *Goshawk* - ACCIPITER GENTILIS

*A*s the very model of killing efficiency, the goshawk has few peers in the world of birds of prey. From its blood-red eye to its chilling talons, this majestic creature is the end product of an evolutionary process that took millions upon millions of years. The result is the last word in bird control. It is a fact of life that all animals – including song-birds – must have population controls. Some people who claim to love birds are horrified by the activities of hawks, but it must be remembered that hawks are part of nature's system. They can do nothing else; hawks are committed to the existence to which they have become adapted.

The goshawk is an *accipiter*, a true hawk. Other birds that we infor-mally call "hawks," such as the falcons, the soaring buteos, and the harriers, all have their distinctive characteristics, and they are not hawks. The true hawks have short, rounded wings and long tails. They are low and stealthy fliers, hedge-hopping toward the unsuspecting target, and show marvelous manoeuvrability in wooded areas, dodging between branches, beneath shrubs, and around thickets with astonishing speed and accuracy for good-sized birds. In unhurried flight, the usual procedure is to take several flaps, sail for a distance, and then flap again. There are three true hawks in Canada; the goshawk, which is larger than a crow, is the greatest.

This fine predator is widespread, but not common. The abundance of birds of prey depends upon the numbers of their prey. Contrary to popular belief, a predator does not usually have any appreciable effect upon the numbers of the animals it eats. For example, a given patch of forest has room in it for only so many flickers. Flickers sometimes lay ten or a dozen eggs. Surplus flickers have to be eliminated one way or another. To be dispatched instantly by a goshawk, as the flicker in the plate was, would seem a kinder fate than some of the alternatives, which include starvation or disease. The very fact that we are not "up to here in flickers" attests to the presence of the goshawk, together with a long list of other predators, parasites, and miscellaneous controlling agents.

This is a fast, agile, and powerful bird, capable of killing prey the size of a pheasant or rabbit. It is much admired by falconers, not only for its efficiency, but also for its legendary ferocity. It is willing to hunt all day, where other species might tire or lose interest after one or two kills.

Length 20-26 inches. Wingspread 3¹/₂-4 feet. Male, Boyle, Alberta, November.

10

Osprey

PANDION HALIAETUS

plate 10   *Osprey* - PANDION HALIAETUS

*T*HE "fish hawk" is found in greater or lesser numbers over a considerable part of the world. Almost as large as an eagle (larger than some), and strikingly marked, this glorious bird is beautifully adapted to its specialty – fishing. It has a strong, hooked beak, the ability to hover in mid-air almost motionless, acute eyesight, and the most unusual feet of any bird of prey. The talons are especially long and curved, and the toes themselves are equipped with short, sharp spines to help the bird grasp and hold its slippery prey.

The osprey hunts by quartering a lake or bay, always on the lookout for fish basking near the surface. Spotting one, it plummets down in a more or less steep dive and hits the water feet first with a spectacular splash. The bird may actually disappear for an instant. As it rises from the water, it usually manages to hold the fish head first, to cut down on air resistance. It then laboriously climbs to cruising altitude and flaps away toward a huge nest of sticks high in the top of an isolated tree.

The osprey's exclusive dependence on fish may be its undoing. Not that there is any shortage of fish; the coarse species that make up the bulk of its diet are in good supply. Unfortunately, the osprey is one of the more frequent victims of the most terrible biotic scourge of all time – the chain-reaction effect of chemical pesticides in our living environment.

Fish and other cold-blooded animals have a low metabolic rate. They are able to build up in their systems substantial quantities of toxic chemicals picked up in their food, but not necessarily enough to kill them. These chemicals are pesticides that are washed from the forests and agricultural lands into our water systems. The fish then pass on a concentrated dose of the poison to the higher, warm-blooded animal that may eat *them*, and whose tolerance may be considerably less. It has been found in recent years that ospreys in areas of high pesticide contamination (river mouths and estuaries) are no longer breeding successfully. Their infertile eggs contain high levels of DDT, its derivatives, and related substances.

Ospreys have dropped alarmingly in numbers. It is quite possible that the age of technology will have claimed this irreplaceable species before many more years have passed.

Length 21-24¹/₂ inches. Wingspread 4¹/₂-6 feet. Female, Coldstream, Ontario, April.

11

Peregrine Falcon

FALCO PEREGRINUS

plate 11   *Peregrine Falcon* - FALCO PEREGRINUS

THE breath-taking aerial performance of the prince of falcons has excited and elated the heart and mind of man for a thousand years. No spectacle in the bird world can surpass the shattering stoop of the peregrine, which has been variously estimated at from 90 to 175 m.p.h. Woe betide the selected duck or pigeon, however swift, struck in mid-flight by a terrible missile that came without warning from out of the depths of the wide blue sky.

The sky is the peregrine's element, the cliff face its home. There are larger falcons, but few are swifter, and, certainly, none is more renowned. This species is the next thing to cosmopolitan. There are a variety of forms; the peregrine of the Queen Charlotte Islands and coastal Alaska, for example, is much darker than the one pictured here.

The peregrine is big-headed, bullet-shaped, and pointed-winged; it is built for whistling speed and crunching impact. No wonder it is the toast of falconers, who are willing to fly lesser species if necessary, but who know no substitute for the genuine article. Falconry is not widely practised in Canada, but there are pockets of it. It is to be hoped that the enthusiasm of the falconers does not have an adverse effect upon the numbers of the falcons. The peregrine can probably no longer withstand nest-robbing for the purposes of falconry, as it is already in grievous trouble from another direction.

Like the osprey, the peregrine stands at the apex of a food "pyramid"; it eats animals which eat lesser animals which eat plants. In many parts of our continent, this food chain is inoculated with deadly poisons which rise through each level to the bird of prey at the top. In the last five to ten years, the peregrine has disappeared as a breeding bird in the eastern United States. The same thing is happening in Britain. Though there is insufficient information on Canadian peregrines, the story would seem to be the same. Chemical pesticides are responsible. Their eventual effects on the whole inter-related wildlife community, in the light of developments with the birds of prey, can only be guessed at.

Length 15-21 inches. Wingspread 3¹/₄-3³/₄ feet. Male, Vernon, British Columbia, October.

12

Pigeon Hawk

FALCO COLUMBARIUS

Pigeon Hawk

plate 12 *Pigeon Hawk* - FALCO COLUMBARIUS

ESPITE its name, the pigeon "hawk" is not a hawk at all, but a small, jay-sized falcon something like a scaled-down peregrine. Its name derives not from the fact that it eats pigeons (it doesn't), but that it looks superficially like a pigeon when in flight. It has the typical pointed wings, longish tail, and rapid, powerful flight of the falcons.

A much better vernacular name for this species is "merlin." It goes by that name in Britain, as it has for hundreds of years — ever since the golden days of mediaeval falconry, when the small merlins were considered appropriate for ladies to fly. Peregrines and the giant gyrfalcon were reserved for top-level males in the complex and iron-clad hierarchy of the sport.

The merlin is found throughout the higher latitudes of the northern hemisphere, breeding as far up as the limit of trees. Though it sticks to the spruce-fir environment for nesting, it is not at all fussy about precise sites. Old magpies' and crows' nests are sometimes used, and even hollows in the ground and the disused excavations of woodpeckers in dead trees. Like the peregrine, this species is quite variable in colour, and again like the peregrine, the form on the Pacific coast is very dark, almost black.

This is a small bird, but a fearless one. It commonly badgers, hounds, and chivvies much larger birds, including crows and great horned owls. Its prey is much more modest; sparrow-sized small birds and large insects account for most of its diet. Among the latter, dragonflies are especially important, plus grasshoppers, butterflies, and others. The merlin sometimes feeds, kite-like, on the wing. It likes to maintain a lookout on a bare twig or high rock from which it can survey the food possibilities, darting after its prey in typical falcon style. It may be the only bird capable of catching swallows on the wing.

The handsome little merlin is not common anywhere, but may be seen most readily during migration, when it often accompanies flocks of longspurs, various sandpipers, and others. Thus it has a food supply for the entire journey.

Length 10-13¹/₂ inches. Wingspread 2 feet.

13

Spruce Grouse

CANACHITES CANADENSIS

plate 13   *Spruce Grouse* - CANACHITES CANADENSIS

THE stiff and ritualized courtship ceremony of the spruce grouse is one of the most magnificent sights of the deep evergreen woods. The strutting, posturing male seems on the verge of exploding as he erects his plumage to the fullest extent and advertises himself unceasingly on his own private parade ground. The drab-coloured hen, seemingly nonchalant about it all, will eventually react appropriately.

This sequestered mating of a woodland species is in contrast with the orgiastic social performances of such open country species as the sharp-tailed and sage grouse and the prairie chicken, all of which indulge in mass courtship and at least some promiscuity. The remote and shaded retreat of the spruce grouse is the perfect backdrop for the male's resplendent plumage.

For all its striking appearance, however, the spruce grouse is remarkably camouflaged. Its apparent blind faith in this method of concealment has earned it the wretched nickname "fool hen." When the bird is disturbed on the forest floor, it promptly flies up into the nearest tree, becomes perfectly still, and lets its protective colouration take over from there. This does not always work, however, and many a starving woodsman has taken advantage of this to knock the bird over with a stick, only to use the ungrateful adjective "stupid" for the bird's providential co-operation.

But the spruce grouse is edible only in an emergency. Its diet consists chiefly of spruce needles and the buds of these and other conifers, which, apparently, is more than evident in its flesh. In summer, it may turn to berries and other such fare, while the young, like those of most birds, stick in the early stages to animal protein in the form of insects and other invertebrates.

This is a sedentary bird; it rarely moves far from its home base, and it is non-migratory. That is a boon to birdwatchers, for prior knowledge of traditional spruce grouse locations saves a great deal of searching for a surprisingly inconspicuous bird.

Length 15-17 inches. Female, Parry Sound, Ontario, October.
Male, St. Fabien de Panet, Quebec, October.

14

Common Snipe

CAPELLA GALLINAGO

Snipe

plate 14

Common Snipe - CAPELLA GALLINAGO

*T*HIS unusual sandpiper is found in appropriate locations throughout the northern part of the northern hemisphere. Its chosen haunts are variable, but there is a common denominator – water. It nests at the borders of marshes and wet bogs. In migration it turns up in roadside ditches, in soggy fields, and wherever there is enough water and damp grassy cover to accommodate it.

Like the related woodcock, the snipe has a heavy-set, stocky body, short legs, relatively large eyes set far back on the head, and a truly enormous bill. The size of the bill is by no means its only peculiarity. It is essentially a probing instrument, for reaching deep into mud and soft soil for worms. Like some item of the most refined surgical hardware, it has a flexible tip for seeking and seizing its evasive target.

Even more remarkable is the snipe's bizarre specialization for purposes of courtship. At night (or by day if it is overcast), the bird flies up to a considerable height, then hurtles earthward emitting a strange, hollow, "winnowing" sound which ceases as it swings aloft again. For many years, the source of this singular humming vibration was unknown; argument surrounded it until relatively recently. It is now known that it is not a vocal note, but an instrumental or mechanical one produced by the tail.

The snipe's tail is specially adapted for the purpose. When it is fanned, its two stiff outer feathers are separated from the rest and vibrate in the air as the bird shoots downward. At the same time, the wings are stiffly agitated and have the effect of allowing air to strike the tail at regular (rapid) intervals. The result is the tremulous *vibrato* music so characteristic of cold bogs in the June darkness.

The snipe does not limit itself to mechanical sound. It has a song of sorts which can often be heard in between "winnows." Not content with aerobatics, the bird also struts like a little turkey on the ground.

Length 10¹/₂-11¹/₂ inches. Male, Puntchesakut Lake, British Columbia, May.

15

Solitary Sandpiper

TRINGA SOLITARIA

plate 15   *Solitary Sandpiper* - TRINGA SOLITARIA

THE overwhelming majority of sandpipers frequent marshes, lake-shores, and other flat, open, water margins. As befits their habitat, they nest on the ground. The attractive solitary sandpiper does neither of these things. It has forsaken the traditional haunts and habits of sand-pipers in favour of the unusual environment of the northern forest; it has defied convention by nesting in trees.

The vast evergreen country of the north abounds in tiny wooded ponds, streams, and forested bogs. This is the retreat of the solitary sandpiper. Like its kind, it is never far from water, but it is satisfied with a very modest supply. It chooses a cool wet swamp more or less heavily overgrown with spruces and tamaracks, and there it seeks out the old, last year's nests of tree-dwelling species such as robins, rusty blackbirds, jays, waxwings, and others. Then, like its close relative of the Old World, the green sandpiper, it proceeds to make the old nest its own. This may be in a tree from four to forty feet high, a most improbable site for a true sandpiper.

Young sandpipers are precocial. They are born fully able to get about by themselves, like young ducks, geese, loons, and many more. Since they must feed themselves, they begin to forage immediately. Presumably the four young solitary sandpipers vacate the nest in much the same way as young goldeneyes are thought to do: they merely fall as gracefully as pos-sible to a soft, sphagnum-cushioned carpet, and under the parent's watch-ful eye set about making a living.

Food consists of all forms of aquatic animal life, including insects, small crustaceans, and many others which it will stir from the muddy bottom of shallow water with its feet. Occasionally the bird will take an insect on the wing, snapping it up as a flycatcher would. There is no shortage of food in the muskeg. This is a good thing, as solitary sandpipers need plenty of fuel in the form of fat for their autumn migration southward. They winter as far from the spruce country as the West Indies, southern Mexico, and Argentina.

Length 7¹/₂-9 inches. Female, Favourable Lake, Ontario, July.

Lesser Yellowlegs

TOTANUS FLAVIPES

plate 16   *Lesser Yellowlegs* - TOTANUS FLAVIPES

THERE are two species of yellowlegs – the lesser and the greater. The two are distressingly similar in appearance, so much so that it is frequently difficult to distinguish them unless they happen to be together for comparison. But there are differences. This species is much smaller than the other. Its bill is quite straight; that of the greater is perceptibly up-turned. Most important, their call notes are distinctive.

This species breeds in open evergreen forests from Alaska to northern Ontario and Quebec. Unlike the tree-nesting solitary sandpiper, which likes the relatively dense thickets around spruce bogs, the yellowlegs prefers muskeg country with more sparse tree cover. Appropriately for a sandpiper, it nests in a hollow on the ground.

Its liking for rather open woods suggests that the lesser yellowlegs might be one of those species which can benefit from forest fire. A mature, dense forest is unsuitable for it; clearings with a pioneer growth of post-fire poplar or aspen saplings are more to its taste.

It is a paradox that some species *must* have at least occasional fire for their very existence. One of these is Kirtland's warbler, which nests only in jack pine of a certain age (and size) in Michigan. Jack pine must have the intense heat of fire for the release of seeds from its cones, so this rare warbler is inextricably bound to conflagration for its survival. The same may be true, to a lesser extent, of the yellowlegs.

Both yellowlegs have loud, shrill cries, and they are very vocal around the nest. Most shorebirds call a great deal of attention to themselves when they have eggs and young, the effect of which is to distract the attention of predators from the brood. Yellowlegs display themselves conspicuously and become exceptionally noisy when an intruder comes anywhere near the nesting site.

All our shorebirds are good fliers, and most are long-distance migrants, moving between forty and fifty miles per hour for remarkable distances. One lesser yellowlegs, banded on Cape Cod, was recovered six days later in Martinique, nineteen hundred miles away – an average of three hundred and sixteen miles per day. This species winters as far south as Chile and Argentina.

Length 9¹/₂-11 inches. Male, Fort Severn, Ontario, June.

17
Great Horned Owl
BUBO VIRGINIANUS

plate 17

Great Horned Owl - BUBO VIRGINIANUS

*I*T is likely that no North American bird has aroused such extremes of human admiration and antipathy as this great owl. Those who know something about the bird hold it in unassailable esteem; many of those who do not are its most implacable enemies. As in all extremes of opinion, the truth lies somewhere in between, although as biological literacy makes slow and laboriously-won inroads among our prejudices, it becomes increasingly difficult — in fact impossible — to condemn any wildlife species.

This is our most powerful and aggressive owl. It will eat any animal it can overcome, and the list of its victims is long. Its menu runs from voles and mice to rabbits, skunks, and even house cats, from insects and small birds to pheasants and grouse. This is what gets the horned owl into trouble. When it eats some item that is equally or even more desirable to man (usually for the purpose of sport killing), loud and strong are the brays of recrimination.

Most predators are lazy. They take the food most readily available, and the prey most easily caught is clearly the species that happens to be most abundant at the time. Populations of grouse, for example, are cyclic; they have dramatic swings through peaks and hollows of abundance on a fairly predictable schedule. In years of grouse "explosions," horned owls take a lot of grouse. In years of vole abundance, owls will depend on them for the bulk of their food. Neither makes any real difference, because the predator depends for its living on the numbers of its prey, and has little if any influence on those numbers. Neither (except in cases of excessive killing, such as that of prairie waterfowl) does the hunter. Both normally take only a portion of natural annual surpluses that one way or another have to be trimmed anyway for the benefit of the wildlife community as a whole.

Yet this excellent bird is persecuted viciously and is legally unprotected in parts of the continent where the traditional pioneer attitudes towards wildlife still prevail. Happily it has no significant enemies save man, and is able to maintain its numbers reasonably well in those wilderness areas where it is undisturbed.

The horned owl breeds very early in the year, usually in the old nest of a crow or hawk, sometimes in a hollow tree. It is not at all rare to see the old bird incubating her eggs with snow lying on her back and all around her. This is our most formidable bird in defence of its nest, and is not content with threats, as most species are. Many a bird bander can testify that climbing to a horned owl's nest is a calculated risk. The bird does not know fear, and is savagely armed to deal with interlopers.

Length 20-25 inches. Female, Algoma District, Ontario, February.

18
Hawk-Owl
SURNIA ULULA

Hawk Owl.

plate 18 *Hawk-Owl* - SURNIA ULULA

EW birds are more appropriately named than this one; although a proper owl in all vital respects, its long tail and hunting technique are distinctly hawk-like. This is a good example of the process called evolutionary convergence. When owls came into being and began to proliferate over the world, there was clearly no need for all of them to be strictly nocturnal. There were possibilities for at least some owls to become crepuscular, or even diurnal. There was an ecological opportunity to be exploited by an owl that would hunt by day, more or less in the style of a hawk. That, evidently, is what happened. An owl found a new niche and occupied it. In the process of becoming adapted to this sort of life, it came to resemble a hawk somewhat, but the two families are not related.

This is an owl of the far north where the summer nights are short. At the season when young must be fed, there is more daylight than darkness to hunt by, so it benefits the bird to work in the daytime, like the snowy owl of even farther north. Just as a merlin or kestrel would, the hawk-owl perches on a tall prominent spike or other vantage point, reviewing the surrounding muskeg. When a small mammal is spotted, the owl launches itself in pursuit. It has everything going for it: the silent, buoyant flight of the owl, the speed of the hawk. It is a singularly efficient, though nowhere common, predator on mice and voles. Probably there are sufficient hawks in the same general line of business to keep the competition healthy.

As you might expect, the hawk-owl's nesting routine is not unlike that of one of the small hawks. It generally nests in a cavity in a tree (often one made by a pileated woodpecker), but it will also use the abandoned nest of a crow or hawk, like many other owls.

Owls can see perfectly well in the daytime. Light blindness is a myth, although some species may see better than others in daylight. The owl's peculiarity is that it can see remarkably well in *minimum* light; its eyes are especially adapted to allow it to take advantage of the slightest illumination. In total darkness, however, with no light source at all, an owl can see no better than any other animal, including man.

Length 14¹/₂-17¹/₂ inches. Male, Big Hay Lake, Alberta, October.

19
Great Gray Owl

STRIX NEBULOSA

plate 19   *Great Gray Owl* - STRIX NEBULOSA

ITH its great puffy head, yellow eyes, and the concentric, "op art" circles of its facial discs, this northern owl is the most striking of them all. It is also the largest over all, because of its unusually long tail, but its size is mostly illusion. Although its measurements are greater than those of either the snowy or great horned owls, the great gray is mostly fluff. It is heavily and thickly feathered, and the body within is quite slight. It weighs considerably less than either of its sturdy relatives.

Since it is not as strong and fearsome as its size would suggest, this species concentrates on smaller food sources than the horned owl. Mice, voles, chipmunks, and other small mammals predominate; it is probably not a serious threat to most birds. Thus its food habits are almost entirely "beneficial," to use an archaism that is happily disappearing from natural history literature. It used to be conventional to categorize wildlife species in this way, but no animal, obviously, is either "harmful" or "beneficial," except in the most subjective human terms, and these are terms that do not apply in nature.

Man does a great deal of rationalizing in his attitudes towards other animals. It is all right to shoot hawks and owls because these birds are "killers." Of course they are killers. That is what they are designed to do; that is their service to the natural system. No other animal has human concepts or human motives; nature knows neither evil nor good. In the complex chain of nature, all living things play their part. No link in that chain is "bad"; each link has its function.

The great gray owl is notably tame. On those rare occasions when one or two individuals turn up during the winter in some settled part of the country, they are nearly always – but not always – approachable and unwary. This has led to an inevitable thinning of great gray owl numbers wherever it has regularly come into contact with man. Luckily for the bird, it is a wilderness species and does not commonly encounter its only enemy.

Length 24-33 inches. Male, Winnipeg, Manitoba, January.

20

Long=eared Owl

ASIO OTUS

plate 20   *Long-eared Owl* - ASIO OTUS

*D*ESPITE its appearance and its name, the ears of this owl are well concealed beneath its feathers and are no longer than those of any other owl. The conspicuous "ears" on the head are only tufts of feathers. Like the "horns" of the great horned owl, they are merely adornments.

This does not mean that owls' ears are not remarkable. They are quite unlike those of any other birds. The ears of some owls have unusually large openings in the sides of the head, to which are fitted flaps that can be raised at will. They work like a cupped hand in reflecting sound waves toward the very large eardrum. Owls are extraordinarily sensitive to high-frequency sounds like the squeak of a mouse and to sounds of very low intensity such as the footfall of a rabbit. In some species the ears are asymmetrical, pointing in different directions, and this is thought to aid the bird in sound location. Since owls can see no better in complete darkness than any other animals can, their ears are of the greatest importance on heavily overcast nights. In experimental situations, in the total absence of light, owls have zeroed in on their prey with astonishing accuracy, by hearing alone.

The eyes of most birds are placed on the sides of the head, so that they have only limited vision to the front. That is why a chicken or a robin cocks its head in the familiar way. But if a bird is going to specialize in catching quick-moving prey, it needs stereoscopic vision in order to be able to judge distances accurately. Placement of the eyes in front, with overlapping binocular vision in an arc up to 70°, makes the owl's pounce precise.

Unlike the eyes of mammals, birds' eyes are fixed in their sockets. They cannot move around. If a bird cannot move its eyes, it must move its head. Owls have developed amazing efficiency in this respect. An otherwise motionless long-eared owl can swivel its head through a full 270° before it must unscrew its neck and go round the other way.

Length 13-16 inches. Female, Simcoe, Ontario, November.

21

Boreal Owl

AEGOLIUS FUNEREUS

plate 21   *Boreal Owl* - AEGOLIUS FUNEREUS

ENGMALM's owl is the Old World name for this northern species which is also known on this continent as Richardson's owl. But it is the same bird – a small, chunky owl of the coniferous forest that is not commonly seen in settled parts of the country.

Since most owls hunt at night or at twilight, they have little to do during the daytime except to digest the meal of the night before. Owls swallow their prey whole or in gullet-sized chunks. Indigestible portions such as skulls, bones, feathers and fur are regurgitated in the form of tightly packed pellets that look as though they were made of felt. (In a sense, they are.) During this digestive process the bird prefers to remain well hidden. Most owls choose a dense concealing evergreen in which to roost, and they usually stay as close to the trunk as possible.

The cryptic camouflage of owls is so excellent that they easily go un-noticed. Both this species and the closely related and even smaller saw-whet owl will sit so tightly and remain so still, relying on their protective coloura-tion, that they can be touched and even caught by hand. This tameness is often their undoing when they are spotted by the wrong party, for the ignorant are still very much with us. Hawk and owl persecution is by no means a thing of the past.

As with other owls (and hawks) the female is the larger of the sexes. This bird nests in a cavity in a tree – usually an old woodpecker dig. An interesting courtship rite has been observed, in the course of which the birds indulge in symbolic feeding. The male does much calling while flying back and forth at the selected nesting hole. When the female is at last in-duced to enter the chamber, there she finds a delectable fresh mouse. Pre-sumably this is difficult to resist.

The boreal owl is a particularly effective hunter, concentrating on small nocturnal mammals. For this kind of life, extraordinary hearing and eye-sight are not the only advantages enjoyed by owls. They have very large wings in relation to their weight, which enables them to fly unusually slow-ly, with a low flapping rate and a very low stalling speed. This allows them great manoeuvrability. Their downy, soft feathers are virtually soundless; the owl's approach and strike are silent and sure.

Length 8¹/₂-12 inches. Male, Port Credit, Ontario, March.

22

Black=backed Three=toed Woodpecker

PICOIDES ARCTICUS

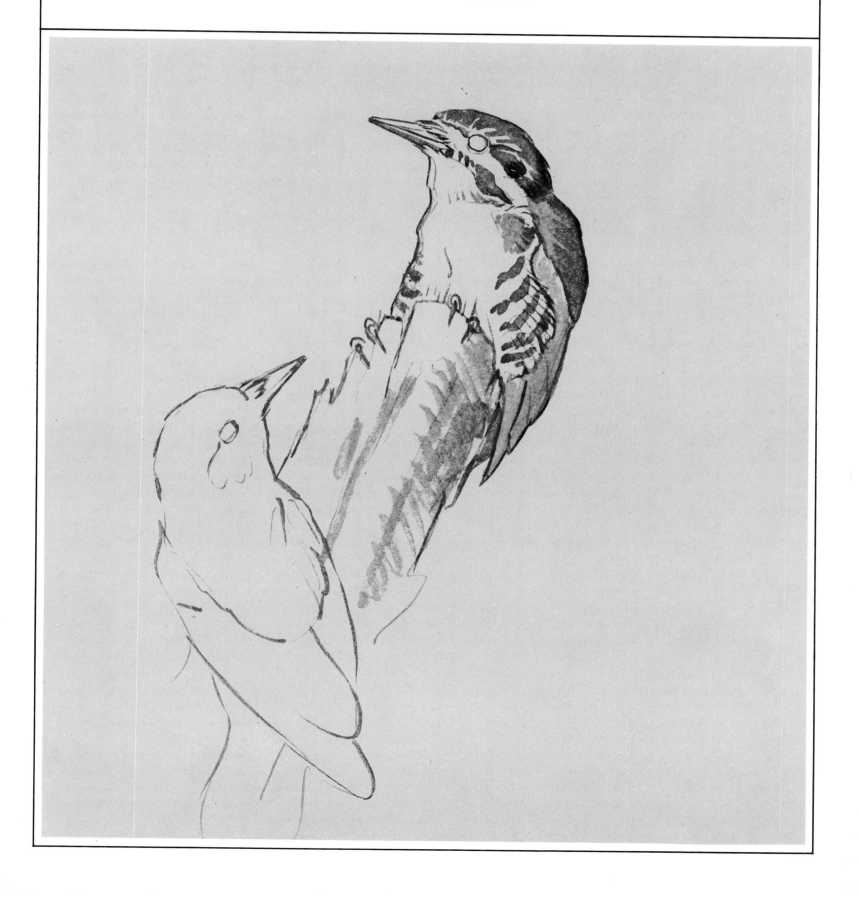

plate 22   *Black-backed Three-toed Woodpecker* - PICOIDES ARCTICUS

*T*HE specific name *arcticus* of this handsome woodpecker is somewhat misleading. The true arctic, a treeless desert, is clearly no place for a woodpecker. In fact this is the more southern in distribution of the two members of this genus, though both are birds of the northern forest of spruce, larch, and fir.

That it has only three toes instead of the normal complement of four does not seem to impair the efficiency of what is otherwise a perfectly typical member of its family. Woodpeckers' feet are stronger than those of many birds, enabling them to feed hour after hour in a near-vertical position, clinging to the bark. One toe more or less does not seem to make much difference. Why one should have been lost in the course of evolution is unclear, though it has been suggested that the elimination of one toe may in some way be an aid to greater pecking force.

In recent years this species has become increasingly familiar to the army of birdwatchers in the southern parts of Canada. At one time the sight of a three-toed woodpecker of either species was a source of great excitement and much agitated communication along the birders' hot lines. This is no longer so in many regions, especially in southern Ontario. Each winter substantial numbers of this species are seen as far south as Lake Ontario – and in the USA, a good distance beyond.

Sporadic, irregular southward movement in some winters is characteristic of several northern birds, including some of the owls, but the appearance of this woodpecker has become an annual event. No one knows what causes the birds to forsake the spruce belt, but there is some evidence to indicate that once in the south, they are kept there for the winter by an abundance of food.

This annual woodpecker bonanza is apparently the result of the widespread ravages of imported Dutch elm disease. Southern Ontario, for example, is now littered with dead and dying elms, and a great many of these trees show conspicuous patches where the bark has been flaked away. This is the normal feeding pattern of this species. The bark layers of dead trees are filled with the larvae of bark-boring beetles and other insects upon which these birds depend for food. Most woodpeckers do not customarily dig in healthy trees; their prey can only occur normally in *un*healthy or dead ones.

Length 9-10 inches. Male, Favourable Lake, Ontario, October.
Female, Lac la Nonne, Alberta, September.

23

Northern Three=toed Woodpecker

PICOIDES TRIDACTYLUS

3-toed
woodpecker

plate 23

Northern Three-toed Woodpecker - PICOIDES TRIDACTYLUS

*L*IKE the preceding species, this woodpecker has strong feet for clutching bark, regardless of the number of toes. It has the typical chisel-like bill of a woodpecker, mounted on a large, heavy skull and driven by a strong and flexible neck. The tongues of woodpeckers are especially designed to penetrate deeply into dead wood. They can be extended for an astonishing length, and carry various types of barbs and bristles for impaling and dragging out their prey. A nice accessory bit of equipment consists of special bristle-like feathers covering the nostrils and protecting them from tiny chips and "saw dust." A woodpecker's tail is notably stiff in order to prop the bird firmly and securely against tree trunks.

Unlike the black-backed three-toed woodpecker, which is confined to North America, this species occurs in Eurasia as well. It is rather more northern in distribution than the other and appears to be much less common. Both depend for their livelihood on the natural mortality of northern evergreens due to such agents as disease, fire, and flooding, all of which occur more or less regularly.

We are too often inclined to think of such tree-killing events as "disasters," and to forget that they have always been a part of the natural process. Without a continuing kill of trees there could be no woodpeckers. Just as fire promotes the spread of white-tailed deer, for example, by providing luxuriant, mixed second growth, it also supplies dead trees and a new larder of wood-boring insects for the woodpeckers. Just as the beaver, by flooding the landscape, improves the habitat for water-loving moose, it also makes drowned trees available to the woodpeckers' insect prey. Rarely does anything happen in nature that fails to bring someone some good. Even the infamous spruce budworm, by thinning the balsam fir forest, promotes a new natural succession of events of benefit to many plant and animal species and of significance to the life cycle of the forest itself.

All woodpeckers excavate their nesting sites in dead wood. They do not line their nests; the chips are let fall where they may, including the bottom of the cavity where the white eggs are deposited. Both sexes take part in the duties associated with nesting. They appear to look after the young for an unusually long period after they have taken to the wing. Perhaps young woodpeckers must take extra time to develop adequate strength in bill, head and neck before they can begin to do their own digging.

Length 8-9¹/₂ inches. Female, Savanne, Ontario, July.
Male, Kenora District, Ontario, June.

24

Yellow=bellied Flycatcher

EMPIDONAX FLAVIVENTRIS

plate 24   *Yellow-bellied Flycatcher* - EMPIDONAX FLAVIVENTRIS

SHY and inconspicuous for a flycatcher, this delicate little species nests in the evergreen forest east of the Rockies. It is one of the bewildering members of the genus *Empidonax*, seven of which occur in Canada (there are two more in the USA), all of which look so much alike that they have long been the despair of both expert field students and (especially) beginners. This one, luckily, is usually identifiable by its yellow underparts and by its yellow throat, which is marked strongly enough to make identification reasonably safe, even though some of its relatives appear somewhat yellowish in the fall.

The more experienced a bird student becomes, the less inclined he is to attempt to separate the *Empidonax* flycatchers in the field, except on the basis of voice; the songs and call notes of the various species are distinctive. This one is so retiring that often its call is the only clue to its presence, although in common with other flycatchers, it can scarcely be called a "singer." Flycatchers' voices are usually harsh and discordant.

This is the only member of its genus that habitually nests on the ground, in a cup-like structure deep in the soft mossy floor of the spruce-muskeg country, so artfully concealed that it is rarely found. There are said to be two cups, or sections, one fitting into the other. The inner cup is described as being well insulated from the constant dampness of the sphagnum bog.

Typically, flycatchers have broad, rather flat bills, surrounded by long bristles which help to trap their prey. Since it regularly takes flying insects on the wing, a flycatcher need not be so much a fast flier as a strong and manoeuvrable one. Its aerial acrobatics in pursuit of winged insects are extremely interesting. At one time it was thought that hummingbirds were the only birds actually capable of flying backward. Flycatchers have been observed to do something very *like* flying backward; certainly they are able to hover in one position, at the same time achieving a variety of subtle movements in apparently any direction.

Length 5-5³/₄ inches. Male, Hamilton, Ontario, May.

25

Olive-sided Flycatcher

NUTTALLORNIS BOREALIS

plate 25   *Olive-sided Flycatcher* - NUTTALLORNIS BOREALIS

*M*ANY flycatchers are strident, vociferous, aggressive birds, and this species is as noisily belligerent as any. It is so competitive about its nesting territory that although it is a common species, it is rather widely scattered through the boreal forest country. Olive-sided flycatchers do not like excessive proximity to their own species, and indeed will frequently drive off other birds as well.

This is an easily identifiable, middle-sized, very sturdy flycatcher with a big head and a drab olive "waistcoat." It likes to station itself bolt upright on the very topmost spire of a spruce or some other evergreen, maintaining a constant watch for passing bees, flies, and winged ants, and watching too for other birds to drive away. When not actually on the wing, it remains quite motionless and would easily go undetected, were it not for its unmistakeable "song," which has been variously expressed from "Hip – three cheers!" to "Hic – three beers!" The verbalization of bird song is a woefully unsatisfactory means of description, as a song can be interpreted differently by every human listener, but in this case at least, the rhythm and phrasing are constant.

Its preferred habitat usually includes water – spruce bogs and muskeg, small forest lakes, streams, and ponds. The nest itself is nearly always in a conifer, often on one of the lower horizontal branches. Incubation of the three eggs takes almost exactly two weeks, and the young are reported to remain in the nest for about three weeks more.

Flycatchers are forced to be migrants; their food demands it. This one winters in Central America and the northwestern part of South America. In the spring, the northward movement of flycatchers must coincide with hatches of flying insects, and thus it is tied to the temperature. This makes the birds vulnerable to sudden drops of the thermometer, and if a cold spell develops during their flight in May, sometimes they are forced to seek insects and other invertebrates on the ground, or even to turn to vegetable food for a meal or two until things improve. However, since this species is so attracted to bees, and some bees often venture forth in surprisingly cool weather, its food supply is reasonably dependable.

Length 7-8 inches. Male, Algoma District, Ontario, June.

26

Gray Jay

PERISOREUS CANADENSIS

plate 26

Gray Jay - PERISOREUS CANADENSIS

OTWITHSTANDING the shocked protests of diehard chauvinists and those of us too old to become unstuck from the nomenclature of our childhood, the Canada jay officially became the gray jay with the 1957 publication of the fifth edition of the American Ornithologists' Union *Check-list of North American Birds*. Actually it was a very good idea, as we already had the blue jay and the green jay. Since this bird breeds in evergreen forests as far south as California, the parochial name really did not suit. Old-timers will continue to call the bird "whiskey-jack" anyway.

This must be one of the most familiar birds of the north country, yet the dark young bird always seems to cause confusion. An adult gray jay looks something like an over-insulated giant chickadee, and is immediately identifiable, but in the immature plumage it looks like a different bird.

No camper in the spruce forest or the western mountains can fail to know this bird. Familiar to the point of contemptuousness, the gray jay will steal anything that is not lashed down, whether edible or not. With a little patience on the camper's part, the bird can often be fed from the hand. It is a true omnivore, taking pretty well anything, animal or vegetable. That its diet runs from hamburger meat and baked beans through bacon rinds to soda crackers and licorice all-sorts has been documented.

In the wild, where camp scavenging is not possible, this jay's fare consists of berries, seeds, and fruits, the eggs and nestlings of other birds, and carrion. But the species seems to have "learned" to associate man with food, and no wilderness traveller is without its company for long. With its loose, fluffy plumage, it can fly as silently as an owl, suddenly appearing over one's head as if from nowhere.

When it cares to, the gray jay can be conspicuously noisy. It has as wide an assortment of notes as any Canadian bird – most harsh, but some soft and whistled. Indeed it is such a polygot that when most observers hear a completely unfamiliar note in the evergreen bush, they charge it to the gray jay and let it go at that.

Length 10-13 inches. Male, Rice Lake, Ontario, October.
Immature, The Pas, Manitoba, May.

Common Raven

CORVUS CORAX

plate 27

Common Raven - CORVUS CORAX

*T*HE raven is the very embodiment not of evil but of wilderness. In Canada we tend to think of it as a "northern" bird; this is merely because our wilderness happens to be in the north. The bird is found from the arctic to Central America, from the desolate tundra to mountain rock slides, desert canyons, and seacoast cliffs. It is a particularly unsociable animal from man's point of view, and confines itself to the most inaccessible parts of the continent. It occurs also in Europe, Asia, and Africa.

A raven is like a hugely overgrown crow, but there are other differences. Its bill is relatively much longer and stouter; its tail is long and wedge-shaped. In its hawk-like soaring, the flight feathers are widely spread apart, almost like those of a vulture. At close range you can see a shaggy "beard" at the throat. The hoarse croak of the raven is quite unlike the call of a crow.

Like its relatives, the jays, crows, and magpies, the raven will eat pretty nearly anything, including carrion. This taste has been the bird's death warrant in those parts of the continent where predator persecution has involved the barbaric use of baits treated with strychnine, "1080," and other poisons. Massive and insensate campaigns have been mounted against wolves, coyotes, and other animals (always under the euphemistic guise of "control"). This deliberate slaughter has arisen from pressure applied by organized interests such as tourist outfitters, farmers, and ranchers. It has cut terrible swaths not only through the target species but many others as well. Eagles and sundry fur-bearing mammals have been victims as well as the crow family.

Ravens, crows, and jays have always been known to be intelligent birds. That ravens have more than the standard bird brain has been demonstrated in laboratory experiments. The species showed the ability to "count," that is, to distinguish accurately between targets with different numbers of spots on them, and to select the right target when presented with an appropriate cue card. The related Old World rook is known to have a kind of traditional learning process in which symbolic elements such as "language" have been detected. This is probably the most fascinating family of birds.

Length 21¹/₂-27 inches. Male, Pefferlaw, Ontario, October.

28

Boreal Chickadee

PARUS HUDSONICUS

plate 28   *Boreal Chickadee* - PARUS HUDSONICUS

CANADA has six of the world family of sixty-four species of titmice. Known variously as the brown-capped, Columbian, Acadian, and Hudsonian chickadee, this species lives in the great conifer belt from Alaska to New England. Except under the pressure of food shortage, it rarely ventures south of the evergreen forest.

When it does come south, however, it is often in staggering numbers. Remarkable irruptions of this species occur once in a while, resulting in movement far beyond its normal range. Once, great numbers of them invaded the unlikely habitat offered by the glass, steel, and concrete of New York City. In common with certain other birds (waxwings and some finches among them) the titmice may enjoy two or three successive years of unusual prosperity when food is in abundance and living (and thus breeding) is easy. The result is a fast and substantial build-up in population. This offers no problem so long as the food supply is constant. But if a food "crash" should develop next year, due to the vagaries of weather or other factors, great numbers of birds are forced to move much farther south in winter than they normally would.

In most years, however, these birds do not move very far in a latitudinal sense. Small bands of them roam about the coniferous forest in winter, searching for insects and other animal protein as they go. It seems incredible that such minute birds can survive the fearful cold of northern winter, but they do.

No bird migrates south because of the temperature; it migrates to find food. There is plenty of food in the spruce forest in the form of overwintering insects, their pupae, larvae, and eggs, and the chickadees manage to find it. So long as their metabolic furnaces are well stoked, insulating fat and feathers do the rest.

But a small bird burns up energy at such a high rate that it must eat very often — almost constantly during the short daylight hours of the northern winter. At thirty below zero, a bird that is hungry at nightfall may not survive until morning; a well-fed bird, no matter what the weather, will be warm, active, and efficient when the next day's foraging begins.

Length 5-5¹/₂ inches. Male, Pottageville, Ontario, October.

Red-breasted Nuthatch

SITTA CANADENSIS

plate 29

Red-breasted Nuthatch - SITTA CANADENSIS

*T*HE nuthatches are a world-wide family of birds that occur chiefly in the northern hemisphere. The name originated with the European nuthatch, which has been alleged to be able to open hazel nuts (hence "nuthack"). This small North American species confines itself to much less formidable challenges.

Nuthatches resemble woodpeckers very superficially; they make their way up and down the trunks of trees, digging in the bark for various items of food. But the two families are not related, and there are important differences. A woodpecker props itself against the trunk with its stiff tail, always in a more or less upright position. A nuthatch does not use its short, stubby tail for support, but depends on its feet, which it usually places one above the other. It commonly descends a tree head first, which no woodpecker does. Its long, sharp bill probes deeply into bark crevices and other hiding places of insects, spiders, and other small invertebrates. Occasionally some nuthatches will take to the air to snap up passing insects.

In winter, this common species concentrates for a good part of its food supply on the seeds of various conifers. In years when the cone crop is poor (and especially if the crop has been good in immediately prior years), great flights come south in winter, as with the boreal chickadee. These irruptions are sporadic and unpredictable; they are not on any definable schedule.

For nesting, the bird uses an existing cavity in a spruce or balsam fir (or a pine in the south), or it will excavate one for itself in a rotten conifer. The nest is lined with wood fibres, soft grasses, and shredded bark. Most peculiar is the bird's habit of smearing evergreen pitch around the entrance to the nesting hole. Spruce, fir, or pine pitch is liberally plastered on all bare wood around or near the opening to the cavity – to what purpose, no one knows. An interesting sidelight on this, though not necessarily related to it, is that the nuthatch can fly directly through the hole and into the nest without stopping or even pausing at the rim. How it brakes in time to come to rest inside is an open question.

Length 4¹/₂-4³/₄ inches. Female, Bruce County, Ontario, September.

30

Winter Wren

TROGLODYTES TROGLODYTES

plate 30

Winter Wren - TROGLODYTES TROGLODYTES

O F the world's sixty-three species of wrens, only this one occurs out-side the Americas. The centre of abundance of the wrens is in South America; Canada has only eight species. The winter wren, however, adaptable and venturesome creature that it is, has made its way over the years across the Bering Strait into Siberia; from there it has fanned across Eurasia and North Africa, finally reaching Iceland. Since it is the only wren in the Old World, it is known there as *the* wren, or, more familiarly in Britain, "Jenny" wren.

This is the next-to-smallest of Canadian wrens. With its very stubby tail and dark plumage, and its reluctance to leave the tangled down-timber and mosses of the forest floor, it often resembles a mouse as it darts and scurries about in the security of its almost impenetrable surroundings. Were it not for its song, most times one would never see it.

The song of the winter wren is one of the marvels of the northern forest. It has no characteristic phrase, no definable structure; it is a glorious welter of pure, crystal notes, a formless babble of tinkling expressions so attenu-ated as to seem endless. It is a particularly high-pitched song; not every listener can pick up all the highest frequencies. But even snatches of it are quite unlike the notes of any other inhabitant of the forest.

In common with many other small birds, wrens are incredibly volatile. Their breeding habits reflect their restless, high-key natures. The male winter wren may build several nests, only one of which may be used. Or, if opportunity arises, he will cheerfully turn polygamist; the extra nests are available for such an eventuality.

The nest is a bulky mass, a structure of mosses and tiny twigs with the entrance usually to one side. It is concealed in tangled roots, under a stump or log, sometimes in a crevice – always very close to the ground. Built as it is of the materials of the forest floor, and nearly always skilfully hidden, it is often very difficult to find.

Despite its name, this species does not winter in most parts of Canada. It migrates to the central and southern states, returning in spring to the great evergreen forest from Newfoundland to Alaska.

Length 4-4¹/₂ inches. Male, Fraserdale, Ontario, June.

31

Hermit Thrush

HYLOCICHLA GUTTATA

plate 31   *Hermit Thrush* - HYLOCICHLA GUTTATA

THE thrush family is nearly world-wide; it comprises more than three hundred species, of which twelve are found in Canada. It includes the familiar robin, the bluebirds, the wheatear of the arctic and the Townsend's solitaire of the western mountains, in addition to the typical brown thrushes such as those pictured here. In the Old World, such notable vocalists as the European blackbird, the nightingale and the song thrush are all members of this celebrated clan, so richly enjoyed by man since the dawn of his acoustic appreciation.

Thrushes inhabit almost every type of Canadian environment from the great cities and lush deciduous forests of the southeast to the arctic barrens. This species, which in many ways is very like its counterpart the nightingale, breeds from Alaska to Labrador and well down into the United States. Unlike some of its relatives, it is not overly choosy about its habitat, although the majority of hermit thrushes live in the evergreen forest.

This is a quiet, inconspicuous bird that sticks very close to the forest floor. Often the only view granted the observer is a flick of its reddish tail as the bird silently darts through the undergrowth to a more secluded hiding place. But if it is secretive and anonymous during the day, the hermit thrush comes into its own at evening, with a pure, flute-like song that some consider the most beautiful and compelling sound in nature – clear, ethereal, and deliberately phrased. But despite the magnificence of its song, the sound is no give-away to the bird's location; it varies so much in volume and pitch that it is almost impossible to get an accurate fix on the singer. It has been learned that no two individuals sing the same pattern.

The hermit thrush is one of our earlier spring migrants; some years it arrives in southern parts of the country before the snow has entirely gone. It shows a related reluctance to move south in the fall. Though some hermit thrushes winter as far south as Central America, most remain in the southern and central USA, and a few occasionally brave the snows of southwestern Ontario's "banana belt" throughout the winter.

Length 6¹/₂-7³/₄ inches. Male, Chapleau, Ontario, June.

32

Swainson's Thrush

HYLOCICHLA USTULATA

plate 32

Swainson's Thrush - HYLOCICHLA USTULATA

O ᴠᴇʀ most of Canada, this species is known as the olive-backed thrush, which would be a much better name if birds of the far west did not have russet backs. As geographically isolated populations of birds often have characteristics distinct from others of their species, it is sometimes difficult on a continent as large as North America to find a descriptive name appropriate to all of a species' local races. So Swainson's thrush it is.

Though it is probably not the equal of the hermit thrush as a singer (what bird is?), this species has much of the musical acomplishment of its family. Its melodious song characteristically spirals upward; that of the related veery, a bird of the southern forest, spirals downward. Like most other brown thrushes, Swainson's usually sings in the evening. During the rest of the day it scarcely utters any sound, and is thus quite awkward to find at the nesting season.

Swainson's thrush breeds from Newfoundland to Alaska and south to the northern tier of states. It is a very widespread and abundant bird over the great reaches of the coniferous forest, favoring low, damp areas near water. It shows a special liking for smaller, young evergreens intermixed with aspens, birches, and other pioneers of second-growth situations.

Like so many other small-to-medium-sized birds, this thrush migrates at night. For the winter, it moves as far south as Peru and Argentina. Most birds that migrate over extremely long distances tend to be blown off course once in a while and to arrive in some unexpected places. Such is the case with Swainson's thrush, which turns up in Europe from time to time.

Though this bird does not look much like our backyard robin in its adult plumage, the relationship of our thrushes is manifest in the markings of the young fledglings, which are heavily spotted. Young thrushes have a way of leaving the nest very early – several days before they can fly. Demands on parental care and watchfulness are thus more onerous than in many other songbird families.

Length 6¹/₂-7³/₄ inches. Male, Nipissing District, Ontario, July.

Gray=cheeked Thrush

HYLOCICHLA MINIMA

Gray cheeked
Thrush

plate 33

Gray-cheeked Thrush - HYLOCICHLA MINIMA

T HIS is the most northerly of our brown thrushes. It breeds through the boreal forest north to the limit of trees and even beyond. At those places on the edge of the vast tundra where stunted spruce trees give way to dwarf willows and birches, the gray-cheeked thrush will venture out onto the barrens as far as there are shrubs of sufficient size to provide cover for nesting.

Since it shows no reluctance to explore the North, even beyond the tree line, it is not surprising that the gray-cheeked thrush has made its way through Alaska to northeastern Siberia. Yet, when winter comes, these birds do not move southward over the Asian land mass. They return each fall by the route their pioneering ancestors used, moving east over what seems an unnecessarily wide arc of the globe before turning south toward their wintering grounds in the tropics of the West Indies and northern South America. Birds are in more of a traditional "rut" than we (sometimes envious) landbound mammals realize.

The nest of this species is built on the ground or in a tree or shrub, and may be situated as high as twenty feet, depending upon the size of available vegetation. Like its relatives, this thrush is a secretive bird — until it begins to sing. It very rarely sings in migration, and few students have heard it; the song is described as being somewhat like that of a veery, but thinner, higher-pitched, and more nasal.

An interesting phenomenon, unusual among birds, is the contribution of the female to courtship song. Both sexes sing, and the voice of the female is said to be nearly as elaborate as that of the male. The two birds may sing either the same song or a different one; they may sing simultaneously (in duet) or alternately. Other Canadian species in which the females sing include the mockingbird, the cardinal, and the rose-breasted and black-headed grosbeaks. In addition, such birds as the South American jacamars and some of the African barbets, among others, go in for duetting.

The gray-cheeked thrush has an interesting pattern of migration in spring. Instead of rushing the season, as the hermit thrush does, this species tarries and dallies in southern latitudes such as the coast of the Gulf of Mexico until almost the last minute. Then, when conditions in the north are suitable, it moves headlong, accelerating as it goes. By the time it reaches the northern half of the continent, it is moving almost twice as fast as it was in the southern states.

Length 7-8 inches. Male, Sandhill Lake, Manitoba, June.

34

Golden=crowned Kinglet

REGULUS SATRAPA

plate 34

Golden-crowned Kinglet - REGULUS SATRAPA

W ITH the exception of certain hummingbirds, kinglets are the smallest North American birds. The European opposite number of this species, the firecrest, is that continent's smallest bird. These minute creatures are members of the Old World warbler family. Presumably they came this way via Siberia and the Bering Strait. But that was very long ago, because the two North American species are no longer identical with their Eurasian relatives; they have changed in the meantime.

This is a very widespread bird, ranging from Alaska east and south to the higher country of South Carolina and Arizona. It winters as far south as the Gulf states, though in general it does not move as far south as the ruby-crowned kinglet. Indeed many birds remain all winter long fairly close to the northern limit of their breeding range. This makes the migrations rather inconspicuous by comparison with those of many other birds.

The golden-crown always nests in a conifer, whether it be a pine, fir, spruce, or hemlock, yet it does not insist upon a pure culture of evergreens in the immediate neighborhood. It likes mixed forest just as long as conifers predominate. Its pendant nest is striking: globular and delicately constructed of mosses, cobwebs, lichens, and bits of leaves. The interior is deeply lined with feathers and has been likened to a cocoon.

This tiny bird lays appropriately tiny eggs, but it produces a lot of them. The average clutch runs to eight or nine, but eleven have been counted. The total weight of a set of eggs may exceed the weight of the bird that laid them! The interior of the nest is small, and in larger clutches the eggs must be deposited in layers so that all may be accomodated.

Natural mortality is high among animals of such fecundity, but the north woods still swarm with golden-crowned kinglets. One is not so much aware of their presence at nesting time as in the off season. Bands of kinglets interspersed with chickadees, nuthatches, woodpeckers, and brown creepers roam the winter woods in an erratic way, sometimes appearing in substantial numbers.

Length 3¹/₂-4 inches. Male, Chapleau, Ontario, June.
Female, London, Ontario, April.

Ruby=crowned Kinglet

REGULUS CALENDULA

plate 35

Ruby-crowned Kinglet - REGULUS CALENDULA

*T*HIS is rather a drab little bird when compared with the preceding one, but the explosive brilliance of the male's normally concealed crown patch, exposed in moments of high excitement, is thus all the more striking. Like so many of the very smallest birds, kinglets seem to be nearly always in a state of high-key agitation, so one does not usually have to wait long for the ruby crown to be displayed.

Kinglets are constantly in motion, flitting and flickering like moths in the shadows of the evergreen forest, darting one way and another in an incessant search for insect food. Small bodies burn fuel quickly, and most of the kinglet's lifetime is spent in a near frenzy of feeding activity. You never see one sitting around doing nothing; only larger birds can afford that luxury.

As does the golden-crowned, this kinglet nests in coniferous forests across the continent, but it is slightly more northern in summer and slightly more southern in its wintering range. Its migrations are therefore more noticeable than those of its relative. Kinglets migrate at night, and on some spring and autumn mornings the dawn reveals hordes of ruby-crowned mites, all energetically foraging in the trees.

This bird has a harsh, wren-like call note, and seems to "talk" a lot while feeding. It has been suggested that in winter, these notes serve not so much to keep the flock together as to keep individuals *apart*; each bird must have plenty of room to work in if it is to pick up sufficient sustenance in the course of the short winter day.

The golden-crowned kinglet has a thin and undistinguished song, but the ruby-crowned is a noted vocalist. When you happen to be standing close to the bird as it sings, it is almost unbelievable that such a volume of sound could originate in such a wisp of a body. The song is an attenuated, varied, and attractive warble, punctuated by short chatters, and remarkably loud. This is one of the several birds that have voice "dialects" — regional variations in song that are sufficiently different to be characteristic of geographic races or populations.

Nesting is like that of the golden-crowned kinglet. The newly hatched young have been described as being little bigger than bumblebees. Both parents are kept frantically busy feeding the large brood.

Length 3³/₄-4¹/₂ inches. Male, Hamilton, Ontario, May.
Female, Coldstream, Ontario, May.

Northern Shrike

LANIUS EXCUBITOR

plate 36   *Northern Shrike* - LANIUS EXCUBITOR

*A*LTHOUGH they are true songbirds, the seventy-odd shrikes of the world are highly aberrant ones. They have become adapted to a hawk-like way of life, and have developed somewhat hawk-like physical features to go with it. Shrikes are found chiefly in the Old World; only one, the loggerhead shrike, is confined to this hemisphere. The northern shrike, known in Britain as the great gray shrike, breeds in the subarctic open forest throughout the northern hemisphere, also occurring in North Africa.

This is a fearless, bold, and aggressive bird that has become almost wholly predatory. It lives on the larger insects (when they are available, insects make up a good half of its food), small mammals and birds, reptiles, and amphibians. The bird in the plate has taken a pine siskin. It catches its prey by dropping on it from above and dealing it a decisive blow with its heavy, robust bill. The bill is hooked, with a tooth-and-notch arrangement for a firm grasp in tearing its food.

Its feet and legs, though strong, are not strong enough to capture prey with, in the way a hawk does. Most of the shrike's work is done with its formidable bill. Occasionally it will lodge a victim in the crotch of a twig, or impale it on a thorn. It is not completely clear whether this is merely an aid in holding the meal firm while it is being cut up, or whether it is a deliberate hanging of food. Certainly the bird will return to these carcasses in times of food shortage. It is this habit which gave the shrike the name "butcher-bird" in Britain. Like hawks and owls, it regurgitates indigestible material in the form of pellets.

All predators, the shrike included, are closely tied for survival to the availability of prey. A major part of this species' food consists of voles; voles, like lemmings, experience population build-ups and "crashes" at more or less regular intervals. The four-year cycle of the voles seems to be reflected in concurrent southward flights of northern shrikes in winter.

The shrike hunts in much the same way as small hawks do: by maintaining a vigilant lookout from some good vantage point (in the north, a spruce spire, in the south, a telephone line) and launching itself in swift pursuit of moving prey. The nest is a bulky, somewhat untidy affair in a conifer.

Length 9-10³/₄ inches. Male, Port Sydney, Ontario, no date.

37

Solitary Vireo

VIREO SOLITARIUS

plate 37

Solitary Vireo - VIREO SOLITARIUS

PHLEGMATIC, slow-moving, and foliage-coloured, the vireos are some of our least conspicuous birds. The family is unique to the Americas, with its centre of abundance in the tropics. Though they look superficially like warblers, vireos are chunkier in build, much less nimble, and have noticeably stouter (sometimes hooked) bills. They are gleaners of dense, leafy vegetation and go about their work with a measured deliberation that is quite unlike the frenetic activity of the warblers.

This vireo shows a preference for mixed forests, ideally with a good representation of evergreens. Usually it will select one of the latter for nest-building. Its nest is a very neatly constructed basket suspended from a low branch by its upper rim, fashioned with birch bark, mosses, lichens, plant down, and bits of dry leaves and spider silk. The inner lining is of fine grasses and slender rootlets.

The sexes share the duties of incubation, and both appear to sing while on the nest. At this time, the birds are remarkably approachable; they are such close sitters that they will sometimes allow themselves to be touched before flying off the nest. The song is reasonably attractive and varied: a series of short phrases, whistled rather than warbled. But all the vireos make up any deficiency in musical ability with sheer persistence; they are among the most indefatigable of singers.

Since it often builds its nest at a low elevation, this vireo is a common victim of the parasitic brown-headed cowbird, which like the Old World cuckoo lays its eggs in the nests of other birds. It is reported that if the cowbird egg is deposited before any of the vireo's eggs are laid, the bird may cover up the strange intruder and lay her own eggs in the upper storey. If she already has eggs, she will continue to incubate, with the inevitable result — a brood of one lumpy cowbird and no young solitary vireos.

This bird is alternatively called "blue-headed" vireo, but the name "solitary" is also appropriate. It is not a sociable or gregarious bird, and is just as likely to be found migrating with a flock of warblers as it is with its own kind.

Length 5-6 inches. Male, Fraserdale, Ontario, June.

Philadelphia Vireo

VIREO PHILADELPHICUS

Philadelphia Vireo

plate 38 *Philadelphia Vireo* - VIREO PHILADELPHICUS

*I*TS name to the contrary, this vireo is a breeding bird of the Canadian forest zone from northern British Columbia to Newfoundland and the upper parts of New England. As so often happens, the bird was described and named from a specimen taken in migration, in this instance at Philadelphia in September 1842.

This is a species that is easily overlooked. It is a night flier in migration, and does not often sing except on the nesting grounds. If possible, it seems to be an even more leisurely feeder than its relatives. Its colour is so much like the surrounding foliage that even when it is in full song it is devilishly hard to spot. Occasionally a sluggish movement will reveal the bird for an instant; if in that instant the plain olive wings (no white bars) and yellowish underparts are evident, its identity is established.

The related red-eyed vireo, a pair of which would seem to inhabit every shade tree north of the southernmost states, has a monotonous robin-like song which is familiar to even the most inexperienced birdwatcher. The voice of the Philadelphia vireo is quite similar, but slower and higher-pitched. It is also something like that of the solitary vireo, but in that species the pacing of the phrases is characteristic. Both sexes appear to incubate and to sing while on the nest.

For nesting, this vireo does not usually select the evergreens of the northern forest, but rather low areas of second growth – sometimes alder thickets or willow jungles, and at others dense stands of young maples. It always demands plenty of leafy cover and usually likes to be near water. The nest itself is like a small cup, neatly woven of lichens, grasses, cobwebs, and birch bark hung from a suitably forked branch.

The origin and evolution of vireos is unclear. Some authorities say they are most closely related to the warblers; others see them as nearer to the shrikes. They behave a good deal like tanagers. But in the time scale of evolution, all of our songbirds are relatively recent. Vireos, warblers, blackbirds, tanagers and finches branched not long ago from the main stream of songbirds and are still, it would seem, in the process of developing new and distinctive characteristics.

Length 4¹/₂-5 inches. Male, Rossport, Ontario, June.

39

Tennessee Warbler

VERMIVORA PEREGRINA

plate 39

Tennessee Warbler - VERMIVORA PEREGRINA

*A*T first glance, this small warbler with its greenish-olive colouration, gray head, and white eye-line might be taken for a vireo. But a second look reveals the fine, sharp bill — needle-thin compared to the stout, curved beak characteristic of the vireos. Above all, its actions distinguish it from the sluggish, deliberate company of vireos. Most warblers are vivacity itself; they are almost constantly on the move in darting, fluttering, nervous activity.

The wood warblers are an American family of some one hundred and fifteen or twenty-odd members, depending upon the authority you consult; forty or so occur in Canada. They are little birds, most of them smaller than sparrows. Many are brightly coloured and boldly patterned; most are energetic if not musical singers on the nesting grounds. Warblers of various kinds range from Alaska and northern Canada to the southern parts of South America, and many are highly migratory. Almost all of them are nearly 100 per cent insectivorous; but, since they must await the right temperatures for hatches of insects, they are not our very earliest migrants in the spring.

Warblers are very widely distributed ecologically; there are few natural environments for which there is not some appropriate warbler species. This is particularly true in the northern Canadian forest, where a wide assortment of these delightful little creatures is enough to guarantee at least one warbler for just about every significant environmental niche.

The Tennessee warbler is not a bird of the deepest evergreen forest; it prefers deciduous and mixed woods and the edges of muskegs and swamps. Its nest is placed on the ground, and is usually made of the north's most ubiquitous commodity, sphagnum. Often this species is remarkably abundant, with many pairs nesting at surprisingly close quarters. The male sings from a high tree; he has a very loud, ringing and emphatic song, with plenty of carrying power. A male is illustrated here; the female is similar, though less contrastingly marked.

The name of the bird clearly has nothing whatever to do with its distribution. The first specimen happened to be taken in Tennessee during migration by Alexander Wilson, the early American ornithologist and bird painter, in 1832.

Length 4¹/₂-5 inches. Male, Nakina, Ontario, June.

Magnolia Warbler

DENDROICA MAGNOLIA

plate 40 *Magnolia Warbler* - DENDROICA MAGNOLIA

*T*HIS magnificent species of the northern evergreen forest got its in-congruous name in the same way so many birds did in the early days of American ornithology. It was shot out of a magnolia tree during migration in Mississippi by Alexander Wilson, and named by him in 1811. (It will be remembered that in those days there were no field guides and no museum collections to refer to; identifications had to be made along the barrel of a shotgun.)

There is little doubt, however, that the next time Wilson saw one of these birds, he recognized it. Few warblers are more distinctively marked. Notice especially the black and white tail; it is diagnostic.

Happily for everyone who enjoys birds (who, once exposed to them, cannot?), this is quite a common species that can be seen in numbers during migration. It winters from the West Indies to Panama, moving in April and May to its distant northern breeding grounds, the evergreen forest of Canada. Its typical habitat consists of fairly open stands of white spruce and balsam fir, with the usual admixture of maples and birches. The nest is normally built in a young evergreen; it is a somewhat loose and untidy construction of little twigs and stout grasses lined with fine rootlets.

At the height of the breeding season, the male is an unforgettable sight. In full display, he fans his striking tail to its greatest extent, flashing its black and white pattern, droops the wings to show their white patches, while his breast glows against the sombre backdrop of the evergreens.

Three to five eggs are laid and are incubated only by the female. When they hatch, both parents are kept busy during every moment of daylight to feed the demanding brood. One student closely observed the feeding process, and estimated that the young were fed, on the average, once every four minutes. When one considers the relatively high density of warblers throughout the northern forest, the number of insects taken must be incalculable. During major outbreaks of spruce budworm in the balsam fir country it has been reckoned that warblers have become so common that there was a pair of one species or another every *tenth* of an acre.

Length 4¹/₂-5 inches. Female, Caradoc, Ontario, May.
Male, Chipewyan, Alberta, June.

Black=throated Blue Warbler

DENDROICA CAERULESCENS

Black-throated Blue
Warbler.

plate 41   *Black-throated Blue Warbler* - DENDROICA CAERULESCENS

*T*HIS elegant species is an eastern specialty, breeding between Nova Scotia and Manitoba. Unlike many of the warblers, the sexes are completely different, but the plain female can nearly always be recognized by a tiny white flash in the wing. The male is impossible to confuse with any other bird.

The black-throated blue is not a true northerner; its usual haunts are the deciduous portions of the "transition" zone between the hardwoods and the evergreens. The mixed forest it likes best consists of mature hardwoods such as maple, with a good dense undergrowth of young trees, including conifers. Thus it is frequently found in cut-over areas where natural succession has begun. The nest is placed on or very near the ground in a shrub, small tree, or fallen tree. It is very bulkily made of bits of wood, bark, and leaves, and lined with animal hair and rootlets. Even fine porcupine quills have been reported.

This is a tame and rather slow-moving bird for a warbler. It is readily approached; when the observer gets too close, it will simply move away to a nearby branch, then resume its deliberate feeding. The bird's husky voice, like its actions, is lazy and unhurried. It has a variety of songs, but the throaty quality is usually detectable.

This species and the cerulean warbler of the south are our only two strikingly blue warblers. This colour is not the product of any blue pigment. Blue in the feathering of birds is a structural or mechanical effect. Just as minute particles in the atmosphere scatter out the shorter wave-lengths of visible light and give the sky its blue appearance, tiny air-filled cavities in the feathers of "blue" birds have a screening effect, eliminating from our vision all wave-lengths save the blue. A "blue" bird, soaking wet, looks black; in anything but reflected light, it looks brown.

Length 5-5$^{1}/_{2}$ inches. Female, Toronto, Ontario, September.
Male, Elmsdale, Ontario, Spring.

42

Myrtle Warbler

DENDROICA CORONATA

plate 42

Myrtle Warbler - DENDROICA CORONATA

THIS, the most rugged of our warblers, is exceptional in several ways. It is possibly the most abundant species and is extremely widespread from Newfoundland to Alaska. It is the first warbler to appear in spring, and the last to leave our latitudes in fall; indeed some myrtle warblers winter a surprisingly long way north. This is because, unlike its relatives, this species is not wholly dependent upon insects. It will eat the fruit of trees and shrubs of various kinds, most especially the berries of the wax myrtle, which grows in such profusion in the heart of its wintering range along the coast of the Carolinas.

In spring migration, the bulk of the myrtle warblers come north by way of the valley of the Mississippi; the birds pour up this great flyway in vast numbers during late March and April. Since this is our only warbler that is able to survive low temperatures, it often arrives in southern Canada in chilly weather with the hermit thrushes and fox sparrows.

When they are on the move, myrtle warblers are dogged foragers, creeping about and around twigs, buds, and leaves, sometimes hanging upside down like titmice, and at other times flycatching. In all their quick, darting movements the yellow rump is conspicuous, and an excellent field mark. Note the white throat. In the west (from Cypress Hills, Saskatchewan, to central British Columbia) there lives the very similar and closely related Audubon's warbler. Except for the fact that Audubon's has a yellow throat and a magnolia-like white wing patch, the two birds are almost identical, and very probably were one species not very long ago. Some authorities will suggest that they are the same species today. Hybridization between them is known.

The myrtle warbler nests at rather low elevations in such conifers as white pine, cedar, hemlock, and white spruce. It favours mixed woodlands, but will usually choose an evergreen to nest in. The nest is composed of small twigs laced together into a cup with strips of bark, fibres, and miscellaneous bits of plants. It is lined with fibres and hair.

Length 5-6 inches. Male, Nakina, Ontario, June.
Female, Toronto, Ontario, May.

43

Black=throated Green Warbler

DENDROICA VIRENS

plate 43   *Black-throated Green Warbler* - DENDROICA VIRENS

LTHOUGH it is a moderately striking bird, this smallish warbler is difficult to see, as it haunts the upper storeys of the evergreen forest. It is not at all shy – indeed, often quite confiding – but since it spends so much of its time at the higher levels of the trees, it is as difficult as an insect to pick out among the dense greenery. It is a very active bird, and one is repaid for a stiff neck by an occasional glimpse of bright yellow cheeks outlined by the black throat and dark crown. The female lacks much of the black throat, but the yellow face identifies both sexes.

The song of this species is quite distinctive: a "drowsy" series of "*zee's*" on changing pitches, drifting down from somewhere in the crowns of the tall spruces and balsam firs it usually selects for nesting. Farther south in its range, it favours hemlock. Though it likes to nest in conifers, it will forage in any trees, including stands of aspen, poplar, and white birch.

While it sings and feeds aloft, the black-throated green warbler seems to build its nest at lower elevations. A horizontal limb is selected, and those who have hunted for this delicate little cup report that it would be frustratingly difficult to find were it not for eye-catching strands of white birch bark that are often interwoven in its sides. The eggs are spotted and number four or five.

This warbler does not breed west of the Rocky Mountains. Between the Great Divide and the Pacific, it is replaced by the closely related Townsend's and black-throated gray warblers. Another very near relative is the golden-cheeked warbler, a species confined to a few counties in Texas. There is a decided family resemblance in the songs of these warblers which, aside from their appearance, leads students of bird evolution to speculate that they have emerged as separate species only quite recently.

In migration, warblers have the habit of travelling in mixed flocks in which several species may be included. Rare is the May warbler "wave" in the eastern part of the continent that does not include substantial representation from the black-throated green.

Length 4¹/₂-5¹/₄ inches. Male, Madge Lake, Saskatchewan, May.

44

Blackburnian Warbler

DENDROICA FUSCA

plate 44 ## *Blackburnian Warbler* - DENDROICA FUSCA

*T*HERE is one instance in which the naming of a bird in honour of a person made some (albeit accidental) sense. This bird was named for one Mrs. Blackburn, an Englishwoman who was interested in birds, in the late 18th century. The coincidence is that the bird has much black about it, and as A. C. Bent pointed out, the throat of the male "burns like a brilliant orange flame amid the dark foliage of the hemlocks and spruces." A fair enough outcome.

Except for the almost artificial radiance of the male's throat, this warbler is not a particularly striking one. But its facial pattern is distinctive even in autumn, when the birds have a generally washed-out appearance.

The Blackburnian warbler is essentially an easterner, breeding from Nova Scotia to James Bay and west to Manitoba. A few may spill over into favoured spots on the prairies, but only a very few. In the Appalachians, however, where the mountain ranges supply the necessary altitude for the right evergreens, this warbler nests as far south as South Carolina and Georgia.

In the south, this is a bird of the pines and hemlocks; in the north, it lives in the spruces. In common with many of its relatives, it likes to sing from the topmost spire of a tall dead spruce or hemlock; the high-pitched zippy song drifts earthward so faintly that it might have been caused by some small insect. Just as individual eyesight varies in man, so does hearing; many people have never been able to hear an incredibly thin and wiry upward-sliding note at the end of the song. The onset of human middle age seems to carry with it the loss of most of the extremely high-frequency bird songs: this one, that of the blackpoll, the bay-breasted, parts of the winter wren's, and several more. For the student interested in warblers, this is bad news, since so many of them (the Blackburnian included) are so many times more often heard than seen. The dense canopy of the forest is ample concealment for these diminutive birds.

The nest may be situated almost anywhere in a conifer (there are records of nests found at from five to eighty feet), but higher levels are most usual. Twigs, plant down of various kinds and *Usnea* lichen are fashioned into a graceful cup which is lined with hair, fine grass, and rootlets.

Length 4¹/₂-5¹/₂ inches. Male, Hamilton, Ontario, May.
Female, Long Point, Ontario, May.

Bay-breasted Warbler

DENDROICA CASTANEA

plate 45

Bay-breasted Warbler - DENDROICA CASTANEA

*I*N a family in which at least some degree of flamboyance in plumage is the general rule, the male bay-breasted warbler is the soul of impeccable good taste. It even wears a pale stiff collar round its neck, which is the best field mark on an otherwise dark, somewhat hefty warbler.

Normally this is not a terribly common bird, by the standards set by some of the other warblers. Yet given the opportunity by favourable nesting conditions and an abundance of food, it can increase to surprising levels. In areas of heavy spruce budworm infestation, its population has been known to rise spectacularly, to the extent that in one such area, eighty-eight pairs of bay-breasted warblers were counted; their territories averaged slightly more than one-third of an acre per pair – a remarkable density for any such songbird.

This is an excellent example of the way in which the economics of nature manage to respond to unusual conditions – outbreaks of one species are balanced, or compensated for, by increases in another. Chemical pesticides reduce both insects and birds drastically – but neither completely. The budworm in particular seems able to pop up again in another part of the forest without much loss of time.

Though it looks so different, this species is very closely related to the blackpoll warbler, which is a much more common bird. This relationship is not evident in the plumage of adult males in spring, but in the autumn the two species (especially the young birds) are indistinguishable to the untrained eye. There *are* differences, however, for which the reader is referred to Roger Tory Peterson's *Field Guide to the Birds*. The familial ties of these two species are apparent also in the fact that they have been known to hybridize.

The song of the bay-breasted warbler is quite monotonous for a member of its family. It is a very high-pitched, sibilant, and thin series of two-syllable notes on the same pitch, not always readily picked up by the inexperienced ear.

This is one of the last migrant warblers to come through southern Canada in spring. But it has a long way to travel: from Panama and Venezuela all the way to the boreal forest stretching from Newfoundland and Labrador to Alaska.

Length 5-6 inches. Female, Lake Attawapiskat, Ontario, June.
Male, Caradoc, Ontario, May.

Blackpoll Warbler

DENDROICA STRIATA

plate 46 ## Blackpoll Warbler - DENDROICA STRIATA

*I*T is a long, long way from the tropics of South America to the Canadian timber-line, but the blackpoll manages this great journey each spring and fall with no apparent difficulty. It is one of the very last warblers to pass through populated Canada on the way north; when the blackpolls appear, the wonderful migration of the warblers is drawing to an end.

The schedule of its northern flight is interesting. The wintering grounds are in Guiana, Brazil, and Peru. From there it moves to Venezuela and across the chain of the West Indies, via Cuba, to Florida. It generally reaches the Florida mainland about April 20, and does not arrive at the latitude of the Great Lakes until May 15 to 20, representing a month more or less for that leg of the journey. Then the flight speeds up. In another ten days or two weeks (or May 30), the birds have arrived on their northern breeding grounds from Newfoundland to Alaska.

At the start of its migration, the blackpoll is moving at the rate of about thirty miles per day; at the end, it is doing two hundred miles per day. This rapid acceleration has been noted in several birds, including the gray-cheeked thrush, which occupies the same far northern environment at the limit of trees. If it is measured in a straight line, the greatest extent of this fantastic trip of the blackpoll adds up to five thousand miles, one way. But it is *not* in a straight line, and it is anyone's guess how much more than ten thousand miles an individual bird may fly in one year.

The blackpoll in spring plumage can only be confused with the black-and-white warbler, but the latter has its crown broken by a white stripe, and it spends most of its time in an un-warbler-like creeping up and down tree trunks. The female blackpoll lacks the black cap. In fall, the blackpoll looks like a totally different bird — very, very like the bay-breasted warbler. At that season the blackpolls move in small flocks; in the spring they are more solitary and seem to travel singly or in groups of two or three. They are not quite so hyper-active as most other warblers, and methodically work spring willow and alder catkins as the migration proceeds.

The song of the blackpoll is excruciatingly high-pitched and thin; one often has to make a deliberate effort to tune in on its frequency before it can be picked up. The average frequency has been worked out at 8,900, "over an octave above the highest tone on the piano"; it can reach 10,225.

Length 5-5³/₄ inches. Male, Kinglet Lake, Quebec, July.

Palm Warbler

DENDROICA PALMARUM

plate 47 *Palm Warbler* - DENDROICA PALMARUM

*W*HY a breeding bird of the northern Canadian forest should have the word "palm" attached to it will become evident when the birdwatcher visits Florida in the winter. He will spend a good deal of time checking local warblers (which are abundant) until he realizes that almost every other bird he looks at is this species. To be absolutely accurate about it, however, the bird does not frequent the palm trees; it seems to be everywhere else *but*. Nonetheless, the name does evoke a picture of that subtropical environment characteristic of half of the bird's life story.

For the other half of the year, this is a bird of the black spruce and jack pine forests of the north and northwest. It likes heavily wooded areas in the southern part of its range, and builds its nest of mosses and grasses on the ground. Farther north, in the subarctic, it nests in the open muskegs where there are scattered spruces and tamaracks.

Unlike most *Dendroica* warblers, this one spends much of its time on the ground, whether on the asphalt of a Florida parking lot or on the sphagnum of the north. It is a conspicuous bird, not only because of its tame and fearless nature, but also because of its habit of perpetually bobbing and wagging its tail up and down. This constant flicking can become an annoyance to the birdwatcher (who by definition has sensitive peripheral vision); try as he will, he cannot help instinctively turning his head to check some movement caught in the corner of one eye. It's always the palm warbler again.

The sexes are similar. In spring, the best marks are the chestnut cap, yellow under the tail, general colouration, and the movements of the tail. Fall birds do not have the conspicuous cap. Like those of so many of its immediate relatives, the palm warbler's voice is thin, weak, and undistinguished, consisting of a repetitious series of six or seven unmusical and sibilant notes, all on one pitch.

There are two well-defined races or subspecies of the palm warbler in Canada. One ranges from the Great Lakes to Hudson Bay and the Mackenzie, the other from the Great Lakes and James Bay east to Newfoundland, Nova Scotia, and northern New England. The western form is illustrated here.

Length 4¹/₂-5¹/₂ inches. Male, Favourable Lake, Ontario, June.

48

Northern Waterthrush

SEIURUS NOVEBORACENSIS

plate 48

Northern Waterthrush - SEIURUS NOVEBORACENSIS

THE unusual warbler genus *Seiurus* includes three species that are any-thing but warbler-like: the well-known ovenbird of the southern forests and two kinds of waterthrushes. "Waterthrush" may or may not be an inapropriate vernacular name; certainly the birds are warblers, not thrushes, but they *look* like thrushes and they definitely like the water.

This species and the very similar Louisiana waterthrush (a bird of the southern forest which barely trickles into Canada) may be distinguished most easily by the colour of the eyebrow stripe. In this species, it is buffy; in the Louisiana, it is white. The ovenbird has an orange crown on its head which is unmistakable.

All three of these ground-frequenting warblers *walk*, instead of hopping. No other warbler does this. Even the palm warbler, which is commonly seen on the ground, never walks. The waterthrushes stride up and down the margins of pools and streams "like mechanical toys," as Peterson describes it, and have the curious habit of bobbing, teetering, and tilting up and down in the way of a spotted sandpiper.

This is a bird of shaded swamps and bogs, favouring deep shrubby tangles at the water's edge. In the heavy underbrush, it maintains a con-stant search for small aquatic animals – such things as insects, worms, and tiny crustaceans – by poking under wet logs, leaves, bits of sodden bark, and mud. Its song is one of the memorable features of the wet woods. It is very loud, emphatic, and ringing, with clearly enunciated and rapidly accelerating phrases, carrying for considerable distances through the dense understorey. (Many birds of the very deep forest have loud, ringing voices of remarkable carrying power; this is especially true in tropical jungles.)

There is plenty of water in the great northern forest, and thus there is ample habitat for the waterthrush. It is distributed pretty well country-wide, from the southern border to the limit of trees. It is also found in appropriately cool and shady retreats in the northern parts of the USA.

Length 5¹/₂-6¹/₂ inches. Male, Favourable Lake, Ontario, May.

49

Rusty Blackbird

EUPHAGUS CAROLINUS

plate 49 *Rusty Blackbird* - EUPHAGUS CAROLINUS

*I*N the Old World, the blackbird is a thrush, very like the American robin. In the Americas, the endemic blackbird family includes many of our most brilliant birds, including the bobolink and meadowlarks, orioles and troupials, caciques and oropendolas, as well as the *black* blackbirds with which nearly everyone is familiar – redwings, grackles, and others. The centre of blackbird abundance is in the tropics; only twelve of the eighty-eight species occur in Canada.

Here is a kind of "oriole," then, that breeds inside the Arctic Circle – the northernmost of its family. Unlike the other black blackbirds, this species shows a strong affinity for water; as often as not its nest will be built beside or even over the water in the trees and shrubs surrounding a forest pond, stream, or bog. Most of our other blackbirds do not care for thickly wooded areas. The rusty nests as far north as the limit of trees and as far south, where habitat permits, as northern New England.

Most blackbirds are gregarious, especially during migration. Massed mixed flocks of redwinged blackbirds, grackles, and cowbirds are familiar to every birdwatcher; this species, though it flocks just as tightly, seems to prefer its own company. It is less likely to mingle with the others. The great spring flight, in which remarkably dense and compact flocks may be seen, begins in the southern states in March and reaches the Great Lakes in April. By May the birds have reached their breeding grounds in the immensity of the wet boreal forest. Only during the nesting period does the rusty blackbird become a solitary species. Soon after the young are on the wing, the flocks, bands, and great companies of birds begin to re-assemble.

The bird gets its name from the rusty-brown winter plumage. The amount of colour is variable among individuals and age groups; it is thought to be brightest in young birds. The bird turns glossy black (slate gray for females) in spring by the simple expedient of losing the rusty tips of its feathers, which break off; underneath, they are the proper breeding colour.

Length 8¹/₂-9³/₄ inches. Male, Hamilton, Ontario, October.
Male, Coldstream, Ontario, May.
Female, Fort Albany, Ontario, June.

Evening Grosbeak

HESPERIPHONA VESPERTINA

plate 50   *Evening Grosbeak* - HESPERIPHONA VESPERTINA

Non-birdwatchers frequently ask what in the world people of our persuasion find to look at in the wintertime. They may be assured that few sights in nature are more arresting than a flock of evening grosbeaks in clear winter sunlight. Their rich plumage has an almost unreal golden glow against glaring snow and the deep blue January sky. That is the season when most Canadians see this splendid bird; at breeding time it withdraws to the remote wilderness of the boreal forest.

The great, stout, conical bill is a beautiful adaptation to seed-eating; it is reminiscent of that of the Old World hawfinch. In summer, on the breeding areas, evening grosbeaks depend to a great extent on softish buds and berries. It is in winter that the specialized beak really comes into its own. Flocks of the birds descend on such trees as the Manitoba maple (box elder), devouring the winged seeds in amazing quantities with amazing speed. Also, in their winter wanderings, grosbeaks are easily attracted to feeding stations.

In *The Birds of Nova Scotia*, Robie W. Tufts has described the evening grosbeaks' feeding technique. "It is interesting to watch them at close range – eight to ten inches – on the window-tray, clipping the edges off sunflower seeds in order to extract the meat. It is done with marked dexterity. Their powerful bills are like shears, the sharp edges of the upper mandible coming down neatly over the side of the lower one, the seed being manipulated by the tongue."

The bill can also be an effective instrument of defence. The bird bander who handles one of these finches carelessly runs the risk of a nip that he will not soon forget. These grosbeaks are sturdy, bellicose birds, and at feeding stations they do not encourage the company of other species, although some lesser fry such as chickadees, nuthatches, and juncos are tolerated. Competitors such as the pine grosbeak, whose winter diet is similar in some respects, nearly always come off second best.

This is a western bird in terms of breeding abundance, but in the off season there is a tendency for it to move eastward. Birds banded in northern Michigan, for example, moved in the autumn not to the south but almost due east to the Atlantic states of New England. Like the boreal chickadee and others, the evening grosbeak experiences periodic population peaks which bring great numbers into southern latitudes. This does not happen on any sort of timetable comparable to the cycle of the northern shrike; it is sporadic and unpredictable.

Length 7-8¹/₂ inches. Female, Rainy River, Ontario, June.
Male, Strickland, Ontario, June.

51

Purple Finch

CARPODACUS PURPUREUS

plate 51   *Purple Finch* - CARPODACUS PURPUREUS

*T*HIS is another of the northern finches with which most people are familiar chiefly in winter, when with several of its relatives it readily patronizes home feeding stations. When a small flock of these erratic wanderers visits a backyard tray of millet seeds, sometimes it is overlooked. The females and young birds look very like some kind of undistinguished sparrows; it is not until a raspberry-red male appears that the flock catches our attention. Usually the fully adult males are considerably outnumbered. There may be more males than one suspects, however, for it takes more than one year for them to reach high plumage, and the males are sexually mature and do breed while still in the "female" garb.

The purple finch is one of the more attractive singers of its family. The song is a highly variable, liquid warble and the bird is a very persistent singer, even in winter. The call note is a short, dull, and metallic *tick*, distinctive enough to immediately draw one to the window overlooking the feeding station.

Males on their breeding territories in summer like to sing from chosen perches high in the tops of evergreens. Often, carried away in the enthusiasm of his courtship, a singing male will flutter from his perch, continuing in full song as he describes an aerial "dance" to his own accompaniment. Song is at its best during morning and evening hours.

Its preferred habitat is forest edge – places where the dense evergreen cover is interrupted by standing or running water or by beaver meadows and the scars of old fires. But there must be evergreens of one kind or another. This is the same country occupied by the goshawk, spruce grouse, hawk-owl, three-toed woodpecker, and the long list of warblers and finches – the great transcontinental belt of conifers that parallels the tundra to the north.

Wintering purple finches sometimes move farther than many of their summertime neighbours, migrating as far as the Gulf states in some years. But, like the others, their wanderings are informal; they are common or even abundant one year, scarce or absent the next, which is one of the charms of so many of the northern birds.

Length 5¹/₂-6¹/₄ inches. Female, Strathroy, Ontario, December.
Male, Fort Albany, Ontario, July.

Pine Grosbeak

PINICOLA ENUCLEATOR

Pine Grosbeak

plate 52   *Pine Grosbeak* - PINICOLA ENUCLEATOR

Our largest finch is also one of the most appealing, with a variety of attractive plumages, a gentle and tolerant disposition, and a pleasant musical voice. It is widely distributed throughout the boreal forest of the northern hemisphere, but only occasionally is it seen in numbers. Like those of so many of the breeding birds of the far north, its appearances in settled areas are unheralded and unscheduled, but they are worth waiting for.

As with the purple finch, fully adult males in their distinctive rose-red plumage are nearly always in the minority when winter flocks visit our latitudes. Sub-adult males are like the females, except that dashes of red make their coloured areas more orange than the dull yellow of the females. Red colouring in these birds is apparently a dietary product; the bird synthesizes red pigment from the contents of the food it eats. Birds raised in captivity often lack the colouration of wild birds.

This is a big, robust bird almost the size of a robin, but it shows some disinclination to tangle with more aggressive species such as the evening grosbeak; although their food habits are somewhat similar, the two species are not often seen together.

Its favoured nesting locations, like those of the purple finch, are the edges and borders of openings in the coniferous forest. Often its nest will be found near water. Buds and seeds are the staple diet; when they come south in winter the birds concentrate on beech nuts and conifer seeds of all kinds. They have also been observed to eat the berries of deadly nightshade (*Belladonna*) with no apparent ill effect.

Nesting pairs keep their distance from each other, but after broods are able to fly, the grosbeaks become gregarious once again, feeding in loose flocks as they aimlessly meander about the forest in late summer. They do not move south as a matter of course; only a food shortage can drive them out of the coniferous zone in any numbers. But when the supply of seeds and berries shrinks, as it occasionally does, the birds move southward, flying by day, to more promising surroundings. When they are on the move, their sweet whistles and deeply undulating, "roller-coaster" flight are reliable field marks.

Length 9-10 inches. Male, Toronto, Ontario, November.
Female, Toronto, Ontario, March.
Immature, Lake St. Martin, Manitoba, October.

Pine Siskin

SPINUS PINUS

plate 53

Pine Siskin - SPINUS PINUS

*H*ERE is one of our smallest finches – a dark, heavily-streaked little bird that may or may not show a certain amount of yellow in its wings and at the base of the tail. Its most noticeable features are its extreme gregariousness and its unpredictably nomadic nature. Small flocks and very large flocks appear one day and vanish the next, never seeming to pop up in one place twice running. The same is true of their populations; in some years they are extraordinarily abundant, in others there will be scarcely one to be seen.

The siskin's closest relative is the much more familiar goldfinch, and the two birds have many things in common. In flight, they both undulate markedly; a tightly-packed flock announces its coming before you can properly see it, with light, twittering flight notes more or less in rhythm with the birds' bouncy progress. In winter, both species like open fields with the seed heads of thistles, dandelions, and other annual plants, and they often join foraging companies of redpolls and crossbills. Goldfinches, however, do not usually build up flocks as large as those of the siskins. When the latter arrive in numbers, those numbers are substantial.

Except when they invade lower latitudes, siskins are birds of the trans-continental evergreen forest and the coniferous slopes and valleys of the western mountains. In summer, their food is mixed: insects of various sorts, buds, and small, tender leaves. Seeds are taken at all seasons, especially those of conifers, alders, and birches. Nesting is in the upper storeys of a tall evergreen. Nestlings of both members of this genus are said to be fed in part by the regurgitation of masses of very small seeds, which may be partially pre-digested.

It is often noted by naturalists that several of the northern finches (including this species, the purple finch, pine grosbeak, crossbills, and others), demonstrate a special fondness for salt. It is a common experience, when you are driving along a country gravel road in winter, to flush small flocks of finches from the bare-scraped shoulders of the road. They are presumably picking up grit, but they also seem to have been attracted by salt deposited by highway crews. The significance of this taste is not understood.

Length 4¹/₂-5¹/₄ inches. Female, The Pas, Manitoba, June.

54

White=winged Crossbill

LOXIA LEUCOPTERA

plate 54   *White-winged Crossbill* - LOXIA LEUCOPTERA

*T*HE great world family of finches, including some four hundred and twenty-five species, is considered to be the most recently evolved group of birds. Among other things, they are characterized by stout, wedge-shaped bills, especially useful for seed-cracking. Though crossbills are true finches, they have developed a further and unique refinement of the bill to allow them to specialize in dealing with evergreen cones, one of the toughest forms of plant food for birds to handle.

The parrot-like mandibles of these birds actually cross at their tips, like a miniature pair of ice tongs. When the bird is not eating, its bill would appear to be the very epitome of awkwardness; it is difficult to imagine how an animal with such an overdeveloped bit of anatomy could possibly survive. In practice, it is a beautifully functioning tool that enables the crossbill to do in an instant what another species might take minutes or hours to accomplish, if indeed it could do it at all.

The bill is opened to its fullest extent as the bird bites into a hard evergreen cone. As it is closed, the tips come together and pass one another, scissors-like, resulting in a form of wedge, or lever, that spreads apart the scales of the cone. The bill, now behind a seed, forces it out; the kernel is extracted with the tongue. As simple as shucking peas, if you're a crossbill.

Quite obviously, this bird and its cousin the red crossbill are dependent upon the annual crop of evergreen cones. But the crop is variable from year to year and from place to place. The erratic, nomadic behaviour of both crossbills is probably yet another adaptation to the pressures of their environment. If they were not confirmed wanderers, they might fail to find alternative sources of food supply in poor years. But since they do have such a tendency to move around almost constantly in the non-breeding season, they are able to find suitable feeding grounds even if the cone crop has been thin over a reasonably large area.

In the great coniferous forest, crossbills concentrate on native spruces and balsam firs. When they move south, they feed on hemlocks and the Norway spruces so widely introduced in farming country.

Length 6-6³/4 inches. Male, James Bay, Ontario, June.
Female, Murrilo, Ontario, July.

Fox Sparrow

PASSERELLA ILIACA

plate 55   *Fox Sparrow* – PASSERELLA ILIACA

*T*HOUGH unobtrusive and wary, this large and handsome sparrow has several distinctions. It is a splendid singer; it is important to students of the evolution of bird species; it is a constant challenge to the alertness of the birdwatcher because of its secretive habits.

The fox sparrow nests as far north as there are trees and from ocean to ocean. It reaches the tree limit in the high mountains as well as in the subarctic; it moves upward just as far as there is undergrowth to accommodate it. This is a bird of the thickets, whether they are dense stands of willow and alder along the banks of streams, or shrubby, young or stunted evergreens.

This bird has made a specialty out of living on the ground. It forages there industriously and vigorously, kicking and lashing out with both feet as it sends leaves flying in all directions and explores the rich humus beneath. Like another ground-dwelling finch, the towhee, this sparrow makes far more fuss, noise, and commotion among the leaves than any bird its size properly should. But despite all this, the bird is unusually shy and self-effacing, and it is by no means easy to observe.

The fox sparrow has one of the better voices and, unlike some, readily sings during migration. We may not be favoured always with the complete song, which the bird usually reserves for its nesting territory, but even the abridged version which we hear in southern latitudes is one of the most rewarding experiences of early spring. The full song is pure virtuosity – rich, musical, and varied; in a way, it is reminiscent of the orchard oriole, but infinitely more lyric.

There are a number of races, or subspecies, of fox sparrows. These have been the subject of much study, particularly on the Pacific coast. It has been found that these races never intermingle, not even on migration or on their wintering quarters. Thus, even at a season when they are not geographically isolated as they are at breeding time, the behaviour of the birds keeps the populations separate and distinct. One day, some of these races may become new species, as different from other fox sparrows as song sparrows are today.

Length 6¹/₄-7¹/₄ inches. Male, Sandhill Lake, Manitoba, June.

Lincoln's Sparrow

MELOSPIZA LINCOLNII

plate 56   *Lincoln's Sparrow* - MELOSPIZA LINCOLNII

*T*HIS very unobtrusive but attractive finch is often mistaken for its much more familiar cousin, the song sparrow. In comparison with its relative, especially in terms of behaviour, it is a most inconspicuous bird, but on close inspection it is anything but drab. It is an unusually tidy and trim little species, finely streaked, with a distinct yellowish-buff band across the breast.

Birds that habitually skulk in the undergrowth as this one does, often pass through in migration largely unnoticed, even though they may be in some numbers. Lincoln's sparrow frequents the densest brushy tangles and thickets on the forest floor, and rarely favours the observer with a good crisp view. This apparent desire for complete anonymity extends to its singing as well; it does not sing in migration to nearly the extent that many of its close relatives do.

This is an extremely widespread sparrow, ranging from Alaska to the lower peninsula of Michigan. In that vast area, only three races or sub-species have been recognized. This is in striking contrast to the ubiquitous song sparrow, of which no less than thirty-one different forms have been described at one time or another. The sexes are alike in plumage, and after the first proper moult the young birds resemble their parents.

The bird is no less secretive on its breeding grounds than it is on migration. For nesting, it chooses low areas such as wet beaver meadows, bogs, and swamps and the borders of lakes, ponds, and creeks. It likes the thickly tangled alder and willow growth in such situations – much the same habitat that is used by the northern waterthrush, among others. In the wide reaches of the boreal forest, wherever impenetrable shrubbery surrounds a marsh or muskeg, there Lincoln's sparrow will be furtively raising its brood of four or five nestlings.

It is a fine singer, delivering a quality somewhere in between that of a purple finch and a house wren; its lively, liquid song is filled with spirit and warmth. The singing perch is usually in a shrub or small tree, but when it is not in voice, the bird inevitably returns to the shaded security of ground level.

Length 5-6 inches. Farquier, Ontario, June.

The birdwatcher is blessed with an extremely wide range of reading, ranging from books especially for the beginner to the vast advanced literature of ornithology. The selection of titles presented here does not pretend to be more than a sample of the sources available; it is offered merely as an introduction to the subject, and includes both elementary and more advanced references. It includes those sources most frequently consulted by the author over the years. Many of the volumes listed contain substantial bibliographies.

Identification

PETERSON, ROGER TORY, *A Field Guide to the Birds.* Boston: Houghton Mifflin, 1947. *A Field Guide to Western Birds.* Boston: Houghton Mifflin, 1961.

POUGH, RICHARD H., *Audubon Land Bird Guide.* Garden City: Doubleday, 1946. *Audubon Water Bird Guide.* Garden City: Doubleday, 1951. *Audubon Western Bird Guide.* Garden City: Doubleday, 1957.

These books are visual aids to bird identification. In many cases, however, the song or call note of a bird may serve as corroboration of a sighting, and occasionally may be even more important than the appearance of a bird. A number of long-play bird recordings of excellent quality has appeared in recent years, and the number is growing. Some are collections of birds of geographic regions; others contain families of birds. For details, the reader is referred to the Federation of Ontario Naturalists, Don Mills, Ontario, Canada.

General and Reference

AMERICAN ORNITHOLOGISTS' UNION, *Check-list of North American Birds* (5th edition). Baltimore: A.O.U., 1957.

AUSTIN, OLIVER L. JR., *and* ARTHUR SINGER, *Birds of the World.* New York: Golden Press, Inc., 1961.

BENT, ARTHUR C., *Life Histories of North American Birds* (20 vols.). Washington: United States National Museum, 1919-1958.

BERGER, ANDREW J., *Bird Study.* New York: John Wiley & Sons, Inc., 1961.

CRUICKSHANK, ALLAN *and* HELEN, *1001 Questions Answered About Birds.* New York: Dodd, Mead & Company, Inc., 1958.

DARLING, LOIS *and* LOUIS, *Bird.* Boston: Houghton Mifflin Company, 1962.

DORST, JEAN, *The Migrations of Birds.* Boston: Houghton Mifflin Company, 1963.

FISHER, JAMES, *and* PETERSON, ROGER TORY, *The World of Birds.* Garden City: Doubleday & Company, Inc., 1963.

FORBUSH, E. H., *and* MAY, JOHN B., *A Natural History of the Birds of Eastern and Central North America.* Boston: Houghton Mifflin Company, 1939.

GRISCOM, L., *and* SPRUNT, A., *The Warblers of North America.* New York: The Devin-Adair Co., 1957.

HICKEY, J. J., *A Guide to Bird Watching.* New York: Oxford University Press, 1943.

KORTRIGHT, F. H., *Ducks, Geese and Swans of North America.* Washington: American Wildlife Institute, 1942.

PETERSON, ROGER TORY *(ed.), The Bird Watcher's Anthology.* New York: Harcourt, Brace & Company, Inc., 1957.

PETERSON, ROGER TORY *and* THE EDITORS OF "LIFE," *The Birds.* New York: Time Inc., 1963.

PETTINGILL, OLIN SEWALL JR., *(ed.), The Bird Watcher's America.* New York: McGraw-Hill Book Company, 1965.

THOMSON, A. LANDSBOROUGH *(ed.), A New Dictionary of Birds.* London: Nelson, 1964.

Canadian

GODFREY, W. EARL, *The Birds of Canada.* Ottawa: National Museum of Canada, (in press 1966).

MUNRO, J. A., *and* COWAN, IAN MCTAGGART, *A Review of the Bird Fauna of British Columbia.* Victoria, B.C. Provincial Museum, Special Publication no. 2, 1947.

PETERS, H. S., *and* BURLEIGH, T. D., *The Birds of Newfoundland.* St. John's, Newfoundland Department of Natural Resources, 1951.

SALT, W. RAY, *and* WILK, A. L., *The Birds of Alberta.* Edmonton, Alberta Department of Economic Affairs, 1958.

SNYDER, L. L., *Ontario Birds.* Toronto: Clarke, Irwin and Company Limited, 1950.

SQUIRES, W. AUSTIN, *The Birds of New Brunswick.* Saint John: The New Brunswick Museum (Monographic Series no. 4), 1952.

TAVERNER, P. A., *Birds of Canada.* Ottawa: Canadian Department of Mines Bulletin no. 72, 1934.

TUFTS, ROBIE W., *The Birds of Nova Scotia.* Halifax: Nova Scotia Museum, 1961.

NOTE: "Page" numbers refer to introduction, "plate" numbers to main text.
Numbers in italic denote accompanying illustration

On the Making of this Book

This book was planned and designed by Frank Newfeld

The type chosen is Palatino,
a design created by Hermann Zapf for
Stempel Linotype, Frankfurt, and first issued in 1950.
It is a Roman face with broad letters and strong, inclined serifs
resembling the Venetian. Named after the sixteenth-century Italian
writing master Palatino, this type is highly legible and
has retained the aesthetic sculptural
form of the Venetian letter.

Type was set in Canada by Cooper & Beatty, Limited

The drawings on pages preceding the plates were repro-
duced from J. F. Lansdowne's preliminary sketches.